D1522905

# EXPLORATIONS IN CHRISTIAN THEOLOGY AND ETHICS

Engaging variously with the legacy of Paul L. Lehmann, these essays argue for a reorientation in Christian theology that better honours the formative power of the gospel to animate and shape doctrine and witness, as well as ethical and political life.

The authors explore key themes in Christian theology and ethics – forgiveness, discernment, responsibility, spirituality, the present day tasks of theology and the role of faith in public life – making plain the unabated importance of Lehmann's work at this juncture in contemporary theology. The internationally recognized contributors draw crucial connections between the gospel of reconciliation, the form of Christian theology and witness, and the challenges of contemporary ethical and political reflection. This book demonstrates why this close friend of Dietrich Bonhoeffer, and author of *Ethics in a Christian Context* and *The Transfiguration of Politics* continues to influence generations of theologians in both the English speaking world and beyond.

# Explorations in Christian Theology and Ethics

## Essays in Conversation with Paul L. Lehmann

*Edited by*

PHILIP G. ZIEGLER
*University of Aberdeen, UK*

and

MICHELLE J. BARTEL
*Trinity United Presbyterian Church, Indiana, USA*

ASHGATE

Published by
Ashgate Publishing Limited
Wey Court East
Union Road
Farnham
Surrey, GU9 7PT
England

Ashgate Publishing Company
Suite 420
101 Cherry Street
Burlington
VT 05401-4405
USA

www.ashgate.com

**British Library Cataloguing in Publication Data**
Explorations in Christian theology and ethics: essays in conversation with Paul L. Lehmann
1. Lehmann, Paul Louis, 1906–1994 2. Theology, Doctrinal
3. Christian ethics
I. Ziegler, Philip Gordon II. Bartel, Michelle Joanne
230'.092

**Library of Congress Cataloging-in-Publication Data**
Explorations in Christian theology and ethics: essays in conversation with Paul L. Lehmann
/ edited by Philip G. Ziegler and Michelle J. Bartel.
      p. cm.
   "A Paul L. Lehmann bibliography"—P.
   Includes bibliographical references (p.      ) and index.
   ISBN 978-0-7546-6358-4 (hardcover : alk. paper) 1. Lehmann, Paul Louis, 1906–1994.
   2. Theology. 3. Christian ethics. I. Ziegler, Philip Gordon. II. Bartel, Michelle Joanne

BX4827.L435E97 2009
230—dc22                                                                                      2008044693

ISBN: 978-0-7546-6358-4
EISBN: 978-0-7546-9379-6

**Mixed Sources**
Product group from well-managed forests and other controlled sources
www.fsc.org Cert no. SGS-COC-2482
© 1996 Forest Stewardship Council
FSC

Printed and bound in Great Britain by
TJ International Ltd, Padstow, Cornwall

# Contents

# List of Contributors

**Michelle J. Bartel** has been Associate Professor of Theology and Chaplain at Hanover College, Hanover, Indiana, USA, and is now Pastor of Trinity United Presbyterian Church, New Washington, Indiana.

**Sally Ann Brown** is Elizabeth M. Engle Associate Professor of Preaching and Worship at Princeton Theological Seminary, Princeton, New Jersey, USA.

**James F. Cubie** is a doctoral candidate at Princeton Theological Seminary, Princeton, New Jersey, USA.

**David E. Demson** is Emeritus Professor of Systematic Theology at Emmanuel College, University of Toronto, Toronto, Ontario, Canada.

**Nancy J. Duff** is Stephen Colwell Associate Professor of Christian Ethics at Princeton Theological Seminary, Princeton, New Jersey, USA.

**Barry Harvey** is Duke University Associate Professor of Theology at Baylor University, Waco, Texas, USA.

**Eunjoo Mary Kim** is Associate Professor of Homiletics at Iliff School of Theology, Denver, Colorado, USA.

**Christopher Morse** is Dietrich Bonhoeffer Professor of Theology and Ethics at Union Theological Seminary, New York, New York, USA.

**Fleming Rutledge** is a priest within the Episcopal Church, USA. After more than twenty years of pastoral endeavour, including 14 years as Senior Associate at Grace Church in New York City, she now preaches and lectures on homiletics across North America.

**Philip G. Ziegler** is Lecturer in Systematic Theology at the University of Aberdeen, Scotland, UK.

# Editors' Preface

It can be difficult to get a purchase upon the wildly disparate and at times dissolute discipline of contemporary Christian ethics. Ultimately, of course, everyone wants Christian ethics to be both useful and faithful – searching reflection upon the grounds of human behaviour which properly reflects the substance of Christian faith. But our analyses of theological precepts, human being, societal dynamics, and our religious, social, and political circumstances all too often evince a sense of floundering. While not suggesting that the legacy of Paul Lehmann provides *the* answer to all the struggles facing Christian ethics in our current clime, we are convinced that the substance, style and distinctive preoccupations of his theological ethic provide impulses which are timely, vital and clarifying. Lehmann's work has staying power; it seems to enjoy abiding timeliness. But more than this, it fixes attention upon that one thing which has the power to steady us amidst ethical turbulence. By his tireless insistence that the form and content of theological ethics be tethered to the dynamic still point that is God's salutary activity – the divine endeavour 'to make and to keep human life human'[1] – Lehmann gives us something 'to stay our minds on and be staid'.[2]

To look to Lehmann's work for 'clarification' can only be done with some sense of affectionate and honest irony. As Nancy Duff remarks in her essay in this volume,

> One of the most commonly reported experiences of those who heard Paul lecture entailed leaving a lecture hall energized by his ability to bring Christian faith alive by examining it through the lenses of scripture, doctrine, philosophy, literature, poetry, and the daily news, and yet also be left wondering what exactly he had said. This intriguing style of speaking also dominated his writing, which, as a result, was both engaging and exasperating.

Its difficult style aside, Lehmann's work represents and so stimulates the necessary exercise of discernment which must always venture to judge the 'significance of the factual'. For Lehmann himself this involved setting forth the contours of the context of God's humanizing activity as a way to sharpen sight and so to see to it that truth unmasks power. Ethical insight and moral will are fostered less by detailing with the logical outworkings of moral calculus than by relentlessly calling

---

[1]    Paul Lehmann, *Ethics in a Christian Context* (New York: Harper & Row, 1963), pp. 23–4.

[2]    Robert Frost, 'Choose Something Like a Star', *The Poetry of Robert Frost: The Collected Poems, Complete and Unabridged*, ed. Edward Connery Latham (New York: Henry Holt and Co., 1979), p. 403.

to mind the determinative theological context within which any given situation arises. This reflective work, Lehmann wagered, served God's own providential and eschatological endeavours to hold open a space for human life to become, and be kept, human.

Fleming Rutledge wrote 'The day after Paul Lehmann's death, I found him in the newspaper. I don't mean the obituary, for I did not find him dead; I found him living. I found him in the news, where the human story is being told in all its terror and wonder every day'. She had come across the story of shootings in a diner in the South Bronx and of the aftermath for the survivors of the community of relatives and co-workers, including many Mexican immigrants.

> Nancy Burgos, the sister of one of the victims, said, 'We want justice, not just for ourselves but for other families who had this in their lives. I see myself as just one person in a million really. I am just a human being.' Do we not immediately recognize here the voice of one whose concerns lay at the heart of the lifelong work of Paul Lehmann, who sought with every ounce of his strength until the day he died to discover the ways in which God was at work in the midst of the carnage of this world to make and keep human life human? who was ever proclaiming the activity of God on behalf of the disenfranchised and disposed of the earth? whose revolutionary theology, even as it ranged across the whole globe of conflict and struggle, always held the individual victim in view, the one in a million? whose passion for justice was not to be played out solely on ideological battlefields but always was to have a human shape, 'a local habitation and a name'?[3] Surely, he has taught us all to read the stories in the newspaper with transfigured understanding, in the light of the shaping and saving power of the biblical story.[4]

This is a rare gift indeed – to articulate an ethic that subordinates neither the individual nor the community to the other, but instead seeks 'the good of all in the good of each' in the midst of everyday life, family dinners, shootings, elections, and all. But, for any ethic that would be of the gospel, the 'good of all in the good of each' can and must only be sought as something already commanded, accomplished and given by God, not as an ideal to be autonomously pursued.

Of course, understanding Paul Lehmann and his work entails appreciating the whole compass of his endeavours. To separate the pastor from the professor or the confessing Christian from the cultural critic would miss the mark. This is because faith that animates the whole of his theological and ethical writing is faith in a *present and living God*:

---

[3]    Rutledge is quoting William Shakespeare, *A Midsummer Night's Dream*, 5.1.17.

[4]    Fleming Rutledge, 'A Tribute to Paul Louis Lehmann', *The Princeton Seminary Bulletin*, 15:2 (1994): 165–6.

As every student of Professor Lehmann will readily recall, all his classes that began as lectures ended as sermons … His poetic fire would start to kindle. He would begin moving away from the lectern. He would begin prowling up and down the aisle, index fingers stabbing the air, eyes blazing and searching the audience of listeners like Jeremiah searching the streets of Jerusalem for 'one that executeth judgment, that seeketh the truth' (Jer. 5:1); if that searchlight caught your own gaze, you were hooked. 'What is truth?' Truth was never a what, but always a Who.[5]

Akin to his friend Dietrich Bonhoeffer's emphasis that knowledge of Christ comes only in encounter with the self-presentation of the person of Christ, Lehmann's work directs theological ethics to take account of the formative presence and identity of One who lives and is at work, here and now. And this One is particular, and devoted to a particular work: 'He unrolled the scroll and found the place where it was written: "The Spirit of the Lord is upon me, because he has anointed me to bring good news to the poor. He has sent me to proclaim release to the captives and recovery of sight to the blind, to let the oppressed go free, to proclaim the year of the Lord's favour"' (Lk. 4:17–19). As Rutledge observes, 'This was the message that seized Paul Lehmann; this was the Lord who had pressed him into service'.[6]

Thanks to students of Lehmann – Nancy Duff, Christopher Morse, Fleming Rutledge and David Demson among them – subsequent generations have been challenged to think and to speak theologically in ways that are beneficially exposed to the 'power of particularity' which Lehmann extols. This volume of essays aims to extend this same challenge more widely yet into the running conversation that is Christian theology and ethics. Following Fleming Rutledge's evocative portrait of Paul Lehmann 'the man and the teacher', the remaining essays are organized and presented in three parts. In Part I, Christopher Morse, Nancy Duff and Barry Harvey trace out the main lines of Lehmann's thought by exposition of his central texts. In Part II, Philip Ziegler, David Demson and James Cubie draw key aspects of Lehmann's thought into conversation with the work of Karl Barth, T.F. Torrance and Paul Ramsey respectively, the last named being a rather provocative and storied critic of Lehmann during his life. The essays by Sally Brown, Eunjoo Kim and Michelle Bartel in Part III then press into the implications and application of Lehmann's work in view of the challenges of contemporary Christian life, formation and proclamation. All the most prevalent themes in Lehmann's *oeuvre* are at issue in the essays collected here: messianic politics, conscience, apperception, the givenness of the reality of the gospel and its formative power upon all human life, the role of the church community in ethical life, and perhaps most consistently *discernment* – these motifs, and many others besides are discussed in relation to the range of particular questions tackled by our authors. It is our hope that by exploring such themes in relation to our

---

[5]    Ibid., p. 168.
[6]    Ibid.

contemporary social, political and ecclesial contexts and in close conversation with the legacy of Lehmann's own work in theological ethics, this volume might contribute usefully to ongoing debates in Christian theology, morals, homiletics and practical theology.

We are very grateful for the support of many whose work does not appear in these pages, including James Kay and Gerhard Sauter. In addition, thanks go to Kent Eilers who assisted with copy editing and to Douglas Denné, Archivist and Curator of Rare Books at Hanover College, who helped compile the bibliographies and index which conclude this volume.

Philip G. Ziegler and Michelle J. Bartel
Ordinary Time, 2008

# Chapter 1
# Introduction: Paul Lehmann –
# The Man and the Teacher

Fleming Rutledge

Paul Lehmann inspired an unusual amount of devotion in many of his students, but even the most devoted of these would have to admit that not everyone 'got' him, not by a long way. Since his conversation, sermons and lectures were laced with untranslated German, Hebrew and Greek, quotations without attribution from Scripture as well as from Shakespeare, W.H. Auden, Samuel Beckett, e.e. cummings and so forth, his listeners were frequently bewildered. Then, too, there was the love of paradox and wordplay, the complicated – some would say tortured – syntax, and the daring leaps of imagination, all of which contributed to the frequent feeling that one simply could not follow him. One of his most adoring graduate students, later a distinguished teacher, heard someone quoting Lehmann and said, 'It sounds just like him – but does it mean anything?' That student was, of course, speaking affectionately for many of us who felt that if we really tried, we could understand perhaps one-third of what he said. We made the effort, because we were pretty sure that he did indeed 'mean something' of ultimate importance and that we were blessed if we could grasp even that one-third.

The most immediately noticeable feature of Lehmann's teaching was the compelling power of his unique voice and presence, which conveyed passion and elicited fascination even though he so often could not be fully understood. Many of us thought that once he had been, in his own habitual expression, 'gathered to my fathers', no one would read him any more, so inseparable was his personality from his communication. It is a singular gift of the Holy Spirit that Philip Ziegler, who never met Paul Lehmann *kata sarka*, has been able to appropriate his meaning and message to a degree equal to the very top rank of the students and colleagues who knew him when he was alive. Better still, Ziegler's relative youth equips him to carry Lehmann's work forward into a new generation – a consequence which would have delighted its author more than anything.

For Paul Lehmann truly cared about students. He was the only one of the Union Seminary faculty in the seventies who invited all of his seminar students to gather after class every week in his grand apartment in Knox Hall, which was spectacularly furnished with a Viennese chandelier, Steinway piano, and Biedermeier sofa. He called these occasions 'sherry and conversation'. Much as he enjoyed ardent spirits – one-hundred-proof *Wild Turkey* being a particular favourite – as well as the pleasures of the table, it was the conversation that was of supreme importance to him. Unlike many professors who have achieved a certain stature, he did not 'hold forth'. It was the exchange that he cared about. He was one of the most *engagé* people imaginable. I never once saw him act dismissively or indifferently toward anyone, either in class or at social occasions. If he was making a point, he would draw a student in by using the student's name, weaving it into his comments, inviting a response. In settings such as these where he felt at ease, he was never threatened by or hostile to any opposing view, but curious about it and eagerly seeking to discuss its merits.

He was utterly consistent in his efforts to encourage students even if he had to use his rapier. I still have a copy of a paper I wrote for Dr Lehmann in an advanced course on Bonhoeffer that I took at Union in 1973. I keep it, not for the content of the quite dreadful paper itself, but for the comments that Lehmann wrote in the margins and on the last page. I was a first-year Master of Divinity student taking an advanced course, had no idea what I was doing, and really did not belong in the class. I cherish the comments, because Lehmann was able to combine quite serious, sharp, and specific criticism with warm encouragement and appreciation. Not only was I not crushed, I was determined to do better.

Lehmann paid virtually everyone the high compliment of talking to them as though they were on the same intellectual level as he. Many people have testified to this: I remember especially the wife of one of his colleagues who spoke feelingly of the way he always paid attention to her with the same keen interest and respect as if she had been a fellow scholar. I often wondered how a man who was so exceptionally gregarious and other-directed could at the same time muster the discipline for scholarly work. His care for people extended to the very 'least of these'. When he left Union, he went around the seminary to say goodbye to all the support staff, from the lowliest assistant in the library to the labourers in the boiler room. Reflecting at the time of Lehmann's death, James F. Kay testified to what many of us had seen: 'He was extraordinarily kindly. One Sunday I accompanied him to church on Madison Avenue, and afterward he told me to wait a moment. He walked half a block to a man without legs in a wheelchair. He gave the man some bills, then lingered and had a genuine conversation. There always had to be a conversation.' This recognition of the humanity of every person linked his theology to his way of life; at the most fundamental level, Lehmann lived what he believed. He worked not only at a political level – for instance as chairman of the American Committee for the Protection of the Foreign Born – but also at the direct human level.

The irony regarding this generosity of Lehmann's lies in the effect that he had on many of his colleagues and some of his students who took great offence at him. There were many reasons for this. To begin with, he came to Union in New York trailing controversy behind him because of his close association with the person and theology of Karl Barth. Union at mid-century represented the high noon of classic liberal American Protestantism, a milieu very much at odds with Barth's – and Lehmann's – radical theology and polemical style. Lehmann's arrival on the faculty in 1963 was therefore an event. The great strength at the seminary in that era was in Biblical scholarship; there had been no powerful systematic theologian for some time. Barth, *in absentia*, loomed over the scene – he had once called Union that place with 'the false Gothic architecture' – and as has always been the case on the American scene, provoked a hostility which as often as not was based in a lack of comprehension.

Lehmann came representing the Reformation that Dietrich Bonhoeffer famously said had never come to America.[1] Some at Union recognized in Paul Lehmann the genuine *theo*logian they had been looking for, and those few who had been drawn to Barth's work rejoiced. Many others were suspicious or hostile. Lehmann enjoyed a battle, however, and waded in with gusto. Often he did not mean his polemics personally, for he was genuinely sociable and did not expect intellectual disputation to deteriorate into attacks on individuals. At other times, it is true, he would indulge in personal animosity; he had a tendency to construct conspiracy theories, and he did not always exercise good judgement. His great passion was for 'the freedom we have in Christ Jesus', and his intemperance at times resembled that of the author of the Epistle to the congregation in Galatia where that very freedom was at stake.

J. Louis Martyn said that he and Lehmann 'recognised one another as comrades in the trenches'. Union in the late 1960s and early 1970s was experiencing upheavals of various sorts, particularly an extended dispute about the shape of the curriculum. It was ironic in the extreme that Lehmann, one of the most revolutionary of all Christian thinkers of his generation, was branded by some as 'conservative'. It must be confessed that Lehmann's combative style did not always help in these disputes. His lightning-quick use of similes and metaphors, often drawn from Scripture, came as naturally to him as do profane epithets to many people today. When a faculty committee reached a decision on an urgent matter, Lehmann said, 'The Philistines have won', and walked out of the room. When a colleague who was enamored of 1960s Esalen-style revisionism had his students lie on the floor for his classes, Lehmann denounced it as 'Ba'alism'. The James Chapel, where such luminaries as Reinhold Niebuhr, Tillich and Muilenberg had preached, became the locus for various experimental liturgies, and Lehmann began to refer to it as 'the Ichabod chapel' – i.e., a place from which 'the glory has departed'.

Needless to say, these sorts of remarks did not endear him to some of the faculty. Lehmann was much more intelligent and far more deeply learned than some of his colleagues, quicker and sharper in debate. This exacerbated the tensions. Some of the most distinguished members of the faculty recognized Lehmann's essential integrity and intellectual stature, and a few were willing to fight. Lehmann's favourite term for these theological allies was 'comrades'. He was very much like his namesake the Apostle in this regard. If the gospel was at stake, then there could be no compromise. Some of the more irenically-minded

---

[1]    Dietrich Bonhoeffer, 'Protestantism Without Reformation' in *No Rusty Swords*, E. Robertson and J. Bowden, eds and trans. (London: Collins, 1965), p. 92ff.

among the traditional faculty were discomfited by his polemical style if not his content, whereas others recognized *the content itself* as radically threatening to all projects centred on human potential.

Here lay the real issue. The theology of Karl Barth, with which Lehmann was essentially in tune – although often arguing with it and seeking to expand it – represented a challenge of the most fundamental sort to the presuppositions of liberal Protestantism. Barth's – and Lehmann's – Pauline-Augustinian emphasis on divine agency in creation and redemption was deemed by American liberals to be ethically defective, encouraging passivity and undermining human responsibility. One of Lehmann's chief purposes was to refute this charge in the most vigorous terms. *The Transfiguration of Politics* was finished and published during these years, and although now dated in certain ways, it is still distinguished by its advocacy of political activism from within a theological and biblical context.

Looking back, it is hard to understand how a man who was dedicated body and soul to the cause of justice for the oppressed and defenseless could ever have been construed as a reactionary. Certainly it was not because he did not work overtime to appreciate the contributions of his colleagues. He went out of his way, in his written work, to quote whatever he could find to approve in the work of others with whom he essentially disagreed. A particular example of this is the section on 'Feminist Repudiation of Patriarchal Co-optation' in *The Decalogue and a Human Future*.[2] In this remarkable discussion he shows that he has read various feminist critiques with the utmost seriousness, seeking to understand what was being said and how it might be instructive. His interpretations of Scripture in the light of the 'new occasions' that bring 'new duties' (in the words of the poem by James Russell Lowell) were often dazzling in their advanced thinking.[3]

If Lehmann had lived another twenty years he would have been at home with the resurgence of premodern readings of Scripture. The poetic imagination and fire that he brought to biblical interpretation is not unlike that of Chrysostom and other Church Fathers, which has risen dramatically in critical esteem in these days of waning respect for purely scientific exegesis. A memorable example of Lehmann's humour arose out of these academic currents. A lot of his twinkling wit sailed over the heads of less learned conversation partners because of its allusiveness, but it was one of his most attractive qualities and was almost never mean. During the late 1970s, a collection of faculty from the biblical and theological fields met together monthly at Union with their graduate students to discuss the Pauline Epistles. The purpose of this gathering, informally called 'the Paul group', was to encourage cross-fertilization between the two disciplines. Lehmann was among comrades in this group and so he was entirely at ease; however, he sometimes confessed himself baffled and frustrated by the scientific strictures of the biblical scholars.

[2]    Paul Lehmann, *The Decalogue and a Human Future* (Grand Rapids: Eerdmans, 1995), pp. 111–44.

[3]    James Russell Lowell, 'The Present Crisis' (1844), in *The Poems of James Russell Lowell* (Whitefish, MT: Kessinger Publishing, 2004), pp. 199–203.

When a section of *The Transfiguration of Politics* was under discussion,[4] he wrote a very funny memo to the members in which he presented himself as 'an untutored and faltering exegetical seeker' who needed to be rescued by the 'illuminati' of the Society of Biblical Literature:

> Having learned from the Society a 'new thing', e.g. that there is a 'Baur (Historicus) principle' (or is it 'Bauer' [Agricolus]?) of exegetical hermeneutics or hermeneutical exegesis (or both), does the exegetical hermeneutical effort set down in Section 5A apply or violate or ignore the 'Baur principle'?

He goes on in this vein:

> Will the *doctores Scripturae ecclesiae* among you please suggest (a) a succinct distinction between *exegesis* and *hermeneutics*; and (b) in how far the exegetical? hermeneutical? or exegetical-hermeneutical undertaking of Section 5A may or may not be allowed? *In* exegetical? hermeneutical? *extremis*, in how far could the discussion of Romans 13:1–10 be warranted by John 14:15–26?

There is some energetic ribbing going on here, but at the same time Lehmann really did seek to understand what others were saying to him, and his earnest inquiring gave much pleasure to those who appreciated his style. Again, it was the *exchange* that meant the most to him and he was always willing to throw all of his considerable energies into it. His humour was fuelled by his dynamism. Lehmann did not hesitate to invoke 'the faith once delivered to the saints' as a criterion by which contemporary theologians – and exegetes! – should be measured, but he would always insist that this faith was 'dynamics on deposit'. This paradoxical combination of *deposit*, suggesting something given, firm, and fixed, contrasted with *dynamics*, connoting something living, active and explosive, was vintage Lehmann.

It would be impossible to overstate the care that Paul Lehmann gave to everything that came his way. He lavished attention on people he cared about, high and low. He remembered children's names, sent greetings to spouses, and inquired anxiously about those who were troubled. Over the years he must have written hundreds of letters of congratulation or sympathy as the occasion demanded, always pouring the full measure of himself into the composition. I treasure one that he wrote to me when I was ordained on June 10, 1975 – five long, heartfelt, handwritten paragraphs concluding with verses from Scripture and a benediction. I cannot resist quoting the first sentence of this letter, which combines so many characteristic Lehmannian touches:

---

[4]    Paul Lehmann, *The Transfiguration of Politics* (New York: Harper & Row, 1975), section 5A, 'Exposing the Disestablishment of the Establishment: Submission – Romans 13:1–10', pp. 35–47.

> It is surely a wondrous incongruity that finds your ordination to the holy ministry of Our Lord in His church being celebrated on the Feast of St. Basil, noted among those liturgically innocent and/or otherwise in pursuit of foreign gods as Flag Day.

This could not have been written by anyone other than Paul Lehmann. The elaborate syntax; the identification of an 'incongruity'; the use of the word 'wondrous' to denote the divine activity; the humour found in the aforesaid incongruity; the utterly serious identification of ministry as 'holy'; the use of 'Our Lord' as a shared personal confession; the capital 'H' to honour Christ and to show that the church is His; the love of proper liturgy; the skewering of national idolatry; the almost imperceptible allusion to Scripture; the punch line held back to the very end – here in one sentence is a rich combination of many of Paul Lehmann's unique qualities. He was endlessly generous with himself in this way.

The great tragedy of Paul and Marion Lehmann's lives was the loss of their only child, born to them in almost Abrahamic fashion relatively late in their marriage. This calamity was borne by him in all the ensuing years with a grace and courage that awed everyone. The fact that the intensity of his suffering was never concealed made the strength of Paul Lehmann's faith all the more striking. He continued for the rest of his life to bear witness to the promise of the Resurrection. When the daughter of a student was stricken with a potentially fatal illness, he sent a lavishly beautiful copy of Dante's *Paradiso*, inscribed by him as 'this surpassing account of our greatest hope'. Such was his faith; such was his care for those foster children that the Lord had given to him by adoption and grace.

When Wilhelm Pauck died, Lehmann wrote 'In Memory of Wilhelm Pauck: Colleague and Friend' to be delivered at Union. The two of them had very different temperaments, but Lehmann's tribute is wholehearted and generous in the highest degree. He put his usual painstaking effort into what he wrote, evoking his colleague's unusual career and his many unique gifts. The tribute is all about Pauck and not at all about Lehmann, but there is one passage in particular that speaks volumes about Lehmann's gratitude for their relationship in Christ that transcended any grievances:

> It belongs to the mystery of selfhood that who Wilhelm was as a colleague should be congruent with Wilhelm as a friend. Our friendship spanned half a century. And as I think of him today, in recollection and remembrance, I think especially of…the experience of his unmistakable being with one, even when one knew that he wished with all his heart that in this, that, or the other respect, one had been or had done otherwise.

The humility implicit in this insight might surprise those who did not know how very much Paul Lehmann wanted to maintain collegial relationships with everyone in his purview. If he often did not succeed in this, it was not because he did not wish it differently. His recognition of Pauck's steadfastness discloses a heart always longing for loyal friendship and a readiness to extend that same friendship to others.

In the end, Paul Lehmann was *simul peccator et iustus*, a man who knew himself to be justified in Christ, a humble servant of the *ministerium Verbi divini*. Once, at a very long ordination service where scores of clergy of all denominations were seated together, Lehmann was observed in prayer while most of the clergy were chatting, fidgeting, and looking around. In fact, one observer said later in awe, the only one who remained in prayer the whole time was Paul Lehmann. This silent but powerful witness took place not long after the acute agony of Peter Lehmann's death. The bereaved father never flagged in his devotion to the Lord of promise. Throughout the subsequent years until at last he entered into the life of the eternal Age, Paul Lehmann continued to embody and show forth the apostolic vocation of his great namesake:

> We have this treasure in earthen vessels, to show that the transcendent power belongs to God and not to us. We are afflicted in every way, but not crushed; perplexed, but not driven to despair; persecuted, but not forsaken; struck down, but not destroyed; always carrying in the body the death of Jesus, so that the life of Jesus may also be manifested in our bodies. For while we [apostles] live we are always being given up to death for Jesus' sake, so that the life of Jesus may be manifested in our mortal flesh. So death is at work in us, but life in you. (2 Cor 4:8–12)

# PART I

# Chapter 2
# Paul Lehmann as Nurturer of Theological Discernment

Christopher Morse

Among Christian theological ethicists of the twentieth century Paul Lehmann remains unsurpassed for having put the news back into the Good News of Gospel proclamation. This is no small achievement as the agitation aroused by such an effort at reading the signs of the times attests. Opposing equally the repristination of tradition and the amnesia of modernity with respect to tradition's present day innovative import, Lehmann's thought has been criticized by conservatives as being too radical, and by radicals as being too conservative. Even the so-called neo-orthodox, or Barthians, with whom he is usually if sometimes superficially classified, have been suspicious of his politicizing emphasis, while the Liberationists more sympathetic to his leftist politics have tended to discount Lehmann's revolutionary claims as being too dependent upon divine agency. Yet, most assuredly, middle of the road he is not. Rather, one is reminded of the Psalmist's recognition that the *hesed* which alone is said to endure as righteous and steadfast forever is, precisely as such, new every morning and faithfully confessed only by 'singing unto the Lord a new song'. It is in this respect that Paul Lehmann may most aptly be characterized as a nurturer of theological discernment. And like his Reformation forebears, Lehmann's nurturing in this instance is to be understood as provocative rather than placative.

## Exposition

Already in 1940 in the first of his four books, *Forgiveness: Decisive Issue In Protestant Thought*, Lehmann stated the *leitmotiv* that would continue to be developed in all his subsequent writings.

> Theologically speaking, the battle now going on in Nationalist Socialist Germany for the life or death of Protestant Christianity is an acute witness to the fact that anthropology and theology are critically integrated. Actually, the affairs of God and the affairs of man are intimately intertwined. And when, in

the present instance, the things of God are threatened by the things of man, eminent importance must be ascribed to a theological anthropology.[1]

Two notes that will become characteristic of Lehmann's thought are sounded here: the emphasis upon what is 'now going on' in 'the present instance', and how the intertwining of God's affairs and human affairs in current events calls for a critically reworked theological anthropology that is different from both the anthropological theology of Enlightenment liberalism and the legitimist orthodox supernaturalism that the Enlightenment rightly challenged.

The argument of this first book contrasts Albrecht Ritschl's theology of forgiveness as representative of Protestant Liberalism with Karl Barth's emerging dialectical theology. While Ritschl is criticized for an over emphasis upon an anthropological standpoint in interpreting the affairs of God, Lehmann questions whether Barth's anti-anthropological polemic in reaction does not risk severing theology in the present crisis from human affairs. Since God's decisive work of forgiveness is the grace of a new creation, neither the newness of this redemption nor the creatureliness of its occurrence can be minimized. 'Clearly, what has happened to Barth is the opposite of what has happened to Ritschl. He has allowed the implications of his doctrine of redemption to imperil the reality of the doctrine of creation, whereas Ritschl has allowed the implications of the doctrine of creation to imperil the reality of the doctrine of redemption.'[2] If the Enlightenment turn to an anthropological theology, reflected in Ritschl, is rightly to be faulted for circumscribing the activity of God in terms of human activity, Barth's emphasis in contrast, Lehmann cautions, intimates a gulf between God and the world that renders God's forgiving grace 'ultimately thinkable only in terms of the supernaturalistic spiritism which destroys the existence and activity of man and the world as a consequence of the existence and activity of God'.[3] Lehmann expresses some encouragement, however, in the fact that Barth appears aware of this problem by more recently publishing tracts for the times under the heading *Theological Existence Today* instead of the earlier title of the theological journal *Between The Times* which was 'in grave danger of becoming a theology above the times'.[4]

In his second and best known work, *Ethics In A Christian Context*, published over twenty years later in 1963, Lehmann expands the reference to anthropology

---

[1]   Paul Lehmann, *Forgiveness: Decisive Issue In Protestant Thought* (New York: Harper & Brothers, 1940), p. 177.

[2]   Ibid., pp. 192–3.

[3]   Ibid., p. 194. Lehmann's critique is based upon his assessment of Barth's writings prior to 1940. Barth's lengthy account of creation doctrine in the *Church Dogmatics* III/1–4, did not appear in German publication until 1945–51. It is worth noting the irony that the 'supernaturalistic spiritism' Lehmann here cautions against in the early Barth sounds not unlike the charge of 'pneumatic exegesis' that will later be levelled against Lehmann himself by some of his critics.

[4]   Ibid., p. 178.

to take more account of its social and political aspects. Now a reading of the signs of the times is said to involve recognition not only of the grace of forgiveness but also of God's political activity. 'The complexity of the actual human situation ... is always compounded of an intricate network of circumstance and human interrelationships bracketed by the dynamics of God's political activity on the one hand and God's forgiveness on the other.'[5] The focus of the theological anthropology here turns from justification to sanctification (Lehmann's preferred term is humanization), a move continuing on from what the Reformers called imputed righteousness to its behavioural consequences. By politics Lehmann explains that he means the communal shaping of the *polis*, or civil society, as defined by Aristotle in his *Nicomachean Ethics* but as described and given content by biblical imagery of 'what God is doing in the world to make and keep human life human'.[6] Lehmann's reascribing of human moral agency by reference to what God is doing in the world, rather than by reference to human virtues as in Aristotle and the philosophical ethics conditioned by him, spells out in much more detail the contrast he is intent to draw between an anthropological theology and the new possibilities of a more biblically discerning theological anthropology that reverses the priority from deriving 'its theological moorings from anthropology'.[7]

Looked at biblically, Lehmann argues, Christian ethical discernment arises from within a community shaped by a particular awareness of what is going on in the current situation. This community, or *koinonia* as denoted in Greek, provides a context for ethical judgements that are not compliant either with a morality prescribed by abstract rules and principles or with an amoral indifference to what is happening. In biblical imagery the present situation is depicted as dynamic and not static. More than human agency is actively involved. The coming of the Lord is viewed as timely and not timeless, formative of human affairs more so than normative. The taking place of a redeemed creation is proclaimed parabolically as in our midst, but not in ways that are commensurate with our antecedent calculations.[8] Lehmann thus prefaces his *Ethics* by writing that 'the main concern throughout these pages is with the concrete ethical reality of a transformed human being and a transformed humanity owing to the specific action of God in Jesus Christ, an action and transformation of which the reality of the Christian *koinonia* is a foretaste ...'.[9]

The *koinonia* ethics profiled and contrasted in this second volume with its philosophical alternatives proposes the replacement of moral principles and directives with considerations of context and parables as the environment for

---

[5]  Paul L. Lehmann, *Ethics In A Christian Context* (New York: Harper & Row, 1963), reprinted (Louisville/London: Westminster John Knox Press, 2006), p. 141.

[6]  Ibid., p. 85. This signature expression of Lehmann's occurs repeatedly throughout the *Ethics*.

[7]  Ibid., p. 120.

[8]  Ibid., p. 87.

[9]  Ibid., p. 17.

responsive (and in this sense, responsible) decision making regarding good and evil that Lehmann characterizes as conscience.[10] Life in such an environment, here designated as 'the fellowship-creating reality of Christ's presence in the world',[11] involves 'imaginative and behavioral sensitivity to what God is doing in the world'[12] that is 'bereft of every prudential calculation'.[13] The unpredictable 'signs of redemption', Lehmann writes, are 'not less real because open only to eyes of faith', and 'not less significant for human apprehension and behavior because they are indicative rather than verifiable', but are as signs indications that what God is doing 'does make a discernible difference in the world'.[14] Hence, 'the theonomous conscience is the conscience immediately sensitive to the freedom of God to do in the always changing human situation what his humanizing aims and purposes require'.[15] Lest readers mistake the reference to 'eyes of faith' to imply a restriction of such ethical sensitivity to institutional Christians, Lehmann takes pains to argue in keeping with Calvin's doctrine of the 'general power of the Spirit' that the unrestricted work of the Holy Spirit does not exclude unbelievers from sharing in 'a common level of imaginative discernment about what the secret of maturity is' – '"I have other sheep, that are not of this fold; I must bring them also, and they will heed my voice. So there shall be one flock, one shepherd." A *koinonia* ethic may thus conceivably dispose of the problem of a double standard by including the unbelievers among the other sheep of the Holy Spirit of God.'[16]

By the time of the publication of his third book, *The Transfiguration Of Politics*, in 1975 the social upheavals of the previous decade had given rise to a revolutionary rhetoric to which Lehmann now directs his attention.[17] This book, we are told, had its origins in an invitation for a series of lectures at Harvard received in 1968, a year of crisis in the United States marked by campus uprisings, anti-war protests, urban race riots, and assassination. What he had initially called 'the intimately intertwined' character of divine and human affairs in his first book, *Forgiveness*, in 1940, and then developed in the *Ethics* of 1963 as 'the dynamics of God's political activity' as known in the context of the *koinonia* as 'the fellowship-creating reality of Christ's presence in the world', Lehmann addresses in *Transfiguration* with more specific regard to current events as signs of 'the coinherence of biblical and revolutionary politics'.[18] The project of a theological anthropology is here directed toward the question, as Lehmann poses it, of what the presence and power of Jesus of Nazareth in and over human affairs has to do with revolutionary times. Once

---

10   Ibid., pp. 347–50.
11   Ibid., p. 59.
12   Ibid., p. 117.
13   Ibid., p. 123.
14   Ibid., p. 112.
15   Ibid., p. 358.
16   Ibid., pp. 158–9, citing Jn 10:6.
17   Paul Lehmann, *The Transfiguration Of Politics* (New York: Harper & Row, 1975).
18   Ibid., p. 289.

again, a sectarian approach is rejected: 'The Gospel is no more for Christians *only* than only Christians are revolutionaries.'[19] Rather, Lehmann argues, 'the coinherence of biblical and revolutionary politics' points to a divine 'pressure of reality upon human affairs, making time and space make room for the freedom and fulfillment that being human takes'.[20] When in the course of human affairs this 'providential-eschatological pressure', as Lehmann characterizes it, erupts at the roots of a radically new humanizing reordering of social and political priorities, no less than a transfiguration may be said to occur of which revolutionary struggle is a sign.[21] Lehmann sums up his position as follows:

> the pertinence of Jesus Christ to the question of revolution is evident from the conjunction of revolution and humanization that generates a dynamics and direction in human affairs, requiring a liberating or 'saving' story. The Christian story records the presence and power of Jesus of Nazareth in and over human affairs, coordinates the human meaning of reality with a humanizing experience and perception of it, delivers revolutionary passion and prospects from a self-destroying fate, and transfigures revolution as the harbinger of a human future through a new beginning of a divinely appointed order of human freedom and fulfillment in this world and the next.[22]

This 'coinherence of biblical and revolutionary politics', as Lehmann refers to it, again is said to involve discernment. 'The power of biblical and theological symbolization ... awakens a redemptive sensitivity to the "signs and wonders and mighty works" (Acts 2:22) of human liberation and formation that are making room in the world for the righteousness of God in action.'[23] Two lines of argument are advanced in this third book to explain the thesis of a 'redemptive sensitivity'. One is exegetical/hermeneutical and provides a reading of the Transfiguration of Jesus pericope in Matthew 17:1–8. The other is social/political and consists of a typology of current revolutions drawn with detailed regard to their histories of colonialism, imperialism and racism. The Matthean pericope is interpreted as offering a political paradigm. The sociopolitical typology is presented as being biblically parabolic. Again the issue of discerning 'the word and will of God in, with, and under the discernment of the times in which we live', and vice versa, amounts here for Lehmann to a call for a theological anthropology in contrast to an anthropological theology. Like Barth, Lehmann both credits Feuerbach's critique of Christianity for seeing that in the Gospel's incarnational frame of reference all theology is indeed anthropology and at the same time notes Feuerbach's failure

---

[19]   Ibid., p. 69.
[20]   Ibid., p. 289.
[21]   Ibid., p. 237.
[22]   Ibid., p. 229.
[23]   Ibid., p. 108.

to recognize that the true *anthropos* of the Gospel message is not ourselves but *Christos*: 'All theology is anthropology as a reflex of Christology.'[24]

The Matthean pericope of Chapter 17 verses 1–8 which gives rise to the term 'transfiguration of politics' Lehmann quotes as follows:

> Six days later Jesus took Peter, James, and John the brother of James, and led them up a high mountain where they were alone; and in their presence he was transfigured; his face shone like the sun, and his clothes became white as the light. And they saw Moses and Elijah appear, conversing with him. Then Peter spoke: 'Lord,' he said, 'how good it is that we are here! If you wish it, I will make three shelters here, one for you, one for Moses, and one for Elijah.' While he was still speaking, a bright cloud suddenly overshadowed them, and a voice called from the cloud: 'This is my Son, my Beloved, on whom my favor rests; listen to him.' At the sound of the voice the disciples fell on their faces in terror. Jesus then came up to them, touched them, and said, 'Stand up; do not be afraid.' And when they raised their eyes they saw no one, but only Jesus.[25]

Lehmann's detailed interpretation, to which a brief synopsis cannot do justice, includes these primary claims. Most importantly, the textual context calls for an apocalyptic rather than a Hellenistic reading of the term 'transfigured' as here used by the Evangelists, one that denotes not simply a psychological change of mind on the part of Peter, James, and John but the imminence of a radically new state of affairs, the promised new world of ancient prophecy now happening 'in their presence'. The setting of this pericope within the sequence of the Gospel narratives marks the convergence between the disclosure of the Messianic identity and the mission of the chosen disciples to engage the sufferings of the present time in the power and presence of the breakthrough that is now taking place. This convergence is epitomized by the appearing on the mount of Moses and Elijah, bringing together the reality of God's law-giving as the making of covenant and the redemption of its eschatological fulfilment. That the voice from the cloud calls the disciples away from the attempt to shelter this convergence by building three booths upon the mountain-top and enables them to stand up, seeing only Jesus through their terror, and listening to him, marks the significant difference, so Lehmann concludes, between 'political messianism and messianic politics'. The revolutionary import of the Transfiguration accounts is that 'the battle with the Establishment is being neither circumvented nor concluded. Instead it is being joined'.[26]

In sum, the transfiguration of Jesus as reported in the Gospels may be taken as a paradigm of a reversed political realism, one in which political activity is transfigured

---

[24]    Ibid., pp. 230–32.

[25]    Ibid., pp. 79–80. Lehmann notes synoptic parallels in Mark 9:2–8, Luke 9:28–36, and a contextual similarity in John's Gospel, which contains no Transfiguration passage, 12:27–33.

[26]    Ibid., p. 91.

from a human initiative claiming divine sanction (political messianism) to a divine initiative claiming human emissaries (messianic politics). Or, in Lehmann's earlier formulation, in the Gospel story anthropological theology is paradigmatically transfigured into theological anthropology at work in current events.

Revolutions are to be seen as signs of this transfiguration now underway where the unconcluded battle for humanization is being waged against the legitimist forces of its circumvention, both within the Church and without, and between the ideological undoing of a political messianism ever threatening its own ranks and the liberating freedom of a messianic politics. The three 'current revolutions' that Lehmann examines in 1975 as 'signs of transfiguration' are, as he phrases them, 'a movement from Marx to Mao and Ho Chi Minh', 'a movement from Fidel and Che Guevara to Camilo Torres and Nestor Paz Zamora', and 'a movement from Frantz Fanon to Martin Luther King, Jr., Malcolm X, and the Black Panther Party'.[27] His treatment is extensive, taking up over a hundred and forty pages of text and documentation, all written at a time when the projected judgement of history upon these three social movements was being hotly contested. The news of the times is in each case considered in relation to the time 'at hand' in the Good News of the Gospel, leading to the conclusion that 'in the world of time and space and things' what is at stake in revolutionary impulses and occurrences 'may be discerned in certain liberating accents that signal the inbreaking in the established order of things of a new order of human affairs and ultimately the transfiguration of revolution itself'.[28]

Lehmann's fourth and final book, *The Decalogue And A Human Future: The Meaning Of The Commandments For Making and Keeping Human Life Human*, was substantially completed just before his death in 1994 and published posthumously in 1995.[29] We have Nancy J. Duff to thank for seeing this text through from initial drafts to its publication and for writing its introduction. Once again a major theme is theological discernment which, as Duff helpfully notes, is here addressed by Lehmann's use of the term 'apperception'.[30] 'Apperception is the experience of retrospective and prospective immediacy,' Lehmann writes, ' – whatever may be its biological and psychological vectors – which shapes and is shaped by the dynamics of human responsiveness to God, world, and society.' At the base of all our feeling, willing, thinking, and judgement there is 'a matrix of humane sensibility that is always there and at hand beforehand'. While Lehmann cites Socrates and Kant for recognizing, in addition to Jesus, a 'soundness of the eye' (Matt. 6:22) or sense of rectitude that is prior to its empirical instances and enactments, his account of

---

[27]   Ibid., p. 109. See Ch. 9, 'A Typology Of Current Revolutions', pp. 103–226, with endnotes, pp. 318–37.

[28]   Ibid., p. 226.

[29]   Paul Lehmann, *The Decalogue And A Human Future – The Meaning Of The Commandments For Making and Keeping Human Life Human* (Grand Rapids: Eerdmans, 1995).

[30]   Ibid. See Duff, pp. 8–9 on 'Discernment Or Apperception'.

this apperceptive *a priori* contrasts sharply with the fundamental ontologies of natural theology that usually appeal to such apriority. Instead, Lehmann here calls for a rediscovery of 'the revolutionary impact' of 'Luther's epochal apperceptive discernment'. The contrast, once again, may be seen as yet a further elaboration of Lehmann's initial distinction between the approach of an anthropological theology and what he now calls 'the nurture of apperception' alternately provided by a theological anthropology.[31] Only in this instance the contrast previously emphasized in a *koinonia* ethics between prescriptive principles and descriptive parables of what God is doing in the world, and between political messianism and messianic politics in a moral or tropological reading of current revolutionary movements, is recast as a contrast between the *praxis* (the uniting of interpretation and behaviour) that is in keeping with a legalistic understanding of gospel and the *praxis* which is in keeping with a gospel understanding of law.

It is this latter gospel understanding of law, and not a legalistic understanding of gospel, which Lehmann finds exemplified in Luther's treatment of the Decalogue in the Large Catechism of 1529 as a work of 'epochal apperceptive discernment'. Lehmann's explication of Luther's insights proposes a sociological reading as an alternative both to the more usual law-abiding notions of 'keeping the commandments' as well as to what he calls 'more enlightened counsels of prudence and virtue'.[32] This alternative views the Decalogue setting forth a structure of responsiveness to what is at work in human interactions constituting the humane reality of our common life. 'Hence the Decalogue is at once parabolic and paradigmatic of what God is doing in the world to make room for the freedom and fulfillment that being human takes.'[33] This 'structural realism', as Lehmann refers to it, recognizes that freedom does not reside either in legitimating hierarchies of inequality or in difference denying egalitarianisms meant to counteract them, but in 'the humanizing relation between heterogeneity and inequality' marked by the 'reciprocal responsibility' which 'the relational sociology of Luther's exploration of the Decalogue' sets forth.[34] Such a structural realism, Lehmann argues, rescues the Commandments from political irrelevance by exhibiting the reciprocal relation between the apperception of freedom and the social structure of power in a nexus of responsibility that constitutes justice. 'Freedom, power, and justice are – as it

---

[31]    Ibid., pp. 23–5.

[32]    Ibid., p. 29.

[33]    Ibid., p. 31.

[34]    Ibid., p. 53. Before turning to the specific commandments and Luther's exploration, Lehmann makes his case for a sociological reading with special reference to the social theories of Peter Blau, *Inequality And Heterogeneity: A Primitive Theory Of Social Structure* (New York: Free Press, 1977), and Louis Dumont, *Homo Hierarchicus*, trans. M. Sainsbury (Chicago: University of Chicago Press, 1970), and *From Mandeville To Marx* (Chicago: University of Chicago Press, 1977).

were – underwritten by the Decalogue and bear witness to the indispensability of the Decalogue to the possibility and prospect of a human future.'[35]

Lehmann spells out the *praxis* congruent with this theoretical position more concretely in the case of the specific commandments. Just as the news of what he in 1975 called 'current revolutions' involving colonialism, imperialism, and racism was specifically addressed in reciprocal relation with the Good News of the Gospel account of the Transfiguration in his third volume, so here in the fourth volume it is the contemporary pertinence of the Decalogue to some of the most crucial issues facing the church and larger society in 1995 to which Lehmann turns his attention.

In short, the first three commandments in Luther's ordering of 'the right tablet of Moses', Lehmann writes, at once place the priority in the nurture of apperception regarding what it means to be human where it biblically belongs: not with any psychological predispositions or capacities first identifiable in us (anthropological theology) but with what it means, in Luther's words, 'to have a God' (theological anthropology). These three commandments, as addressed by Luther, Lehmann lists as, first, 'You shall have no other gods besides me'; second, 'You shall not go about with the name of God as though it made no difference'; and third, 'You shall make a day for celebration holy'.[36]

The first command identifies and names only the One who is wholly trustworthy as the subject for a wholly human trust. For the heart, in Luther's words, to 'cling' to less or any other is never to find human wholeness or satisfaction.

The second command leads to a consideration of what Luther, as Lehmann infers, sees as present day 'co-optations' of this identity and name of the wholly trustworthy One. Under the rubric of this second command Lehmann thus enters remarkably into critical alliance with feminist critiques of patriarchal and misogynistic co-optations represented by Phyllis Trible, Elisabeth Schüssler Fiorenza and Carol Christ by defending, neither the repristination of traditional Christian God-talk, nor a failure to discern such God-talk's innovative revolutionary import beyond the textual captivity of a univocal literalism 'impervious to metaphorical transfiguration'.[37]

The third commandment, as Luther rightly perceives by recognizing that the Sabbath was made for being human and not being human for the Sabbath (Mk. 2:27) with his striking translation – '*Du sollst den Feiertag heiligen!*' – brings the first two commandments to bear upon what Lehmann calls 'the responsibility for creation' in our common life. The trivialization of Sabbath observance as legalistically prescribed is hereby rejected along with the despoiling of its humane purposes. What is at stake, as discerned in Luther's 'structural realism', is instead the issue of 'the correlative limits that the nonhuman order of the world sets to its use for purposes of human freedom and fulfillment'. Thus, Lehmann concludes,

---

[35]   Ibid., pp. 66–7.
[36]   Ibid., p. 95.
[37]   Ibid., p. 139.

the command 'to make a day of celebration holy' relates Sabbath observance to such urgent matters affecting the common good as 'the ecological and energy crises of our day'. In doing so it thereby rejects any 'ideological reduction(s)' of the Gospel call to do no 'harm on the Sabbath' (Lk. 6:9) that disregard 'the responsibilities reciprocal to an order of freedom that joins God and humanity and nature in a humanizing concern of *authority* and *gratitude* and *trusteeship*' as it is environmentally structured and delineated in the first three commandments.[38]

This discerning of no other than the wholly trustworthy One as the *authority*, or author, of our freedom to respond with *gratitude* to all creation, not in possessive exploitation of the other, but in a *trusteeship* of the diversity of gifts and a heterogeneity that is biblically celebrated as creation's Sabbath good, leads directly in Lehmann's accounting to consideration of the fourth, fifth and sixth commandments of what Luther envisions as the tablet in Moses' left hand. 'You shall honour your father and mother' is explicated as recasting cultural notions of traditional family values in terms of reciprocal responsibilities rather than heteronomous obligations or patriarchal rights. 'You shall not kill' addresses the taking of life by the state and by individuals and asks how the fifth commandment applies today with respect to war and the disputed issue of abortion. 'You shall not commit adultery', heard as gospel in view of the One who authors reciprocal responsibility in humanizing freedom, extends the gratitude for, and trusteeship of, the nonadulterous good of creaturely otherness in differentiation and mutual fidelity beyond the legalistic norm of an exclusive and discriminatory heterosexuality. Lehmann's prescience here of sexual issues increasingly facing the churches and civil society, and his radically transfigured sense of what constitutes adulterous consequences, is again quite remarkable. 'Since Luther notes that this commandment is concerned specifically with the estate of marriage, I venture to suggest that his exposition of the commandment does not exclude a move from heterosexual to homosexual married life, as well as "others whom [God] has released by a high supernatural gift so that they can maintain chastity outside of marriage"', quoting words from the Large Catechism.[39]

With each of these commandments, when the news of the day is heard as coincident with the news of the Gospel proclamation of what is apocalypsed as 'at hand', and vice versa, Lehmann proposes ways in which today it becomes more than a platitude to conclude in a society marked by heterogeneity and inequality: 'I cannot pursue my own righteousness in disregard of my neighbor. As surely as the letter kills, the spirit gives life' (2 Cor. 3:6).[40]

This theme is illustrated as well in the final chapter of the fourth volume where Lehmann addresses, partly through papers previously published in other venues, commandments seven to ten under the rubrics of 'property, false witness, vocation, and belonging'. 'You shall not steal' provides the occasion for reflecting

---

[38]   Ibid., pp. 147–8.
[39]   Ibid., p. 173.
[40]   Ibid,, p. 171.

upon the current strengths and weaknesses of the Reformers' attitudes toward ownership and the rights and responsibilities attendant upon use and possession that go with belongings. 'You shall not bear false witness against your neighbour' recalls Luther's foremost concern for the public integrity of the civil courts in upholding justice for the accused and the deprived and comments in this light upon the celebrated trial and execution of Julius and Ethel Rosenberg in 1953 and 'the almost genocidal inhumanity that characterizes the treatment of the Haitian refugees by past and now present government officials of the U.S. through its Departments of Justice and State'.[41] As the ninth and tenth commandments in Luther's ordering concern covetousness – 'You shall not covet your neighbor's house' and 'You shall not covet his wife, man-servant, maid-servant, cattle, and anything that is his' – Lehmann takes up the issue of vocation in a commodity-oriented society where 'Willie Loman lives out the whole of his adult life always being somebody else',[42] and where 'for the inheritors of the sexual revolution' the transfigured sense of sexual meaning and spousal belonging occurs in the gospel freedom to venture reciprocity in commitment beyond the isolation of both dehumanizing repression and promiscuity.[43]

'For Luther', Lehmann concludes, what is at stake is nothing less than that 'the Decalogue is, in fact and in sum, an apperceptive description of what the gospel – and indeed, the Bible – affirms about life in this world and about what a realistic assessment of life in this world involves'.[44] As such it provides us not

---

[41]    Ibid., p. 204. It is important to note here that Lehmann not only wrote and spoke about such matters, he also otherwise acted. As a founding member of the Emergency Civil Liberties Union, organized during a time of rampant McCarthyism when the established American Civil Liberties Union refused to defend those accused by the McCarthy hearings, he sat, as he once told us, through many an all night meeting to prevent Communists from seizing control of the organization and its justice agenda. He never forgot that during this trying period it was the theological conservative John Mackay of Princeton who supported his civil justice efforts while more liberal colleagues such as Reinhold Niebuhr and others strongly cautioned against his risky involvement. The *Decalogue* volume is dedicated to Mackay. Also, Lehmann remained active in Haitian immigrant affairs through his participation in the Committee on the Foreign Born. One could point to such other social events reflective of his theories as his going to meet with student groups in Brazil during a time there of great civil unrest, his participation in the Columbia University campus uprising of 1968 in which he wore a 'Strike Now' button to the consternation of academic administrators, and the delight reported by former students when they happened upon him in his retirement marching in a Civil Rights demonstration in Nashville. Temperament is a factor in all *praxis*, of course, and Lehmann's stances and interactions while inspiring to many were also not without their painful estrangements. If there was still such a thing in the last half of the twentieth century as high Protestant culture Lehmann embodied it, but precisely because of this his concerns were never sectarian.

[42]    Ibid., p. 210, with reference to Arthur Miller's play *Death of a Salesman.*

[43]    Ibid., p. 224.

[44]    Ibid., p. 225.

with a prescribed legalism to be kept but 'with the limits that point us toward the freedom for a human future coming our way'.[45]

## Assessment

*'The limits that point us toward the freedom for a human future coming our way'* – these final words from Lehmann's last book reiterate the consistent focus upon 'what a realistic assessment of life in this world involves' that he variously elaborated throughout his four major works and provide us with a gauge for assessing his own account of theological discernment. The construal of what he has called 'biblical imagery', 'saving story', and 'commands' of the Decalogue as descriptive and not prescriptive 'limits that point toward freedom' involves consideration of the role of *parable* in gospel renderings of what is now at hand and raises the question of current parabolic significance. The construal of freedom as a dynamic inbreaking in human affairs of a righteousness not stipulated as normative but rather 'apocalypsed' (Rom. 1:17) and taking place as a formative 'future coming our way' involves consideration of biblical *apocalyptic* and raises the question of current apocalyptic significance. At stake is the central issue for any theological ethics, the relation of divine and human agency. Whatever critical evaluation is made of Lehmann's claims for a theological anthropology and ethics, and in whatever sense they are finally judged either to make sense or not make sense, will therefore also reflect the critic's own assumptions about how 'realistic' in today's world one finds eschatological talk of biblical parable and apocalyptic.[46]

Such talk by definition is unfamiliar. In gist, to envisage things apocalyptically is to view current events as the scene of a dynamic inbreaking of the established order by that which is '*at* hand' and not reducible to that which is already established or, so to speak, *in* hand. Taken in canonical context with the rest of the New Testament scriptures the gospel parables of the coming of the kingdom of heaven may be said to tell of such inbreaking by pointing to things proximate and, in Johannine terms, *en sarki* ('in the flesh', 1 John 4:2), as having meaning that is not approximated by any prior conceptions – that is, in the words of Paul, not known *kata sarka* ('according to the flesh', 2 Cor. 5:16). In such an apocalyptic and parabolic frame of *en sarki* but not *kata sarka* reference, the unprecedented takes precedence and there occurs a reading of events that involves, as Lehmann puts

---

[45]   Ibid., p. 227.

[46]   On this point (as on other issues regarding Lehmann) see especially Nancy J. Duff, 'The Significance of Apocalyptic for Lehmann's Ethics', in her *Humanization and the Politics of God: The Koinonia Ethics of Paul Lehmann* (Grand Rapids: Eerdmans, 1992), pp. 117–52.

it, 'an imaginative juxtaposition of what is incommensurable'.[47] It also involves polemics for 'the axe is laid to the root of the trees' (Lk. 3:9).

Lehmann's own imaginative and polemical juxtapositions of the incommensurable obviously resonate much more with some than with others. Responses to them have more often been hot or cold rather than lukewarm. Where many may indeed hear a 'new song' of the Psalmist's *hesed* that endures forever, others confess to having less ear for what sounds to them at times more hyperbolic than substantiated – or if a bad pun may be allowed – more akin to clanging symbols. To his credit Lehmann recognized this latter complaint and in his teaching never ceased energetically to engage it. When a summer school class, in which I was his tutor assistant, made up mainly of college and secondary school teachers of ethics, many of whom were Roman Catholic, affectionately but tellingly presented him with an inflated beach ball with the surface of the moon drawn on it to indicate their sense of dislocation as to where exactly his moral thought was taking them, Lehmann delightedly responded at the next class session by distributing and extolling these lines from Rilke:

> When catching what you throw yourself, it all
> is mere dexterity, dispensable attainment;
> only when all at once you catch the ball
> which she, eternal fellow-player,
> has flung to you ... only then
> ability to catch becomes achievement –
> not yours, a world's.[48]

Yet it would be mistaken to conclude, as some have, that Lehmann's recourse to poetry throughout his work and objections to what he calls 'philosophical ethics' amounts simply to a filling in of the logical gaps with idiosyncratic word plays or poetic citations. His rhetoric, though sometimes cryptic and enamored with a turn of phrase, is not without a sturdy cogency. This becomes evident when one recognizes that Lehmann inhabits the Reformers' discursive world of biblical allusion where what Luther called the *claritas* or perspicuity of scripture's focus serves as Calvin's 'spectacles' or corrective lens to see what is actually taking place all around us in creation. Far from inhibiting the use of divinatory imagination, as even a cursory reading of Luther and Calvin reveals, the conviction that God has made some things abundantly plain (Rom. 1:19) serves to release imaginative wonder. This *claritas* thus changes the ethical dilemma from not knowing what to do, to not doing what we know. It has been said, with probably only slight exaggeration, that at the time of the Reformation Luther had virtually memorized the Bible. The Reformers were steeped in the idiom of the scriptures in a way

---

47     Paul Lehmann, *Ethics In A Christian Context*, p. 87.
48     Rainer Maria Rilke, 'When Catching', *Modern European Poetry*, ed. Willis Barnstone (New York: Bantam, 1966), p. 118.

most of us moderns are not, and Lehmann's claims make little sense abstracted from this background. But against this background of biblical literacy they do make sense and are accountable. Thus a seemingly (and syntactically, admittedly!) convoluted characterization of 'apperception' as 'the uniquely human capacity to know something without knowing how one has come to know it, and to bring what one knows in this way to what one has come to know in other ways, and, in so doing, to discern what is humanly true or false',[49] may only be said to defy all logic if one is oblivious to Romans 1, or unaware that 'the wind [*pneuma*] blows where it chooses, and you hear the sound of it, but you do not know where is comes from or where it goes', and, 'So it is with everyone who is born of the Spirit [*pneumatos*]' (John 3:8).

A theological sensibility shaped by the prayer, 'Thy kingdom come, thy will be done, on earth as it is in heaven' (Matt. 6:10), will not fail to recognize that for Christian ethics the question of what is done this day on earth arises in conjunction with news of what is done and coming from heaven. This news of a heavenly 'doing' is conveyed in the New Testament through parables in which 'the earthly picture has a heavenly meaning'.[50] Or better, since the direction of the kingdom's coming is said to be from heaven, 'the heavenly coming has an earthly bearing'.[51] Parabolic significance with respect to this heavenly coming involves a reversal of the terms of analogy so that what is taken to be 'the real world' is not a state of affairs in which heaven (demythologized or otherwise) is considered analogous to earth, but a state of affairs in which earth comes to be made analogous to heaven. A similar kind of significance is present as well in New Testament passages other than those explicitly designated as parables of the kingdom, especially in testimony to the coming of Jesus Christ and the Holy Spirit. Divine agency, as the forthcoming of heaven, is parabolically signified and apocalyptically realized.

Lehmann's appeals to parabolic discernment are consistent with this matrix of meaning. Such a matrix also informs the role apocalyptic plays in his thinking and how it differs from what often is associated with so-called apocalyptic versions of events today. Insofar as fundamentalist scenarios of the end time consist of univocally literalistic construals of biblical prophecy as predictions of 'real historical happenings' they reduce 'real happenings' to conformity with established conceptions of what qualifies as 'historical' and thus are neither eschatologically parabolic nor biblically apocalyptic. Obviously, this is not what Lehmann's *en sarki* but not *kata sarka* discernment of the signs of the times is about, and his thought may be seen to provide a uniquely critical alternative in its attentiveness to the cruciality of present day apocalyptic significance.

What this significance has to do with a theological ethics is a question pointedly raised by J. Louis Martyn in his commentary on Galatians. Observing that 'the

49    Paul Lehmann, *The Decalogue And A Human Future*, p. 23.
50    John Drury, *The Parables In The Gospels: History And Allegory* (New York: Crossroad, 1985), p. 33.
51    I am indebted to Paul Meyer for this suggestion.

picture Paul presents in Gal. 5:13–24 is so thoroughly permeated by apocalyptic motifs as to be seriously domesticated when it is pressed into the categories usually associated with morals and ethics', Martyn writes that Paul's picture, 'rather than being basically hortatory, is in the first instance a description of daily life in the real world, made what it is by the advent of Christ and his Spirit'.[52]

Such domestication, from this perspective, can certainly be seen in Elizabeth Anscombe's claim that Christianity has a 'law conception of ethics' derived from the ethical notions of the Torah that was (in her judgement, lamentably) 'substantially given up among Protestants at the time of the Reformation'.[53] Lehmann's account of contextual ethics thus differs emphatically. Yet it is equally the case, though not as generally recognized, that Lehmann's position also differs emphatically from the so-called utilitarian 'consequentialism' Anscombe criticizes as an alternative to a law governed conception. This may be plainly seen in the difference between Lehmann's contextualism and the situation ethics of Joseph Fletcher where emphasis is placed upon the human maximizing of love as a normative principle within the constraints of a situation without reference to God currently 'doing' anything actively within the situation.[54] What is clear is that neither Anscombe's influential discussion of deontological and virtue ethics, nor Fletcher's more popularized situation ethics, acknowledges the importance of divine agency in biblical apocalyptic and its significance for Christian ethics that Lehmann's thought represents.[55] A subject that did not receive sufficient notice in these earlier debates over rule governed, situational, and virtue ethics is how closely agency is associated with references to 'heaven' in the gospel accounts and the difference one's hearing of heaven makes for what one considers to be 'the real world'.[56]

---

[52]  J. Louis Martyn, *Galatians: A New Translation with Introduction and Commentary* (New York: Doubleday, 1997), p. 502. See also his *Theological Issues In The Letters Of Paul* (Nashville: Abingdon, 1997), p. 233ff.

[53]  See G.E.M. Anscombe's 1958 essay, 'Modern Moral Philosophy' in *Virtue Ethics*, ed. Roger Crisp and Michael Slate (Oxford: Oxford University Press, 1997), pp. 26–44 (30–31).

[54]  Joseph Fletcher, *Situation Ethics: The New Morality* (Philadelphia: Westminster, 1966).

[55]  This does not mean that Lehmann's own views did not meet with biblical criticism. After the publication of *Transfiguration* he was chagrined to receive the respected Ernst Käsemann's friendly letter of response that, while he had high personal regard for Lehmann's political concerns, he found his exegesis '*nicht möglich*'. In characteristic fashion the dismayed Lehmann promptly convened an 'Ad Hoc Society For Exegetical Discussion' at Union, asking biblical colleagues (one of whom was J. Louis Martyn) and students, 'Will the Käsemann *illuminati* please step forward to the rescue of an untutored and faltering exegetical seeker?'

[56]  See, for example, James M. Gustafson, 'Moral Discernment in the Christian Life', *Norm And Context In Christian Ethics*, eds Gene H. Outka and Paul Ramsey (New York: Charles Scribner's Sons, 1968), pp. 17–36, where Gustafson in a parenthesis questions

The Kantian attempt to activate human agency by de-activating divine agency entails a rejection of all gospel claims to a righteous forthcoming apocalypsed from heaven. Eschatological parables of the kingdom of heaven are thereby reduced to moral maxims. The mood shifts from the indicative to the imperative, leading to the 'hortatory' character of the anthropologically grounded ethics that Martyn finds so contrary to the Apostle Paul. As Susan Owen, from another arena of moral reasoning, has aptly put it: 'the sinner Kant identifies cannot be assured by the God Kant allows'.[57] Nor does the reascribing of agency from a theological *virtus* denoting an efficacious power of God's Spirit, notably in Calvin,[58] to an anthropological *virtue* within the power of human disposition, 'up to us and voluntary', as Aristotle characterizes it, allow for a virtue ethics that is any more adequate than a deontological ethics in specifically this parabolic and apocalyptic regard.[59] To Paul Ramsey's criticism that Lehmann's ethics allowed no place for the virtue of prudence, Lehmann's reply was that those who begin with prudence never get to prophecy.

The deeper issues at stake were three: (1) how gospel traditions distinguish what is coming to pass from what is passing away, (2) how what is proclaimed in this biblical frame of reference to be *at hand* may be said to reveal what currently is and is not, so to speak, *in hand* (within our power), and (3) what it means responsibly to be *on hand* (able-to-respond in love and freedom) to the reality of what's happening at the present time. In consideration were the words of Paul that 'the form (*schema*) of this world is passing away' (1 Cor. 7:3) and the testimony that the Lord's coming from heaven is 'at hand' (Phil. 4:5).

If the presupposition of Christian decision making is that indeed there is in some sense a 'presence and power of Jesus of Nazareth in and over human affairs' to be reckoned with, then the question becomes whether 'the world come of age' is one in which this presence and power is passing away, perhaps as the form of

---

'the current celebration of the openness toward the future' in the eschatological interest of the time and writes, 'Much of this celebration refers primarily to human *attitude* in any case, and as such is insufficient to determine what men ought to be doing in particular instances. Attitude alone does not determine act. To be open to the future is not to discern what one ought to do in it' (p. 35). For a model of how a scholar with decidedly differing views can nevertheless provide a most fair-minded and accurate account of another's position see also Gustafson's insightful review of Lehmann's *Decalogue And A Human Future*, 'Commandments For Staying Human', *Christian Century*, December 20–27, 1995, pp. 1247–9.

[57]   Susan Owen, *Forgiveness And A Return To The Good*, Ph.D. Dissertation, Department of Religious Studies, University of Virginia, August 1997, p. 19.

[58]   See John Calvin, *Institutes Of The Christian Religion*, IV.17.10, where Calvin discusses how Christ by the immeasurable *virtus* of the Holy Spirit 'truly presents and exhibits his body' (*quin vere praestet atque exhibeat*) in the Lord's Supper. For Calvin's rejection of Aristotle's and 'the philosophers' attribution of virtue to our powers see *Institutes* II.2.3 and II.5.2.

[59]   Aristotle, *Nicomachean Ethics*, III. 5. 1113b.

a waning religious symbol, or rather is now actually coming to pass. If the latter, it does not follow that this is a world without rules or limits, but that as parabolic instantiations the rules and limits are pointers and promises signalling a 'future coming our way' that does not conform to what antecedently is taken for real.[60] How the divine agency of a heavenly doing and coming calls forth and relates to our human agency and ethical responsibility on earth through the enabling of discernment leading to action finds expression in words of Paul in the Philippian letter that might be taken as a discursive précis of Lehmann's consistently argued position. When Paul writes to the community at Philippi that 'our *politeuma* (citizenship or commonwealth) is in heaven, and it is from there that we are expecting a Savior, the Lord Jesus Christ, who will transform our lowly body to be like his glorious body, by the power which enables him even to subject all things to himself', his prayer for them is 'that your love may overflow more and more with knowledge and full insight to help you to determine (*dokimazein, discern*) what is best, so that in the day of Christ you may be pure and blameless, having produced the harvest of righteousness that comes through Jesus Christ for the glory and praise of God' (Phil. 3:20–21, 1:9–11). The ethical determination of what love seeks as best in any concrete situation is neither axiomatic nor autonomous if that love is of an arriving power and presence to which all things are subject. 'Getting what's coming to us' bespeaks a very different moral judgement if what is coming is heard to be the redemptive arrival of a living Lord. In such a hearing of the Gospel watchful waiting is never a passive inertia because the arrival is promised to take place always and concretely in relation to what is happening with those who are currently being considered 'the least' (Matt. 25:45).[61]

Lehmann's reading of events does not paint a rosy scenario. It has its dark side, though it is the darkness of the Cross illumined by the light of Resurrection morn. When the beloved son Peter, and only child, of Paul and Marion Lehmann died at age 27, Lehmann said to his class that sooner or later we all find ourselves living between the two prayers of Jesus, 'My God, why?,' and 'Father, into Thy hands

---

[60] Those who question the philosophical sophistication of such a perspective today may find interesting some more recent and intriguing parallels in the philosopher Alain Badiou's self-described atheistic and assertively non-theological materialist claims that the 'truth' in St. Paul's 'regime of discourse' declaring the resurrection of Christ is to be seen in its nonconformity to any previous states of affairs, or 'prior markings' and 'pre-constituted historical aggregates', as Badiou expresses it. See Alain Badiou, *Saint Paul: The Foundation of Universalism* (Stanford: Stanford University Press, 2005), pp. 4–6.

[61] In moralistic and 'hortatory' treatments of this text quite often the reverse point is ignored; doing unto 'the least' is stressed without any contextual regard for the Son of Man's coming in glory with all the angels (Matt. 25:31). Preaching on the politics of God from this Matthean passage Lehmann could not resist reminding the congregation that the separation of the sheep on the right hand and the goats on the left meant that for those of us facing the glorious throne of judgement it was the left that would be accounted righteous!

I commend my spirit'. Such times, he added, confirm the saying that 'the dark is light enough'.[62]

Obviously, no ethical theory adequately addresses all problems, and Lehmann's ethics of discernment is no exception. Matters of government and politics involve legislation and legal statutes, and social justice requires both the enactment and enforcement of law. But as experience shows, simple appeals to natural law or following commands does not necessarily make for justice. There is always a sensibility shaping the sense of justice from which legislation proceeds. The idea of justice 'apocalypsed' seems quite inapplicable, for example, in a courtroom setting or a legislative body. Yet insofar as judicial discretion, prudence, a sense of proportion, and mitigating circumstance are seen to enter into legal deliberation some such awareness of a sensitivity to what's really happening in human affairs cannot responsibly be discounted. John Calvin, the lawyer theologian, refers to 'the many dangers and evils to which [those] expose themselves who obstinately prefer to demand the letter of the law (*summum ius*) rather than to act out of equity and goodness'.[63] Earlier writers of antiquity had emphasized the point about legal *equity*, and Calvin cited Seneca's *De Clementia* (c. 55–56 C.E.) as well as the scriptures in writing that a fair judgement requires *clemency*, 'that best counselor of kings' and 'the chief gift of princes'.[64]

At the present time, when a 24-hour news cycle brings late breaking confirmations daily from somewhere in the world of the Psalmist's 'terror of the night ... and the destruction that wastes at noonday' (Psalm 95:5–6), the question is whether there is also any 'new song' of *hesed* to be sung that does not circumvent the real struggle but empower its engagement. To those who ask that question the work of Paul Lehmann continues to bear witness.

---

[62]   The title of a play by Christopher Fry, *The Dark is Light Enough: A Winter Comedy* (Oxford: Oxford University Press, 1954).

[63]   Calvin, *Institutes* III.5.7.

[64]   Calvin, *Institutes* IV.20.10. Calvin had earlier published a commentary on Seneca's *De Clementia* in 1532.

# Chapter 3

# The Commandments and the Common Life –
# Reflections on Paul Lehmann's
# *The Decalogue and a Human Future*

Nancy J. Duff

## Introduction – A Personal Account

On 29 March 1979 Paul Lehmann delivered the Warfield Lectures at Princeton
Theological Seminary.[1] The title of his series of six lectures, which he planned
to edit into a book, was 'The Commandments and the Common Life'. He
continued working on the manuscript for the book by giving similar lectures in
various locations, and giving copies of the manuscript to friends and colleagues
for critique. I may have been the only one among that group who preferred the
original title, 'Commandments and the Common Life', with its alliteration and its
focus on the place of the Ten Commandments in the life of the community and,
therefore, in terms of relationality. Others preferred the richer theological meaning
behind the title he chose, i.e., *The Decalogue and a Human Future*.[2] In addition
to its reference to eschatology the phrase 'a human future' invokes the concept for
which Lehmann is best known, i.e., 'making and keeping human life human' (the
subtitle even uses this phrase explicitly). Lehmann's work, therefore, ends where
decades earlier his best known book, *Ethics in a Christian Context*, began: with
the affirmation that divine revelation creates a space in which human beings are
free and empowered to *be human* as God has created and redeemed them to be.

As time went on Paul was distracted by other responsibilities and returned to the
book manuscript when he could. By the time he was able to turn his full attention
to the project, his health began to fail, and it looked as if the book would never be
published. In the academic year 1992, I spent my sabbatical working with a rather

---

[1]   Paul L. Lehmann, Annie Kinkaid Warfield Lectures at Princeton Theological
Seminary in Princeton, New Jersey, March 26, 1979. See my Introduction to Paul L.
Lehmann, *The Decalogue and a Human Future: the Meaning of the Commandments for
Making and Keeping Human Life Human* (Grand Rapids: Eerdmans, 1995), p. 1. He had
been on faculty at Princeton Theological Seminary from 1947–56.

[2]   I believe the others were right – this is the better title. I have, nevertheless, chosen
to use Paul's original title for this essay.

daunting collection of manuscripts, aiming to piece them together to complete the book. I soon found, however, that two problems plagued the project.

First, the manuscript needed more serious editing than either Paul or I anticipated. Ensuring that grammar and form appropriate to lectures was translated into the more formal style for publication presented only part of the problem. The real editorial challenge arose from parts of the manuscripts that significantly lacked clarity. That this was so should not have come as a complete surprise. Paul's favourite fan and critic, his wife Marion, said that Paul had never learned to write a clear sentence in English, having spoken German until he started first grade.[3] While her charge was certainly exaggerated, Paul did have an unusual style of speaking and writing that projected an ethos as powerfully creative as the content of what he had to say. He loved to play with words, finding hints of their meaning in etymology that few others would have perceived, and he drew images and ideas from an impressive breadth of knowledge that few others could match. His own distinct form of reasoning would take him down side paths that lead to historical, literary, political, and any number of other illustrative ends. While Paul never lost his train of thought, always arriving back at the main path precisely at the point where he had diverged from it, the same could not always be said of his listeners, who could lose their way while seeking to follow his unfolding argument. One of the most commonly reported experiences of those who heard Paul lecture entailed leaving a lecture hall energized by his ability to bring Christian faith alive by examining it through the lenses of scripture, doctrine, philosophy, literature, poetry and the daily news, and yet also be left wondering what exactly he had said. This intriguing style of speaking also dominated his writing, which, as a result, was both engaging and exasperating. Each book, from *Forgiveness: Decisive Issue In Protestant Thought*, to *Ethics in a Christian Context*, to *The Transfiguration of Politics*, became more difficult to decipher than the one before, but for most readers making one's way through them was well worth the effort.[4] Now, this final project threatened at significant points to be so puzzling as to render it indecipherable. Fearing that his significant insights into the Commandments would be lost, I asked Paul if I could do more serious editing than simply sorting through the manuscripts and finding appropriate transitions, suggesting that I actually change some of his wording, omit paragraphs, and rearrange pages. I fully understood when he

---

[3]    Paul was born in the United States to German speaking parents. On Lehmann's biography see, Horace T. Allen, 'The Life and Minstry of Paul L. Lehmann', *The Context of Contemporary Theology: Essays in Honor of Paul Lehmann*, eds A.J. McKelway and E.D. Willis (Atlanta: John Knox, 1974), pp. 15–24, as well as Nancy Duff, 'Paul Louis Lehmann', *Theology Today* 53:3 (1996), pp. 360–69. For a moving account of Paul Lehmann's life and character see Fleming Rutledge, 'A Tribute to Paul Louis Lehmann (Sept. 10, 1906–Feb. 27, 1994)', *The Princeton Seminary Bulletin*, 15:2 (1994): 165–9.

[4]    Paul Lehmann, *Forgiveness: Decisive Issue in Protestant Thought* (New York: Harper & Brothers, 1940); *Ethics in a Christian Context* (New York: Harper & Row, 1963); *The Transfiguration of Politics* (New York: Harper & Row, 1975).

refused, explaining that he would do that editorial work himself after I had pieced the whole book together. Unfortunately, and as I feared, his health prevented him from ever turning to this editorial task.

The second problem arose when I discovered that for all the work he had done on the lectures and book manuscript, Paul had never made his way through *all ten* commandments. The lectures ended with a quick summary of the sixth commandment (as Martin Luther numbers them) with no reference to those that follow. Only when I was ready to edit material on the seventh commandment and began searching through the piles of papers at my disposal did I realize that there was no material on the last four commandments. The project, even in draft form, was incomplete. In desperation I considered turning in the manuscript at hand and letting it stop where Paul had stopped. Christopher Morse dashed that idea when he told me what I already knew but hated to admit: there are *ten* commandments and no book on the Decalogue can address only six of them.

I finally resolved this second problem by locating essays that Paul had published earlier in his career that could be used to illuminate each of the last four commandments. A 1947 essay on the Reformed understanding of property was well suited for the commandment against stealing.[5] An essay on the trial and execution of Julius and Ethel Rosenberg in 1953, written originally for a memorial service in 1978, fit perfectly under the commandment against lying, which Lehmann, following Luther's lead, had interpreted as having primarily to do with those who are falsely accused in court.[6] A 1953 essay on vocation served the command against coveting.[7] These older essays had not been in publication for years, but rather than sounding stale, they were brought back to life by being read in the context of one of the Ten Commandments. With these essays, the book manuscript was completed and the book published in 1995.[8] Sixteen years after that first Warfield lecture, and thanks to Mr. William B. Eerdmans, people were able to read Paul Lehmann's reflections on the meaning of the commandments for making and keeping human life human.

Unfortunately, too many of those readers have found it impossible to make their way through the book. The first problem that plagued the manuscript – its need for more serious editorial work than Lehmann wanted to entrust to someone else – resulted in a book that some find impossible to read. Those who knew Paul's earlier work appreciate the familiar brilliance and insight that arise throughout the book, and even readers who never knew Lehmann are intrigued by his

---

[5] Paul Lehmann, 'The Standpoint of the Reformation', *Christianity and Property*, ed. J. Fletcher (Philadelphia: Westminster Press, 1947), pp. 100–123.

[6] Paul Lehmann, 'Rosenbergs, Then and Now: History's New Light', *Christianity and Crisis* 38:11 (1978): 185–7.

[7] Paul Lehmann, 'Biblical Faith and the Vocational Predicament of our Time', *The Drew Gateway* 23:3–4 (1953): 101–8.

[8] Although Paul died before the book was released, he knew that it was in the hands of the publisher.

reflections. Everyone, however, agrees that the book is in places nearly impossible to understand. The extremely important argument Lehmann sets forth in *The Decalogue and a Human Future* is too often lost in his brilliant, but sometimes enigmatic and sometimes outright unintelligible reflections.

It is one of my greatest regrets as a friend and former student of Paul Lehmann and as a scholar who has been enormously influenced by his work that I did not push harder for his permission to make more radical editorial changes to the manuscript. I have often wondered if he had been given a more capable assistant for putting this last project together whether the final text would read more smoothly. Those doubts, however, simply have to be set aside. The book 'is what it is' as the popular saying goes. I hope that this current essay will bring some clarity to those who have read or hope to read *The Decalogue and a Human Future*. The second section of this essay – Lehmann's Contextual Ethic – will address Lehmann's approach to Christian ethics, which is essential for understanding the *Decalogue* book, and the third section – The Decalogue – will turn to the book itself. While the primary goal is simply to help readers understand what Lehmann sought to accomplish in his last book, it is also to analyse and evaluate how successfully he reached that goal.

## Lehmann's Contextual Ethic

In his 1967 book, *Ethics in a Christian Context*, Paul Lehmann set out to hew a path for Christian ethics that would avoid, on the one hand, a legalistic ethic where absolute moral law can ignore specific circumstances and, on the other, an antinomian ethic where relativized moral law allows specific circumstances to dictate moral action. This goal does not in itself set Lehmann's ethic apart from others. Most ethicists, in fact, seek to avoid the pitfalls of both legalism and moral chaos, but what appears to be legalistic or morally lax to one person does not so appear to another. Furthermore, some ethicists intentionally bend more towards one approach than the other, in part, because they fear the pitfalls of one over another. Hence, in a slightly different context Lehmann notes John Calvin's fear of anarchy, when Calvin claims, 'It is indeed bad to live under a bad prince with whom nothing is permitted; *but much worse under one by whom everything is allowed*'.[9] Lehmann suggests that perhaps we need to recognize the wisdom of reversing Calvin's fear, so that the saying reads, 'It is indeed bad to live under a prince with whom everything is allowed *but much worse under one by whom nothing is permitted*'.[10] Lehmann is more suspicious of the threat posed by legalism than by moral chaos, though he certainly recognizes the dangers of the latter and seeks to avoid them. The approach to ethics that he presented and defended was a *contextual* one.

---

[9]    Lehmann, *The Transfiguration of Politics*, p. 42 (emphasis mine).

[10]   Ibid. (emphasis mine).

It would, however, be a mistake to say that Lehmann promoted a contextual ethic because he examined different types of ethics and concluded that contextualism was superior. He was, in fact, opposed to the identification of different types of ethics followed by the application of one of those types to the Gospel.[11] He believed one should search for the ethic that arises from the Gospel itself.[12] There are, of course, other Christian ethicists who claim to be searching for the ethic embedded in the Gospel but who find therein an ethic of duty and an emphasis on moral law. Lehmann's insistence that a contextual ethic is consistent with God's revelation in Jesus Christ points, therefore, to a christological difference between his interpretation of Christian ethics and that of his opponents.

Lehmann's theology and ethics emphasize divine revelation in Jesus Christ, which makes known to us *the living God* whose will cannot be reduced to, summarized in, or correctly interpreted by an abstract formula or an absolute command.

> The fact is that the dynamics of the divine behaviour in the world exclude both an abstract and a perceptual apprehension of the will of God. There is no formal principle of Christian behaviour because Christian behaviour cannot be generalized. And Christian behaviour cannot be generalized because the will of God cannot be generalized.[13]

The focus on the context of moral reflection and action is for Lehmann grounded in christology. Because God chose to be incarnate in Jesus Christ 'in this world of time and space and things', Christian ethics cannot ignore the specific contexts that demand a morally responsible decision or act, for to do so would also require one to ignore the ongoing activity of God in this world. In other words, if one summarizes or reduces the will of God to absolute moral laws or to universal laws embedded in nature one actually no longer needs recourse to God, at least not for the purpose of defining responsible Christian thinking and acting. One can insist that God is the *source* of moral laws, but once the laws are known, God is scarcely needed. Lehmann, however, insists that because God's activity is dynamic and ever present in this world, the divine will cannot be captured within or summarized by the formulation of an absolute standard of conduct.

In turning his attention to a contextual ethic, Lehmann identifies three meanings of 'context' for Christian ethics. The first context for Christian ethical reflection is the activity of God. Unlike his teacher, Reinhold Niebuhr, for whom Lehmann maintained unflinching, though not uncritical, respect, Lehmann does not base his ethic on Christian anthropology. While the doctrines of creation and the human person are operative in Lehmann's work, christology is central. The meaning of

---

[11]   Lehmann, *Ethics in a Christian Context*, p. 15.

[12]   Lehmann was, in fact, appreciated by biblical scholars, such as J. Louis Martyn, for his willingness to read and study the biblical texts in their original language as he wrote about theology and ethics.

[13]   Lehmann, *Ethics in a Christian Context*, p. 77.

God's saving work in Jesus Christ is often described by Lehmann as 'making and keeping human life human', a phrase that will be discussed below. Second, Lehmann identifies the Christian church, or *koinonia*, as the context of Christian ethics. Divine revelation is a community-creating event or a 'fellowship-creating reality' and, thus, brings into existence the Christian community, the body of Christ in the world.[14] Hence, human relatedness, as will be discussed below, becomes essential for Lehmann's understanding of Christian ethics. Finally, the contextual nature of Christian ethics leads us to seek God's will in each particular situation. Lehmann's contextual ethic only arrives at an emphasis on each particular moment of decision making *after* exploring the nature of divine activity and the Christian *koinonia* as essential for the discipline of Christian ethics. These first two meanings of 'context' – divine activity and the Christian *koinonia* – prevent Lehmann's ethics from falling into moral chaos even though he rejects absolute moral law. The moral agent never enters a situation of moral decision-making 'empty handed' or ready to allow the situation alone to dictate moral decisions. The activity of God and participation in the *koinonia* inform the identity of the moral agent prior to entering the dynamics of a particular situation of moral concern.

Understanding this three-fold meaning of 'context' should enable readers to avoid the confusion that has sometimes arisen between Lehmann's ethic and that of his contemporary, Joseph Fletcher, who published *Situation Ethics* not long after the publication of *Ethics in a Christian Context*.[15] Although both Fletcher and Lehmann argued against the absolute and universal nature of moral law, Fletcher's ethic is distinctively utilitarian; Lehmann's ethic is not. Fletcher argued that because an ethic that emphasizes the absolute character of moral law can lead to cruel consequences, Christians should seek to promote the greatest good for the greatest number of people by defining the 'good' as New Testament agape. Using a method called 'act utilitarianism', Fletcher proposes that each moral decision should be made and evaluated according to how well it serves to promote *agape*.[16] Lehmann's reasons for rejecting absolute moral law differ from Fletcher's. For Lehmann it is not just the consequences of applying an abstract law to particular cases that is problematic, although he too was concerned with the cruelty and arrogance that can sometimes accompany such an approach to ethics. More important for Lehmann, however, is that abstract, absolute moral laws and principles are inconsistent with divine revelation even when revelation takes the form of divine command. Furthermore, he does not propose a calculus

---

[14]    One finds numerous references to the 'fellowship-creating reality' of divine revelation in *Ethics in a Christian Context*. See, for instance, pp. 47, 49 and 59.

[15]    Joseph Fletcher, *Situation Ethics: The New Morality* (Philadelphia: Westminster Press, 1966).

[16]    Act utilitarianism applies the rule of utility (doing the greatest amount of good for the greatest number of people) to each particular moral situation. Rule utilitarianism applies the rule of utility to more general rules or laws that are in turn applied to each particular situation.

for determining the greatest amount of good produced by moral decisions. He does not, in fact, initially emphasize the specific moral decision or act at all. By beginning with divine action and then moving to the Christian *koinonia* that results from it, Lehmann emphasizes the identity of the moral agent and only then moves to the specific context of moral decision-making. Then, in that context one seeks to discern the will of God.

In examining the contextual nature of Christian ethics from the perspective of divine revelation, Lehmann believes that Christian ethics seeks to discern what God is doing in the world 'to make and to keep human life human'.[17] Those who know anything at all about Paul Lehmann's work know this phrase. It is the line most often quoted from his work, and understanding it along with his frequent reference to 'humanization' can mark the difference between rightly interpreting his theological approach to ethics and misinterpreting his work altogether. 'Humanization' is *not* a principle that Lehmann applies to determine the morality of human action, nor is 'making and keeping human life human' the ideal goal toward which we strive. Furthermore, his focus on humanization does not indicate that the doctrine of the human person forms the foundation of his ethics. The meaning of both the phrase and the word is filled out *christologically.* According to Lehmann, God's revelation in Jesus Christ creates a space in which human beings are free and empowered to be human as God has created and saved them to be. Our task as Christians is to live within that space and give parabolic expression to the grace of God that created it.

Lehmann poses the fundamental ethical question as, 'What *am* I, as believer in Jesus Christ and as a member of Christ's church to do?'[18] He purposely forms his question as, 'What *am* I to do?' rather than 'What *ought* I to do?' to emphasize the indicative rather than imperative nature of human action, i.e., to stress that *who we are* precedes and informs what we are called to do. The action of God in Jesus Christ has determined *who* we are, i.e., we are creatures, forgiven sinners, and believers by the saving grace of God.[19] We are children of God who know that God has already reconciled the world to God's self. Hence, we are to act in ways consistent with who we are as believers in Jesus Christ and members of Christ's church. This indicative character of ethics will be reflected again in Lehmann's understanding of the Ten Commandments.

---

[17]   This phrase and variations on the word 'humanization' are found throughout *Ethics in a Christian Context*, beginning on p. 14.

[18]   Lehmann, *Ethics in a Christian Context*, p. 25 (emphasis mine).

[19]   See an early series of three essays, which identify the significance of understanding human beings as creatures, sinners, and believers. Paul L. Lehmann, 'The Christian Doctrine of Man, I: Man as Creature', *The Journal of Religious Thought* 1:2 (1944): 140–56; 'The Christian Doctrine of Man II: Man as Sinner', *The Journal of Religious Thought* 2:1 (1944): 60–77; and 'The Christian Doctrine of Man, III: Man as Believer', *The Journal of Religious Thought* 2:2 (1945): 179–94. Although there are still hints of natural theology in these essays, which Lehmann later rejected, they are insightful and worthy of attention.

## The Decalogue

*The Decalogue and a Human Future* was initially written to celebrate the 500th anniversary of the publication of Luther's Large Catechism. Lehmann's reflections, therefore, draw frequently on Martin Luther, and he follows Luther's ordering of the Ten Commandments, which differs from the numbering used by Calvin and others. What many of us, who are not Lutheran, count as the first two commandments ('Have no other gods before me' and 'Make no graven images') are considered by Luther to be the first commandment only. What many of us count as the tenth commandment against coveting, Luther divides into two, making them the ninth and tenth. Because most people seem unaware that different religious traditions number the Commandments differently, readers, who are not Lutheran, may be puzzled by this numbering in Lehmann's book. This confusion is easily clarified; there are, however, places in the book where lack of clarity is not so easily remedied. The remainder of this essay will explain three key aspects of Lehmann's work that have caused the most difficulty for his readers. Clarifying Lehmann's concepts of (1) apperception, (2) the descriptive (as opposed to prescriptive) character of divine commandments, and (3) the 'structural realism of the Decalogue' may help readers make their way through *The Decalogue and a Human Future* with fewer roadblocks.

### Apperception

The most blatantly confusing concept in Lehmann's book, *The Decalogue and a Human Future*, occurs very early on in his use of the term 'apperception'. A quick reading of the definition – even when followed by a very careful reading! – confirms for many critics the persistent claim that Lehmann was often unable to provide precise and clear definitions of terms. Lehmann defines apperception as 'the uniquely human capacity to know something without knowing how one has come to know it, and to bring what one knows in this way to what one has come to know in other ways, and, in so doing to discern what is humanly true or false'.[20] After untangling the sentence's syntax most people find at least a hint of natural theology in it. The reference to knowing something about truth 'without knowing how one has come to know it', surely points to some innate human capacity to know the truth, which certainly for a theologian means to know something about God. Lehmann, however, insisted he did *not* intend to make *any* reference to natural theology in his use and definition of apperception. Only in Lehmann's earliest work does one find positive references to natural theology, a concept that he, like Karl Barth, soon rejected. By the time he publishes *Ethics in a Christian Context* he no longer employs natural theology and occasionally argues

---

[20]    Lehmann, *The Decalogue and a Human Future*, p. 23.

against it.[21] No matter how much his definition of apperception – which most readers of the early manuscript urged him to discard – may *sound* like a reference to natural knowledge of God, this last book does not reflect a return to a concept he had previously rejected and long argued against.

In everyday use apperception often refers to a process whereby one can make connections between things newly known and things long understood. For instance, an existing concept can be related to past experience, or, new ideas can be related to existing ones, resulting in new insight and understanding. Apperception, then, allows seemingly disparate objects of knowledge to be connected into a meaningful whole. Borrowing from music, one could consider this connection among diverse bits of knowledge serving the same purpose as the *cantus firmus*, which connects polyphonic parts (i.e., independent melodies) and holds them together in such a way as to avoid mere cacophony. As Dietrich Bonhoeffer said, 'Where the *cantus firmus* is clear and plain, the counterpoint [polyphony] can be developed to its limits'.[22] Apperception, as Lehmann uses it, can be understood as the process by which we are enabled to recognize the 'cantus firmus', or the single, stable connection of meaning among all the diverse things we know.

Apperception, then, is best understood to mean *discernment*, a term Lehmann uses within the definition itself. A key question for Christian ethics has to do with how Christians *discern* the will of God in the world. While it may be true, as some theologians claim, that there is a natural capacity to know the truth and, therefore, some ability to discern the will of God just by virtue of being human, Lehmann, like Calvin, believes that this capacity has been rendered virtually useless through humanity's fall into sin. Although we *should* be able to look at the world and recognize it as the handiwork of God or rely on human conscience to reveal the will of God, our capacity to know and do the will of God is so tainted by human sin that it now serves only one use, and that is to convict us. The ability that would allow us to gain knowledge about God just by virtue of being human has been incapacitated by sin. Therefore, Lehmann agrees with Calvin that we must put on Scriptures as we would eyeglasses, so that we may correctly see what is clearly there to see, but obscured by sin.[23] Apperception brings one to self-understanding whereby 'one is drawn into the heritage and the reality of what it takes to be and to stay human in the world'.[24] Furthermore, according to Lehmann, that heritage

---

[21]   For critical comment on natural theology, see Lehmann, *Ethics in a Christian Context*, pp. 120–21, 158, as well as a roughly contemporary essay, 'A Christian Alternative to Natural Law', *Die moderne Demokratie und ihr Recht: Festschrift für Gerhard Leibholz zum 65. Geburtstag*, eds K.D. Bracher et al (Tübingen: J.C.B. Mohr Siebeck, 1966), pp. 517–49.

[22]   Dietrich Bonhoeffer, *Letters and Papers from Prison*, Enlarged Edition, ed., E. Bethge (New York: Macmillan, 1971), p. 303.

[23]   See John Calvin, *Institutes of the Christian Religion*, I.vi.1.

[24]   Lehmann, *The Decalogue and a Human Future*, p. 23.

and reality are always *there* beforehand, but apart from Scripture they remain unknown to us.

One cannot, however, simply read the Bible, and more specifically the Ten Commandments, and claim to have gained the apperceptive power to recognize God's humanizing activity in the world. Although the saving story does not arise from the human story, the saving story, according to Lehmann, and the biblical story are not entirely identical either. It is only when the biblical story encounters the human story that the saving story can truly be discerned.[25] Hence, Lehmann describes the relationship between Scripture and the world we live in as one of movement. Within Scripture one discovers a world of 'origin and destiny, of purpose, possibility, and promise'.[26] From the world of Scripture one moves into this world of 'time and space and things', which is a world in which God has already created the space or environment for human flourishing.[27]

> This connection between the biblical story and the human story defines Christian praxis and provides evidence for the fact that life at a human level is always and at the same time life in two worlds; it is always on the move from the world of origin and destiny toward and within the world of human story; and from the world of human story it moves under and toward the destiny purposed at and by its origin.[28]

Scripture is a world into which we are drawn and from which we are sent forth, not just once and for all – though to some extent this is also true – but repeatedly as we hear the stories proclaimed again and again. It identifies our origin, which is from God, and our destiny, which is toward God's promised Kingdom, and sends us into the world of lived human experience with our identity intact: we belong to God; we are God's people. The emphasis, then, is upon who God is and *therefore* who we are, upon what God has done for us and *therefore* what we are called and empowered to do for one another and for the world whose care has been entrusted to us. Apperception draws us into the 'heritage and reality of what it takes to make and keep human life human'.[29] Apperception is not, however, an innate human capacity whereby we come to discover God on our own. On our own, we are lost, as Robert Penn Warren knew: 'Yes, message on message, like wind or water in light or in dark. / The whole world pours at us. But the code book, somehow

---

[25]    Although I heard Lehmann make this claim about the biblical story and the human story bringing about the saving story, I have not been able to locate it in any of his writings. I continue to suspect, however, that it can be found within one of them.

[26]    Lehmann, *The Decalogue and a Human Future*, p. 16.

[27]    Lehmann often used the phrase, 'time and space and things'. One instance of it can be found in *Ethics in a Christian Context*, p. 74.

[28]    Lehmann, *The Decalogue and a Human Future*, p. 16.

[29]    Lehmann, *The Decalogue and a Human Future*, p. 23.

is lost.'[30] With our reading of the Decalogue, Lehmann believes that the codebook has been found. The Decalogue understood as a codebook, however, does not mean that the Ten Commandments provide a manual for living that prescribes how we ought to live. Rather, the Decalogue as codebook *describes* how God would have us live.

## The Descriptive Character of the Commandments

Lehmann rejects the commonly held notion that biblical commandments can prescribe the obedience that arises from faith.[31] He believed that a prescriptive interpretation of the commandments narrows their scope and leads both to legalism, which destroys the freedom that being human requires, and, surprisingly, to moral laxity. Rather than serving as imperatives that prescribe behaviour, divine commands *describe* the 'pathways and patterns' of human life.[32] The Commandments are not, Lehmann insists, 'a repository of regulations', but the 'clue to responsibilities'.[33] They do not organize Christians under the power of rules; they draw us into parables.[34] They do not *prescribe* what God would have us do in the world, but *describe* the lives God would have us live. 'The tone is not, "This is what you had better do or else!" The tone is rather, "Seeing that you are who you are, where you are, and as you are, this is the way ahead, the way of being and living in the truth, the way of freedom!"'[35] Lehmann's understanding of the Decalogue is, therefore, consistent with the indicative nature of Christian ethics, because it responds to the question, 'What *am* I as a believer in Jesus Christ and a member of his Church to do?' Initially and for the most part, what we are to do is *to be who we are*, i.e., be who God calls us to be. The prologue, each commandment, and all of the commandments taken together with the prologue, tell us who we are.

Many readers find Lehmann's distinction between prescriptive and descriptive interpretation of the Commandments – which he views not as rules, but as parables – nothing short of nonsense. The Commandments are, after all, *commandments*. They are written in imperative form. They do not tell a story, but command certain behaviours and prohibit others. Furthermore, not only is Lehmann's denial of the prescriptive nature of the Commandments nonsensical, it also threatens the rigorous and disciplined demands regarding moral behaviour required by Christian

---

[30] Lehmann, *The Decalogue and a Human Future*, p. 42. Lehmann is quoting Robert Penn Warren, 'The Code Book is Lost', *Now and Then* (New York: Random House, 1978), pp. 43–4.
[31] This, he says, is especially true when such programmes serve primarily to validate opinions one already holds. See Lehmann, *The Decalogue and a Human Future*, p. 18.
[32] Lehmann, *The Decalogue and a Human Future*, p. 18.
[33] Lehmann, *The Decalogue and a Human Future*, p. 85.
[34] Lehmann, *The Decalogue and a Human Future*, p. 85.
[35] Lehmann, *The Decalogue and a Human Future*, p. 85.

discipleship. If the Commandments are not prescriptive, if they are understood as stories rather than rules, has Lehmann simply made Christian ethics so ambiguous as to render it useless?

The critics, of course, are right. The Decalogue is not a narrative account; it is a list of commandments. This list, however, is completely transformed from narrowly perceived prescriptions about what we are to do and refrain from doing by the prologue, which reads, 'I am the Lord your God who brought you out of the land of Egypt, out of the house of slavery' (Deut. 5:6).[36] These words in the prologue – which, it should be noted are *not* typically included on the monuments that have been strategically placed on court house lawns or in municipal buildings – bring to mind the covenantal context in which the Ten Commandments were delivered. We misunderstand the Decalogue if we overlook the prologue, which invokes the *story* of what God has done for us.

As early as *Ethics in a Christian Context* Lehmann says that it 'cannot be too strongly stressed that the Decalogue presupposes the covenant'.[37] Lehmann points the reader to Deut. 6:20, which tells the Israelites how to answer the question that will invariably be posed by their children, i.e., 'What is the meaning of the decrees and the statues and the ordinances that the Lord our God has commanded you?' The Israelites are instructed to answer their children by saying, 'We were Pharaoh's slaves in Egypt, but the Lord brought us out of Egypt with a mighty hand'. The Deuteronomic response locates the meaning of the decrees and statutes and ordinances of God in *the story of what God has done for the Israelites*. What is the meaning of the decrees? That God has liberated the Israelites. Only *after* invoking the story of what God has done, does the author of Deuteronomy say, 'Then the Lord commanded us to observe all these statutes, to fear the Lord our God, for our lasting good, so as to keep us alive, as is now the case'.

It is a weakness of Lehmann's book on the Decalogue that he omits direct reference to the prologue, although a short chapter bears that title. In *The Decalogue* book the covenantal context of the Ten Commandments is assumed by Lehmann and does, in fact, further the same understanding of ethics he held in 1965. His failure, however, to make that covenantal context explicit by directly addressing the prologue obscures his argument about narrative and the descriptive character of the commandments, though it does not destroy it: readers can and must bring this forward from *Ethics in a Christian Context*, for it illuminates Lehmann's argument as a whole, as well as its particulars. Perhaps most significantly it stands behind Lehmann's insistence that we should stop aiming to *keep* the Commandments and instead seek to *obey* the One who gave them. We keep the Commandments whenever we follow the letter of the law with little or no regard to the humanizing presence and activity of God in the world. In contrast, we obey the One who gave the Commandments by seeking to understand through them what God has done

---

[36]   Cf. Deut 6:10ff., 7:7f., *inter alia*.

[37]   Lehmann, *Ethics in a Christian Context*, p. 77.

for us to make and keep human life human and what God now calls us to do for others as well as for ourselves.[38]

Ironically, while Lehmann's ethics has often been charged with moral laxity, it is in fact the narrow, prescriptive understanding of the commandments that leads to a more truncated and therefore finally less rigorous understanding of Christian responsibility. A prescriptive rendering of each commandment invites self-deception, for it can make it seem easy to fulfil the law and to enter the church of the self-righteousness and the self-satisfied. For instance, many of us can claim that we have not broken the Sabbath commandment because we attend church at least on a fairly regular basis. We haven't taken anyone's life, so we have fulfilled the law against killing, and since we could not justly be thrown into jail as a thief, we have kept the commandment against stealing. When, however, we turn to a broader descriptive understanding of the Commandments, which includes their trajectory into future biblical texts and into the complexity of life itself, we realize that we break the Sabbath commandment when we do not allow people or animals (specifically mentioned in the text) or the earth itself to rest. Lehmann believed that the commandment for Sabbath rest describes something necessary for life, namely *rest*. Hence, he could even interpret crop rotation – which prevents fields from being worked to death – as a response to the commandment regarding Sabbath rest. All of the commandments can be similarly expanded when understood descriptively.[39]

Rather than keeping the commandments – i.e., rather than following the letter of the law apart from the story of what God has done for us – Lehmann insists that we need to *obey* the One who gives them, the very same One who brought us out of the house of slavery. Only in that way do the Commandments apply to the whole of life. Lehmann's descriptive interpretation of the Bible, therefore, supports Luther's claim that the whole Bible is summarized in the Decalogue and, in turn, rescues the Commandments from disregard and disarray. The Decalogue speaks to the whole of human life, not just to isolated moments. Furthermore, it describes the structure of human relatedness that serves to keep human life human.

*The Structural Realism of the Decalogue and the Structure of Human Relatedness*

According to Lehmann, when the Decalogue is understood descriptively within the context of God's covenant with humanity, it does not proffer abstract rules and regulations for the ordering of human life and relationships, but sets forth

---

[38]  Lehmann, *The Decalogue and a Human Future*, p. 15ff.

[39]  One finds a similar interpretive move in Dietrich Bonhoeffer's brief reference to the Ten Commandments. According to Bonhoeffer, we break the commandment to honour our parents when we idolize youth. We break the commandment against stealing when we silently tolerate the exploitation of the poor and the simultaneous enrichment of the strong. Dietrich Bonhoeffer, *Ethics*, Dietrich Bonhoeffer Works 6, trans. I. Tödt et al. (Minneapolis: Fortress Press, 2005), pp. 139–40.

'concrete purposes, directions, patterns, and boundaries of human relations and interrelations'.[40] These purposes, patterns, and boundaries encounter the reality and problem of power between and among human beings. While the first three Commandments (as Luther orders them) define our relationship to God whose transcendent power defines us as creatures who are to have no other god than this God, all of the commandments also have to do with how power is wielded among human beings – whether that means labourers who need time to rest, elderly parents who need to be honoured, or the poor who have been falsely accused and need to be defended in court. To describe the humanizing as opposed to dehumanizing structure of power in human relationships, Lehmann turns his attention to the work of sociologists Peter Blau and Louis Dumont, believing that here he finds a coincidence between the truth revealed in the Bible and truth uncovered by social science.[41]

Lehmann describes three ways that power can be structured among human beings, two of which he finds problematic, i.e., hierarchy and egalitarianism. According to him neither hierarchical nor egalitarian structures can further 'the freedom that being human in this world requires'.[42] In spite of their inadequacies, however, each recognizes something essential about human relations. Hence, while hierarchy weds power with privilege in a self-justifying and self-perpetuating way so that injustices are overlooked or quite consciously defended, it also recognizes 'the facts of differentiation and variation' that are simply part of human relationality; not all people are the same, and to treat them as if they were can lead to cruelty.[43] Egalitarianism, on the other hand, tends to mistake equality with sameness, failing to acknowledge the real differences that exist among people, including differences in abilities and power. Positively, however, egalitarianism recognizes the 'facts of shared identity' among all people. We share a common humanity, which includes common needs and desires as well as contributions to make to the good of the whole.

Lehmann insists that the structure of human relatedness that will best promote human freedom described in the Decalogue needs to recognize both differentiation (which hierarchy over-emphasizes and egalitarianism overlooks) and shared identity (which hierarchy overlooks and egalitarianism over-emphasizes). He refers to this structure of power in human relatedness as 'reciprocal responsibility'

---

40    Lehmann, *The Decalogue and a Human Future*, p. 31.

41    See Peter Blau, *Inequality and Heterogeneity: A Primitive Theory of Social Structure* (New York: The Free Press, 1977) as well as Louis Dumont, *Homo Hierarchicus: The Caste System and Its Implications* (Chicago: University of Chicago Press, 1970) and *From Mandeville to Marx* (Chicago: University of Chicago Press, 1977).

42    Lehmann, *The Decalogue and a Human Future*, p. 32.

43    Lehmann also acknowledges that hierarchical systems are not completely devoid of the recognition of equality among people. This equality, however, tends to divide people into groups. Hence, faculty members, even though divided by rank among themselves, would be considered to have more in common with one another – to share an equality with one another that they would not share with members of the grounds crew, who would, in turn, share a certain equality among themselves.

and believes that it provides 'the humanizing relationship between heterogeneity and inequality'.[44]

In one of the most difficult sections of the book Lehmann engages both Blau and Dumont in order to explain the difference between nominal and graduated parameters in social structures. A social structure, according to Peter Blau, is 'a multidimensional space of different social positions among which a population is distributed'.[45] This structure has parameters that define it. Some examples of parameters are gender, religion, wealth and power. These parameters can be divided into two types: nominal parameters and graduated ones.

Nominal parameters divide people into social groups with distinct boundaries, but with no *inherent* or *essential* rank ordering among the groups. Nominal parameters include gender, religion and race. Confusion can arise here, because we know that gender, religion and race are indeed factors in ordering people by rank, very often in unjust ways. Men tend to have more power and privilege than women; Caucasians in the United States have wielded destructive power over Native Americans, Blacks and people of other races since its inception. The point is, however, that the status attached to nominal parameters such as gender and race is *not inherent* to those parameters. There is, for example, nothing about the white race that makes it *inherently* superior to other races. The same can be said for gender. Nominal parameters, therefore, can be misused to create hierarchal abuse of power within the group, but in reality these parameters are 'nominal', i.e., in name only. That we are male and female, African-American and Caucasian is significant to our respective identities, but carries no inherent need for us to be divided into status groups. To thwart the abuses of hierarchical power, we can seek to overcome the value judgements that have been wrongly attached to nominal parameters, hence moving closer to that equality that comes with the recognition of shared identity.

Graduated parameters, on the other hand, differentiate people in terms of status that *is inherent*. Graduated parameters include income, education and intelligence. What is being claimed here is *not* that educated people are more valuable than people without formal education, but that increased power typically accompanies higher levels of education. The adage that 'knowledge is power' cannot be ignored. There are, of course, different forms of education. In a classroom discussion of Shakespeare, the person with a PhD in English Literature could wield power over the farmer who dropped out of high school, but would be at the mercy of the farmer's power in the field, which requires knowledge about growing and cultivating crops. Refusing to acknowledge the inherent differences in status that accompany graduated parameters can be detrimental to human well-being. An example which can help us grasp this notion is found in the relationship between an adult and a child. Adults have more experience, more knowledge, and more power than children. To ignore this difference and treat the child as equal to the

---

[44]    Lehmann, *The Decalogue and a Human Future*, p. 53.

[45]    Lehmann, *The Decalogue and a Human Future*, p. 50.

adult would be cruel. The same is true in a relationship between employer and employee, because the former has the power to hire and fire. How much more power is appropriate to the employer can be debated, but not to recognize that the difference in power exists no matter how modified is dangerous and naive.

The humanizing response to hierarchy (the inherently uneven distribution of power among human beings) and inequality (the unjust values assigned to categories of people based on these differences) is reciprocal responsibility. Reciprocal responsibility seeks to acknowledge the differences among human beings by transforming hierarchy into heterogeneity in a move to eliminate the unnecessary abuses of hierarchy. It also seeks to acknowledge the shared identity among human beings without assuming that everyone is the same. The aim, according to Lehmann, is to structure society so that we can appreciate differences and take responsibility for differences at the same time that we seek to overcome artificial and unjust differentiation. According to Lehmann, these insights from macro-sociology coincide with the concern for justice in human relationships that is reflected in the Decalogue.

With this explanation of the structural realism of the Decalogue laid out, Lehmann moves to discuss each commandment. While for the most part these reflections on the individual commandments are easier to follow than the first section of the book I have been expounding, one will still run into road blocks. Yet in a time when the voices for *keeping* the Commandments in a public show of strength and a private show of judgement and self-righteousness sometimes speak louder than the voices encouraging us to *obey* the God who gave the Commandments and who acts on our behalf to make and to keep human life human, Lehmann's difficult book is well worth our attention.

## Concluding Thoughts

In a recent conversation, after I had explained that Paul Lehmann had been my mentor and friend, someone said to me, 'Interest in Lehmann's work is dead, isn't it?' to which I responded, 'Not to some of us'. With this relatively brief explanation of how *The Decalogue and a Human Future* came into being, along with this summary of Lehmann's method for ethics and an explanation of some of the most potentially confusing concepts in *The Decalogue and a Human Future*, perhaps readers can approach Lehmann's book better able to understand what he was about. In substance Lehmann's last book is as insightful as *Ethics in a Christian Context*, published thirty years earlier. One can hope that this essay and more importantly this book of essays about Paul Lehmann's work will encourage others to join those of us for whom Lehmann's work is still very much alive.

Chapter 4

# The Laboratory of the Living Word – Paul Lehmann on Conscience, Church, and the Politics of God

Barry Harvey

Perhaps more than any other theologian in the twentieth century, Paul Lehmann's life and work eluded convenient stereotypes. In secular settings he was often considered too Christian, and in many Christian circles he was suspected of being too secular, even a dangerous radical.[1] He placed great emphasis, for example, on the Eucharist, going so far as to call the abiding substance of the church a eucharistic achievement. Yet he did not see participation in the liturgy as an end in itself, but always as integral to the church's mission 'to be the vanguard of the presence of Christ in his purposed liberation (or, salvation) of all people for full participation in human fulfillment'.[2] He pointed also to the pivotal place that politics occupies in human life, though not in the first instance in connection with the institutions and practices of the nation-state, but in association with the redemptive activity of God in the world as it takes visible form in the fellowship of the church. In Lehmann's capable hands, the traditional words and acts of the church, which Dietrich Bonhoeffer saw as 'so difficult and so remote that we hardly venture any more to speak of them', once again did seem 'new and revolutionary'.[3]

During a career that spanned six decades Lehmann addressed the full range of theological topics, but at the heart of his writings was the question of what God has done and continues to do in Jesus Christ to make and to keep human life and behaviour human. A satisfactory answer from his perspective necessarily has to do with conscience, which he defined as the 'delicate conjunction of the inner springs of human motivation and of human judgment'. In a fallen world, motivation and judgement are beset by ambiguous generalizations that frustrate its human

---

[1]    Horace T. Allen, 'Introduction', *The Context of Contemporary Theology: Essays in Honour of Paul Lehmann*, eds A.J. McKelway and E.D. Willis (Atlanta: John Knox, 1974), p. 21.

[2]    Paul Lehmann, *The Transfiguration of Politics: The Presence and Power of Jesus of Nazareth in and over Human Affairs* (New York: Harper & Row, 1975), p. 168.

[3]    Dietrich Bonhoeffer, *Letters and Papers from Prison*, enlarged edition, trans. R.H. Fuller, J. Bowden et al. (New York: Macmillan, 1971), pp. 299–300; cf. Lehmann, *The Transfiguration of Politics*, p. 20.

significance and diffuse its power to shape the practice of everyday life. By itself, then, it is incapable of discerning 'the aims and the direction, the motivations and the decisions, the instruments and the structures of human interrelatedness' that sustain a style of life that is fully and completely human. 'What is required', he wrote, 'is a context for conscience which conjoins the focus of divine activity and the focus of human responsiveness in such a way as to provide behaviour with direction and decisiveness'.[4] According to Lehmann, that context was the church as the body of Christ, and more particularly, the basic pattern of relatedness that constitutes the church's *koinonia*, its fellowship.[5] This fellowship, he maintained, is an essentially *political* association, albeit one that is ordered to the politics of the triune God.

In what follows I shall attempt to sketch Lehmann's understanding of the relationship between conscience, church and the politics of God. I shall then conclude with a few observations that hopefully will indicate ways that theologians can continue to build upon Lehmann's profound insights.

### The *Koinonia* of the Church as the Context for Conscience

It would be difficult to overstate the significance of Lehmann's selection of the church as the point of departure for a theological account of what God is doing to make and to keep human life human. As he put it in discussing the significance of the *filioque* clause in the creed, 'it involves the question of whether "history" or "nature" is the key to the understanding of God's self-revelation in Christ'.[6] By beginning with the social and historical reality of the church, Lehmann positioned conscience, and thus human existence in all its relations, as a *social and historical performance*. 'The whole complex, conflictual, unstable process of human history', says Nicholas Lash, thus becomes 'a matter of the production and destruction of the "personal". [And] Christianity ... at once discloses that this *is* the character of the process, serves as a 'school for the production of the personal".'[7] No field of human endeavour and inquiry, whether domestic, artistic, literary, social, scientific, economic or political, is thus excluded from theological scrutiny.

In his most well known work, *Ethics in a Christian Context*, Lehmann identifies four aspects of the church that distinguish it as the formative context of conscience.

---

    4    Paul L. Lehmann, *Ethics in a Christian Context* (New York: Harper & Row, 1963), pp. 288, 316; cf. Paul Lehmann, 'On Doing Theology: A Contextual Possibility', in *Prospect for Theology: Essays in Honour of H.H. Farmer*, ed. F.G. Healy (Digswell Place: James Nisbet and Co., 1966), p. 233 (n. 10), and Paul Lehmann, 'Messiah and Metaphor', in *Religious Studies in Higher Education*, ed. E.I. Abendroth (Philadelphia: The Division of Higher Education of the United Presbyterian Church, 1967), pp. 25–6.

    5    Lehmann, *Ethics in a Christian Context*, p. 85.

    6    Ibid., p. 110.

    7    Nicholas Lash, *Theology on the Way to Emmaus* (London: SCM, 1986), p. 153.

The first derives from its nature as the body of Christ, which is that the church is the '*fellowship-creating reality* of Christ's presence in the world'. As Jesus' life and ministry take shape, 'the records implicitly or explicitly indicate an increasing identification of himself with the Messiah, who is unintelligible apart from the covenant community, the corporate structure of God's activity in the world'. There is thus 'no real presence of Jesus in history without or apart from the true people of God which as the work of the Holy Spirit is always at the same time a spiritual and a visible reality'.[8] It is only in the *koinonia* of the church and due to it, then, that humans are concretely and inescapably involved in God's humanizing activity.

The link between the Messiah and the church's basic patterns of relatedness not only identifies the historical context within which the formation of conscience takes place, it also locates this process within the inner life of God, in which humans are not merely products, but 'also, in different ways ... *cherished*'.[9] The incarnation, classically articulated in the formula of Chalcedon as the union of the divine and human natures in the person of Jesus, thus incorporates 'inconfusedly and inseparably' the community which the Holy Spirit gathers about him. Humanity's participation in the divine activity is thus not extrinsic to human nature, but thanks to what may legitimately be called the sacrament of the church coheres within the trinitarian relations of God as divine gift.

As the corporate structure of God's messianic activity in the world, says Lehmann, the *koinonia* is generated in and though the liturgy of the Eucharist. The pattern of life cultivated among the communion of saints is thus principally a eucharistic achievement: 'To "go to communion" is to engage in a twofold act: an act of receiving and of sharing. The celebration of the sacrament is the celebration of the miracle of authentic *transubstantiation*, "which means", in [Luther's] unforgettably vivid phrase, "through love being changed into each other"'. Communication, in this sense of the term, cannot be limited to, nor grounded in something like Jürgen Habermas's concept of communicative action,[10] but partakes of the New Testament and Elizabethan sense of the word, according to which a person actually exists only in relationships with others, and in which each shares of oneself with the other.[11] The use of 'transubstantiation' to describe the production of persons within the corporate humanity of the eucharistic community was thus crucial on Lehmann's part.

Communion is not limited, however, to the liturgy. With his inauguration of the eucharistic feast, Jesus 'was also inaugurating a new order of community of life. Contrary to existing political, social, and ecclesiastical authority and procedure, the community of the kingdom of God, the fellowship of believers in Him would be signed and sealed by the bread and the cup which signified his presence in

---

8    Lehmann, *Ethics in a Christian Context*, pp. 47, 58, 112; cf. 68, 72, 74, 80, 284.

9    Lash, *Theology on the Way to Emmaus*, pp. 164–5.

10   See, for example, Jürgen Habermas, *The Theory of Communicative Action*, vol. 2, trans. T. McCarthy (Boston: Beacon Press, 1987).

11   Lehmann, *Ethics in a Christian Context*, p. 65.

the community as one who serves'.[12] This intimacy of communication within the *koinonia* takes in our everyday relationships with the other members of Christ's body. Lehmann, citing Luther's mystical description of Christ's atoning work, asserted that our fellowship with one another is grounded in Christ's eucharistic presence, through which he takes on our estate and strives with us against sin, evil and death, while we assume Christ's estate and dwell faithfully in his righteousness, life and blessedness.[13] The eucharistic nature of Christ's presence thus conveys to the members of his body the *servant* character of the atonement: 'The atoning sacrifice of the sacrificial lamb has been dispensed with and displaced by one oblation, once-offered, one for all. The "sacrifice form", if we may put it this way, has been superseded by the "servant-form".'[14]

A second aspect of the *koinonia* has to do with the way the church articulates for itself and for others the reality of Christ's presence in the world. There is a 'line of revelation' – a prophetic-apostolic line – which is illumined in and to the fellowship by the Spirit.[15] Lehmann highlighted in this prophetic-apostolic line of revelation the early church's depiction of itself as an eschatological fellowship and therefore as 'the people of the "Age to Come", the people who are under a new covenant and hold membership in the true Israel. But so marked is the proleptic sense of reality in the New Testament that the "inheritance of Christ" is viewed not only as a transforming membership in a brotherhood which is to be but also as the fruit and function of the Spirit's operation here and now'.[16] Though its consummation still lies in the future, the messianic age is now also a present reality.

Lehmann unpacked the content of this prophetic-apostolic line of revelation in terms of a running conversation between the biblical narrative and the church. The activity of the Holy Spirit is the presupposition and foundation of this dialogue, informing the exercise of judgement within the *koinonia* and re-directing the practice of everyday life in keeping with basic motifs of the biblical narrative. The messianic community, therefore, forms that point where the 'prophetic-apostolic *witness* and the *response* of the fellowship in the Spirit coincide'.[17] The emphasis for biblical interpretation thus falls upon the active, obedient, and liberating response of conscience to the mystery of the divine activity, in which 'the conceptual is always instrumental to the concrete, and the concrete is never self-authenticating but always being fashioned by the dynamics of the self-authenticating activity of God in, with, and under the forms of man's humanity to man of which man's language speaks'.[18]

---

[12]   Paul L. Lehmann, 'Betrayal of the Real Presence', *The Princeton Seminary Bulletin* 49 (January 1956): p. 23.

[13]   Lehmann, *Ethics in a Christian Context*, pp. 64–5.

[14]   Lehmann, 'Betrayal of the Real Presence', p. 23.

[15]   Lehmann, *Ethics in a Christian Context*, pp. 50–51.

[16]   Ibid., pp. 14, 45–6.

[17]   Ibid., p. 51.

[18]   Ibid., pp. 80, 248.

The *koinonia* is, thirdly, a fellowship of diverse gifts: 'There is no uniformity, no monotony in the *koinonia*. These diversities of gifts are themselves part of the Creator's purpose according to which Christ functions in the world.'[19] The diversity of gifts thus exhibits the differences that mark the goodness of creation within the purposed activity of God. But then in characteristic fashion Lehmann linked the gifts of the Spirit to God's activity to make and keep human life human. In particular, he employed the notions of reciprocity and reciprocal responsibility, on the one hand, to articulate the distinctiveness and integrity of every woman and man, and on the other, to emphasize the irreducible interrelatedness of selfhood that characterizes the corporate fabric of human existence in the *koinonia*.

The fourth and final aspect of life in the *koinonia*, which is also its goal and *esprit*, is the cultivation of human maturity and wholeness, what Paul referred to as the new humanity in Christ, and according to which 'all of us come ... to the measure of the full stature of Christ' (Eph. 4:13). These traits describe the complete development of the human person and of all persons in their mutual relations, owing to their obedient response to, and participation in the triune God's reconciling activity. What is fundamental to being human, wrote Lehmann, 'is the gift to man of the power to be and to fulfill himself in and through a relationship of dependence and self-giving toward God and toward his fellow man. Thus, maturity is self-acceptance through self-giving'. Maturity is therefore a gift given by Jesus Christ to the members of the *koinonia*, and through them is offered to all humankind: 'This is the meaning of the New Testament claim that Jesus Christ is both Redeemer and he "in whom all things hold together", both prototype and bestower of the new humanity.'[20]

Taken together, these four aspects of the church establish in the world *a laboratory of the living word* constituted by the Spirit to be the bearer 'of the mystery (secret) and the transforming power of the divine activity, on the one hand, and, on the other, of the secret (mystery) and the 'stuff' of human maturity'. The use of 'laboratory' is a revealing image, particularly in light of the fact that its etymological roots, as well as those of 'liturgy', are grounded in the idea of labour. Thus in the *koinonia* the habits and relations that rightly configure the labour of everyday life are concretely set forth, as 'God sets up the conditions for human maturity and makes available to all men the power of human wholeness'.[21]

## Church, Society and Conscience

The fellowship of Christ and believers that forms the context of conscience rested for Lehmann on a *societal* rather than a strictly *sacredotal* understanding of God's relation to the people of the covenant. The basic sense of *leitourgia* in the New

---

[19]   Ibid., p. 52.
[20]   Ibid., pp. 16–17.
[21]   Ibid., pp. 101, 112, 131, 345.

Testament, from which we derive the idea of liturgy, is predominantly ethical: 'Work and worship are correlative forms of behavioural service to God. The laborer is the philological precursor of the worshiper.'[22] The Eucharist is the liturgical celebration of this servant reality, and apart from it the liturgy defeats itself by obscuring the dramatic presentation of God's redemptive presence in the world in Jesus Christ. The divine activity gives to the eucharistic liturgy its occasion and significance, and 'the ethical reality of the *koinonia* gives to the celebration of the Eucharist its integrity'.[23]

As this statement suggests, Lehmann principally characterized genuine selfhood in terms of the concept of integrity rather than with the notions of freedom or autonomy. Integrity is only achieved *in and through* the interrelatedness of the communion of saints. He uses the Pauline image of the organic unity of the physical body to depict the connection between integrity and interrelatedness, stating that 'the interrelatedness between Christ, the head, and the several members of the fellowship of diverse gifts which is Christ's body is structured in the world in a pattern of integrity in and through interrelatedness. And participation in this pattern is at once the mark and the means of that organic vitality which carries forward toward wholeness, or maturity'.[24]

The identification of the *koinonia* as the context of conscience raises important questions regarding the relation between the spiritual (or socio-ethical) and the empirical (or institutional) dimensions of the church. Lehmann argued that the spiritual character of Christ's body, which as the work of the Holy Spirit issues from God's specifically purposed activity in the world in Jesus Christ, is dialectically linked to the empirical church, the visible *ekklesia*. Just as there is no real presence of Christ in history apart from the fellowship of the *koinonia*, apart from the historical continuity embodied in the institutions, traditions and practices of the visible church there is no *koinonia*.[25]

For Lehmann the most satisfactory account of the connection between the *koinonia*, 'the redeemed family of the Lord Christ', and the institutional reality of the church, 'the pilgrim city of King Christ', was Augustine's *The City of God Against the Pagans*. According to Augustine the reality-creating fellowship of the *koinonia* is dialectically related to the institutional nature of the *ekklesia*: 'The *koinonia* is neither *identical* with the *visible* church nor *separable* from the visible church. *Ecclesiola in ecclesia*, the little church within the church, the leaven in the lump, the remnant in the midst of the covenant people, the *koinonia* in the world – this is the reality which is the starting point for the living of the Christian

---

22    Ibid., p.102; cf. *Theological Dictionary of the New Testament*, s.v. 'leitourgeo, leitourgia', by Hermann Strathmann and Rudolf Meyer.

23    Lehmann, *Ethics in a Christian Context*, p. 103.

24    Ibid., pp. 54–5.

25    Ibid., p. 70.

life.'[26] Once again he insisted that the two aspects of the church should neither be confused nor separated.

This dialectical reciprocity between the invisible and the visible church gradually degraded over time into a hard and fast distinction, with the invisibility of the church being consigned to a realm beyond history. Whenever the dialectic between the invisibility and the visibility of the church is weakened or lost sight of, attempts were made to safeguard the integrity of the church by emphasizing its invisibility, which inadvertently accelerated the secularization of the visible church: 'It is a kind of vicious circle in which the more invisible the church becomes, the less it visibly becomes the church.'[27] By the sixteenth century, then, Augustine's sense of the dialectical reality of the church was in urgent need of restoration in order to re-establish the proper relationship between the church's empirical and spiritual dimensions, between the church as institution and the church as event.

The church must never exclude one possibility that emerges 'precisely in the context and course of God's action in Christ in the fellowship of believers in the world'. The divine activity, though disclosed in and through the *koinonia*, cannot be confined to or exhausted by it. While bound in covenant *to* what has been accomplished in the church, God is not bound *by* it, so that God is free to work in the world as it pleases the divine will. 'It may therefore always be possible', wrote Lehmann,

> ... that the distinguishable, though inseparable, relation between the *koinonia* and the church may be strengthened, or corrected, or even set upon an entirely fresh track, by the unexpected eruption into visibility of the invisibility of God's purposed fellowship in Christ. If and when such a marginal possibility occurs, it can only be welcomed by those who belong to the *koinonia* anywhere.[28]

## Conscience, the Politics of God, and Eschatology

Lehmann contended that these divinely instituted patterns of maturity and reciprocity within the fellowship-creating reality of the church are best described in terms of the 'politics of God'. He was fully aware that he was putting forward a conception of politics that differed sharply from its customary use in modern political discourse: 'The present adoption of the word "politics" as applied to the activity of God has to do, not with ... pragmatic and passing manifestations of political behaviour, but with that to which the word "politics" fundamentally and

---

[26]   Ibid., p. 72. While he states that the German Pietists drew too sharp a distinction between the 'little church' and the 'larger church', the phrase *ecclesiola in ecclesia* enunciated for Lehmann the concern for the integrity of the historical relation between visible and spiritual facets of the church 'as a fellowship of which Christ is the head and in which Christ is really present and at work in the world'. Ibid., pp. 50–51, n. 1.

[27]   Ibid., p. 71.

[28]   Ibid., pp. 72–3.

centrally refers.' In this most basic sense of the term, one should say that God is a 'politician'.[29]

Lehmann arrived at this concept of politics by combining an Aristotelian *definition* with a biblical *description*. According to Aristotle, politics is both a science and a practice that attends to the historical possibilities for human existence as they are realized within communities.[30] These associations exist as 'the precondition for and the expression of the fulfillment of human life'.[31] Men and women do not therefore exist as 'persons' prior to being members of a *polis*.[32] Politics thus names that 'activity, and reflection upon activity, which aims at and analyzes what it takes to make and to keep human life human in the world'.[33] Everyday life, lived out in response to the creative and redemptive activity of God, thus becomes a primary focus for theological inquiry. The corporate structures and dynamics of human life – economic, moral, legal, cultural, political, scientific and, not least of all, ideological – are therefore not incidental to what is essentially human, but intrinsic to the historical (that is to say, the political) vocation of human creatureliness. The task of theology is therefore in large part to exhibit, in, with, and under these activities, 'the formative and particular activity of God'.[34]

The human response to God's formative activity in Christ, namely faith, can therefore not be reduced to creedal assent, liturgical repetition, or personal trust (though all of these contribute to a well-formed faith). At bottom it is '*involvement*, with heart and mind and soul and strength, in and with a formative way of looking at life and of living it',[35] that is to say, 'the involvement of man in the freedom of God to be God for man and in man. In this freedom all things are made new'.[36] As a performative activity, faith always entails an act of obedience, thus bringing us back to the reality of conscience. In conscience 'the risk of faith is the risk of

---

[29]    Ibid., p. 83.

[30]    Ibid., p. 85; cf. Aristotle, *The Politics*, III.9, trans. C. Lord (Chicago: The University of Chicago Press, 1984).

[31]    Lehmann, *Ethics in a Christian Context*, p. 85. Aristotle's definition is at variance with modern conceptions of politics, according to which individuals contract with each for the mutual protection of life and property. See, of course, Thomas Hobbes, *Leviathan*, ed. E. Curley (Indianapolis, IN: Hackett, 1994).

[32]    The notion of *polis* or 'city' thus functions as a synecdoche, by which a species stands in for the genus, 'political association'.

[33]    Lehmann, *Ethics in a Christian Context*, p. 85. Lehmann observes that the starting point for Aristotle's political theory is the *koinonia* of the *polis*, 'the same word that markedly and specifically conveys the New Testament understanding of the phenomenological consequences of God's activity in Christ in the world'. Ibid.

[34]    Lehmann, 'On Doing Theology', pp. 123, 130–31.

[35]    Lehmann, *The Transfiguration of Politics*, p. 84, emphasis mine.

[36]    Paul Lehmann, 'Jesus Christ and Theological Symbolization', in *Religious Studies in Higher Education*, ed. E.I. Abendroth (Philadelphia: The Division of Higher Education of the United Presbyterian Church, 1967), pp. 22–3.

obedience to what Jesus did and is still doing today. This is to invite men and women, in the power of their humanity for which He has set them free, to engage in the struggle for the liberation of any and all who are oppressed and enslaved; and thereby sharing in the saving risk of creating a new humanity'.[37] Faith thus has no reality apart from the politics established by the Spirit in and through the *koinonia*: 'Participation in this [divine] disclosure and its human prospects [is] open to "as many as received him" in a community of discernment and commitment whose dynamics and direction pointed toward the inclusion of all mankind'.[38]

It is at the point of its descriptive content that Aristotle's account of what is required for the realization of human life in a political association diverges sharply from that of the church. The formative biblical images that describe the divine activity in the world provide the principal clue to the nature and intent of the divine politics. Beginning with the story of Abraham and Sarah, God chooses a people with whom to be in fellowship, redeems their offspring from slavery, covenants with them in an everlasting commitment of reciprocity, provides for them a promised land, gives to them a law that spells out the directions of, and dangers to, the practice of everyday life, and after leading them into this land raises up leaders to administer this covenant life. '[A]nd then, under circumstances that are as fluid and complex as the policy is dubious – dubious to God as well as to the "people" – God gives them a "king".'[39]

Kingship, wrote Lehmann, is in actuality the focus of the politics that shapes the life of the covenant people. The realization of the divine kingship is nothing less than 'the beginning and the end (*das Proton und Eschaton*) of Israel'.[40] A preoccupation with the 'complete kingly rule of God' generates the paradoxical character of Israel's distinctive understanding of theocracy. The theocratic paradox, seen 'already in Gideon's refusal to rule, and more explicitly in the Sinai covenant and in the historically formative event and memory of the Exodus', manifests itself in humanity's desire and constant striving to be free from the domination of others. This desire for freedom, however, is not for the sake of individual autonomy, but for the sake of the highest bondage, that of covenant with God. 'The existential depth of this paradox', said Martin Buber, 'is evident in this, that the highest bondage knows no pressure, that its implementation is uninterruptedly entrusted to the believing behaviour of him who is bound, who under theocratic authority either strives toward a perfect fellowship in freedom, a kingdom of God, or under

---

[37]  Paul Lehmann, 'Black Theology and "Christian' Theology"', *Black Theology: A Documentary History, 1966–1979*, eds G.S. Wilmore and J.H. Cone (Maryknoll, NY: Orbis Press, 1979), p. 151.

[38]  Paul Lehmann, 'A Christian Alternative to Natural Law', *Die moderne Demokratie und ihr Recht*, eds K. Dietrich Bracher et al. (Tübingen: J.C.B. Mohr, 1966), p. 534.

[39]  Lehmann, *Ethics in a Christian Context*, pp. 90–91, 95.

[40]  Martin Buber, *Königtum Gottes*, 3d ed. (Heidelberg: Lambert Schneider, 1956), p. 118, cited by Lehmann, *Ethics in a Christian Context*, p. 93.

cover of this aspiration can succumb to an inert or wild disorder.' The theocratic paradox thus constitutes the historical 'stuff' of Israel's faith and tradition.[41]

The theocratic paradox in Israel's history culminates in a political crisis that brings with it the first 'tremors of eschatology'. These tremors first erupt in the conflict between the advocates of monarchical unification and the proponents of the traditional political ethos of exclusive divine kingship. This conflict leads to a deeper crisis in which the human king of Israel emerges as the Anointed One, the Messiah. This becomes the crucial image of the politics of God: 'The "tremors of eschatology" never cease their rumbling beneath the surface of Israel's historical and political life. From David's line he comes, the "Anointed of God", on an appointed "day of the Lord".' The day of his coming, however, is delayed time and again, 'as "exile" and "captivity" and "restoration" and "revolt and the wars of independence" lead the "covenant-people" through virtual abandonment of their hopes for his "kingdom" to an abortive attempt to "take it by force"'.[42]

The fellowship-creating reality of the church is predicated upon its confession that the Messiah, the inaugurator and consummator of the kingship of God, has come in the person of Jesus of Nazareth. In this one Jewish man the power and pattern of God's eschatological rule, 'the "God-man" structure of reality' has intruded on the present. Consequently, the disclosure of the messianic politics of God in the life, death, resurrection and ascension of Jesus forms the centre and criterion of life in the basic patterns of life among the members of Christ's body, and in Christ the church recognizes 'the revelation of God in and through whom all other apprehensions of God's activity are to be criticized and comprehended'.[43]

Eschatology, 'the connection between the *course* and the *consummation* of human experience *in this world*', is therefore a key element within the messianic politics of God. Lehmann rejected as 'speculative and irrelevant' all eschatological thinking that is divorced from the activity of the divine politics in the present: 'It makes no sense to talk about the "last things" apart from what is going on here and now. And what is going on here and now ... is primarily a matter of behaviour, of what God is doing in the world and of what in consequence man is involved in [through the Holy Spirit], of what man is to do and can do.' The practice of politics and the eschatological framework of God's messianic presence in Jesus Christ thus mutually condition each other: 'Politics provide the terms and the structures by which the fulfillment of history invades and transforms the labyrinth of human involvement in history.' The fellowship of the church thus offers to the world a sign and a foretaste 'that God has always been and is contemporaneously

---

[41]    Lehmann, *Ethics in a Christian Context*, pp. 91–4; Buber, *Königtum Gottes*, p. 118.

[42]    Lehmann, *Ethics in a Christian Context*, p. 94.

[43]    Lehmann, *The Transfiguration of Politics*, pp. 91, 279; *Ethics in a Christian Context*, p. 89; cf. pp. 94, 105.

doing what it takes to make and to keep human life human'.[44] The vanguard of a new humanity, of maturity and wholeness, exists within the *koinonia*, making it possible to discern what makes and keeps human life truly human.

According to Lehmann, the transfiguration of Jesus is the paradigm for this convergence of politics and eschatology.[45] This story, located in the synoptic gospels between Peter's confession of Jesus' messianic status at Caesarea Philippi and Jesus' announcement that he was going to Jerusalem, becomes in the prophetic-apostolic line of revelation 'the crucible of messianic identity, function, and destiny' in which 'Jesus' relations to God and to man, to Israel and to the church, to principalities and powers and to new and fulfilling times and seasons of creativity and consummation, converge'. This event thus forms the dramatic mid-point between 'the imminent exposure – one might almost say, explosion – of the messianic secret and the imminence of a messianic exodus. It is as though the whole history of Israel had gone into a sudden inversion'.[46]

Everyday life within the *koinonia* thus undergoes an eschatological transfiguration as the presence and power of the future ruptures the temporal chain of cause and effect in everyday life (and especially of the effects of death): 'The Christian lives neither by his "Adamic" past nor by his "Christian" past, but by the future, of which his present is an exhilarating foretaste.' In the transfiguration of Jesus the fulfilment of the Law and the prophets (testified by the presence of Moses and Elijah) is adumbrated in the messianic reign: 'The Maker, Sustainer, Redeemer and Fulfiller of heaven and earth, and of all things visible and invisible, has come awesomely and transformingly near the turmoil and travail of the human story: its sin and suffering, its exploitation and enmity, its promise and possibility, its forgiveness and fulfillment.'[47]

Lehmann developed in connection with the notion of transfiguration an ascending typology of power, and of the forms of knowledge that accompany significant shifts in power within the political context of human life. A *transformation* of power signals a relatively straightforward exchange of one form of power for another, e.g., when nations use negotiations rather than military might to resolve their disputes, or when arbitration replaces a lockout or strike in labour relations. A *transvaluation* of power involves a more radical shift, inverting an accepted value or sentiment in response to the unrelenting claim of humanness upon it. A classic example of transvaluation occurs in the teaching of Jesus when the love of one's enemy displaces hatred. Finally, a *transfiguration* of power (and therefore of knowledge) indicates an ingression of the 'things that are not' (1 Cor. 1:28–9)

---

[44]    Paul L. Lehmann, 'Evanston: Problems and Prospects', *Theology Today* 11 (July 1954), p. 149; *Ethics in a Christian Context*, p. 101; cf. pp. 117–18, 121–2 as well as 'Evanston', p. 149.

[45]    Mt. 17:1–8; cf. Mk. 9:2–8, Lk. 9:28–36.

[46]    Lehmann, *The Transfiguration of Politics*, pp. 81–2.

[47]    Lehmann, *Ethics in a Christian Context*, p. 123; *The Transfiguration of Politics*, pp. 13, 83.

into the present configuration of the world, an intrusion so urgent and dialectical that it signals that history has reached its divine-human moment of truth.[48] Thus transfiguration, unlike the other two, is not strictly a historical possibility, but presupposes that the eschaton has broken into history.[49]

For Lehmann power and knowledge are closely linked with the Eucharist. The transfigured character of the church's fellowship is constituted in the liturgical celebration, as Jesus anticipated with his followers the coming banquet with the Messiah when he will assume his role as earth's ruler: 'the Lord's Supper becomes a celebration both of Christ's sovereign presence and activity in and over the church and the world and an anticipation of the consummation of his work in the new heaven and the new earth and the new humanity'. The church's political nature thus provides the Eucharist with its direction and integrity, while the eschatological transfiguration of politics gives to the liturgy its occasion and significance.[50] To paraphrase Barth's construal of the relation between gospel and law,[51] the liturgical celebration is the necessary form of the messianic community, and the messianic transfiguration of politics comprises the irreducible content of the eucharistic celebration.

**Assessment and Conclusion**

In the space remaining I shall comment on just a few of Lehmann's wise insights. I find his claim that the church's fellowship is a eucharistic achievement particularly striking, for as a Protestant he articulated a theme that was being developed independently by Catholic theologians associated with the *nouvelle théologie* movement that was instrumental in many of the reforms promulgated by the Second Vatican Council. In his groundbreaking work to retrieve the patristic meaning of the Eucharist, Henri de Lubac describes the Eucharist as that which gives concrete form to miracle whereby the ecclesial body becomes the body of Christ: 'Literally speaking ... the Eucharist makes the Church.' By its hidden power the members of the church are united to each other by becoming more fully members of Christ, such that their unity with one another cannot be separated from their unity with the risen Lord is the head of that body.[52]

48    Lehmann, *The Transfiguration of Politics* pp. 73–8; cf. p. 271.

49    Paul Lehmann, 'The Metaphorical Reciprocity Between Theology and Law', *The Journal of Law and Religion* 3 (1985), p. 187; cf. Paul Lehmann, 'The Politics of Easter', *Dialog* 19 (Winter 1980), p. 38.

50    Lehmann, *Ethics in a Christian Context*, pp. 100, 103.

51    Karl Barth, 'Gospel and Law', in *Community, State, and Church*, trans. A.M. Hall (Gloucester, MA: Peter Smith, 1968), p. 80.

52    Henri Cardinal de Lubac, SJ, *Corpus Mysticum: The Eucharist and the Church in the Middle Ages*, trans. G. Simmonds CJ, R. Price and C. Stephens (Notre Dame: University of Notre Dame Press, 2006), p. 88.

This convergence with these Catholic thinkers becomes all the more significant when combined with the emphasis Lehmann placed on the Eucharist's political character, especially in the reciprocity of gifts that prevails in the *koinonia*. Through their participation in Christ through the sharing of bread around the table in the manner of the family, the members of Christ's body are reconstituted by the Spirit as 'a new order of community life' which lives and acts in a manner '[c]ontrary to existing political, social and ecclesiastical authority and procedure'.[53] In the community fashioned in the Spirit around the Eucharist, then, a different mode of exchange is established, one that binds us to the risen Christ and to one another by drawing our relationships, including those having to do with earthly goods, into the infinite plenitude of God's triune life. The gift of Christ's body sets aside both the primacy of contractual exchange and the marginalization of gift-giving to the private sphere, where the recipient is rendered passive and the giver experiences giving as an alienation of property. In God's gift of the Son to the world, the Father is not alienated from the gift, but goes with the gift, is in the gift.[54] In return an exchange of sorts is expected of the recipient, though not one that presumes to return to God something that might be lacking in the divine life, 'since there is nothing extra to God that could return to him'.[55] This shared meal prefigures the hope of the messianic age, when – as Mary's song magnifying the Lord puts it – the rich will give up what we now call their capital, and the poor will be well fed (Lk. 1:53).

Equally significant is Lehmann's threefold typology of power. The distinction between transformations and transvaluations of power, on the one hand, and a transfiguration of power on the other, is rich with interpretive possibilities that have yet to be explored. For example, this distinction helps to preserve the Christological nature of the church's participation in the social, political, economic and cultural circumstances of the earthly city. A form of life based on the transfiguration of power, that is to say, on the incursion of the future into the present through the habits and relations of the *koinonia*, allows the body of Christ to be involved fully in the world, while at the same time calling into question purely sociological conceptions of the church.[56]

---

[53]    Lehmann, 'Betrayal of the Real Presence', p. 23.

[54]    William T. Cavanaugh, 'The City: Beyond Secular Parodies', in *Radical Orthodoxy: A New Theology*, eds J. Milbank, C. Pickstock and G. Ward (New York: Routledge, 1999), p. 195.

[55]    John Milbank, 'Can A Gift Be Given? Prolegomena to a future Trinitarian Metaphysic', *Modern Theology* 11 (January 1995), p. 133, cited by Cavanaugh, 'The City', p. 195.

[56]    See, for example, Rowan Williams' critique of this tendency in the work of F.D. Maurice in 'Incarnation and the Renewal of Community', in *On Christian Theology* (Malden MA: Blackwell, 2000), pp. 225–38, and also Paul Martens' insightful analysis of the later work of John Howard Yoder in 'The Problematic Development of the Sacraments in the Thought of John Howard Yoder', *Conrad Grebel Review* 24.3 (Fall 2006): 65–77.

One more aspect of his thought deserves to be highlighted in this regard. Long before it was popular to speak at length about 'difference', 'alterity' and 'the other', Lehmann emphasized the diversity of the *koinonia*, and in the process helped to recover what had been a long-standing emphasis in the tradition.[57] What is distinctive about his presentation of this topic, however, is that he linked it, not to the views of cultural anthropology (which has its own shortcomings[58]), but to the Pauline notion of the gifts of the Holy Spirit. It is within the *koinonia*, then, that the mystery of the diversity of creation is truthfully exhibited. With their incorporation into the body of Christ women and men receive their spiritual gift that constitutes the distinctive singularity of their existence in the body of Christ. Difference is therefore not embraced for its own sake, but so that in the giving and receiving of their gifts all might share in one calling – to be for the sake of the world sign, foretaste and herald of the destiny of all things in God's new creation.

I am no longer persuaded, however, that the concept of conscience can bear the doctrinal and moral weight that Lehmann put on it. To be sure, his use of the term does stand within a tradition that employed it to great effect. Both Martin Luther and John Calvin (to whom Lehmann constantly deferred) made considerable use of the notion. Much of Luther's theology in particular was built around this concept, such that Karl Holl could say that in the final analysis, 'Luther's religion

---

[57]    St. Thomas Aquinas, for example, argued that 'superabundant variety' was at the heart of God's creative intention: 'For He brought things into being in order that His goodness might be communicated to creatures, and be represented by them; and because His goodness could not be adequately represented by one creature alone, He produced many and diverse creatures, that what was wanting to one in the representation of the divine goodness might be supplied by another. For goodness, which in God is simple and uniform, in creatures is manifold and divided; and hence the whole universe together participates the divine goodness more perfectly, and represents it better than any single creature whatever.' – St. Thomas Aquinas, *Summa Theologiae*, Ia. 47, A. 2. This appreciation for diversity extended to the manifold customs, creations, convictions, rites and habits of humankind. As St. Augustine put it, the achievements of human industry, agriculture, navigation, the arts, drama, hunting, weapons, medicines, culinary arts, communication, oratory and poetry, astronomy, even the ingenuity of philosophers and heretics in defending their errors and false doctrines, are wondrous and astonishing – see Augustine, *The City of God Against the Pagans*, XXII.24, ed. R.W. Dyson (New York: Cambridge University Press, 1998).

[58]    In the words of Bernard McGrane, 'We think under the hegemony of the ethnological response to the alienness of the Other; we are, today, contained within an anthropological concept of the Other. Anthropology has become our modern way of seeing the Other as, fundamentally and merely, culturally different.' In other words, the concept of difference has been democratized, which permits us to insert the other into 'our' present, to transform her or him into 'our' contemporary, always of course on 'our' terms. The other is now '*merely*' different. (Bernard McGrane, *Beyond Anthropology: Society and the Other* (New York: Columbia University Press, 1989), p. x.)

is a religion of conscience in the strictest senses of the word'.[59] Apart from a rich theological context, however, the idea of conscience invariably becomes (to borrow an expression from Evelyn Underhill) 'strange, vague, or merely sentimental'.[60] Witness for example, Jean-Jacques Rousseau's description of conscience: 'Divine instinct, immortal voice from heaven; sure guide for a creature ignorant and finite indeed, yet intelligent and free; infallible judge of good and evil, making man like to God!'[61] In our secularized circumstances a wide variety of connotations attach themselves to this notion that run counter to Lehmann's intentions.[62] Given the ethos of our time and place, the odds that his conception of conscience would prevail, even in churches, seem slight, and in the process the wealth embedded in his work would be tragically overlooked.

---

[59] Karl Holl, 'Was verstand Luther unter Religion?' *Gesammelte Aufsätze zur Kirchengeschichte*, vol. 1 (Tübingen: J.C.B. Mohr, 1923), p. 35.

[60] Evelyn Underhill, 'The Future of Mysticism', in *Evelyn Underhill: Modern Guide to the Ancient Quest for the Holy*, ed. D. Greene (New York: SUNY Press, 1988), p. 66.

[61] Jean-Jacques Rousseau, *Émile*, trans. Barbara Foxley (London: Dent, 1911), p. 254.

[62] One thinks here of 'Sheilaism', a name that one woman gave to her own personalized faith: 'I believe in God. I'm not a religious fanatic. I can't remember the last time I went to church. My faith has carried me a long way. It's Sheilaism. Just my own little voice.' Robert Bellah argues that Sheilaism is a perfectly natural expression of current American religious life. Robert Bellah et al., *Habits of the Heart: Individualism and Commitment in American Life* (New York: Harper & Row, 1985) p. 221; cf. Charles Taylor's discussion of the 'Age of Authenticity' in *A Secular Age* (Cambridge, MA: The Belknap Press of Harvard University Press, 2007), pp. 471–504.

# PART II

Chapter 5

# Creation, Redemption and Law – Toward a Protestant Perspective on the Question of Human Law

Philip G. Ziegler

'The concept of the natural must be recovered from the gospel itself.'[1]

## Introduction

In this chapter I explore two distinct efforts within more recent Protestant theology to ask and to answer the question of the 'consequences of the Christian faith for establishing and observing law'.[2] My aim is chiefly to analyse the dogmatic descriptions within which the question of human law is set, and which also ultimately underwrite the answers which are proposed. The work of the American theological ethicist Paul Lehmann, and the Scottish theologian T.F. Torrance serve as my exemplars. Both are Reformed Christian thinkers of substance and influence; and both approach the question of human law on the basis of themes close to the material heart of their respective projects – Torrance in relation to an understanding of the contingency of creaturely reality, both physical and moral upon the divine; Lehmann within a christologically concentrated and eschatologically inflected theological ethic. Each is, in his own way, centrally concerned to connect the actuality of human law to the decisive and salutary reality of divine sovereignty, though they differ significantly regarding how this connection is best acknowledged and described. The difference concerns the proper dogmatic location of the question of human law, a difference which, in turn, trades upon a wider disagreement over the dogmatic location of the 'world' within Christian theology. Each, however, is convinced that much is at stake – both Christianly and humanly – in doing theological justice to the question of the basis and nature of human law.

---

[1]   Dietrich Bonhoeffer, *Ethics*, Dietrich Bonhoeffer Works 6, trans. I. Tödt et al. (Minneapolis: Fortress Press, 2005), p. 173.

[2]   The phrasing in that of Wolfhart Pannenberg, 'On the Theology of Law', *Ethics*, trans. K. Crim (London: Search Press, 1981), p. 23.

## T.F. Torrance – The Reality of Law within Creation

We do not commonly think of T.F. Torrance in connection with the theme of theology and law. Yet, the historical and dogmatic theologian turned his hand to the question of the nature of law in two significant essays: the first a small monograph entitled *Juridical Law and Physical Law* (1982) – characterized by one reviewer as 'a pungent tract for the times'[3] – the second his 1995 Warburton Lecture delivered at Lincoln's Inn and published the following year as 'Revelation, Creation and Law'.[4] A common aim encompasses both texts, namely to diagnose and then venture a theological alternative to the positivism of contemporary British legal science. Taken together, legal positivism and the constructivism and utilitarian rationality which are its close colloraries are adjudged the cause of the 'highly volatile state' of contemporary legal institutions. Torrance contends that this regnant philosophy of law sees to it that the 'laws we formulate and put into effect are ultimately no more than patterns of self-centred human subjectivity within which we imprison ourselves'.[5] For the idea of 'truth in law' has long since been displaced by pursuit of 'impeccable logical correctness', the object of legal science having been reduced to 'law as it is' and thus jurisprudence constrained to adjudication of 'what is formally right'.[6]

All this, says Torrance, is a 'recipe for frustration and lawlessness' a long time in the making.[7] Arising on the ground of early modern nominalism and dualism, the theoretical contributions of first Locke and then Bentham bequeathed to British legal science a thoroughly conventional and external view of laws as the utilitarian outworking of that 'first and fundamental positive law' of the nation, namely the sovereignty of legislative power.[8] The common law tradition, despite its salutary inertia, was progressively overtaken by this trend. Over time it became a commonplace that law is simply *made* – rather than being discovered or articulated – and 'in so far as legislation is the sole source of law, it is a self-contained and self-grounded system'.[9] Of a piece with this is the loss of any distinction between law and rules of social organization. This has and continues to fuel a vast multiplication of laws whose sheer volume tends to diminish the

---

[3]    W.A. Whitehouse, review in *Scottish Journal of Theology* 36:3 (1983): 243.

[4]    T.F. Torrance, *Juridical Law and Physical Law* (Edinburgh: Scottish Academic Press, 1982) and T.F. Torrance, 'Revelation, Creation and Law', *Heythrop Journal* 37 (1996), pp. 273–83.

[5]    Torrance, *Juridical Law*, p. xi.

[6]    Torrance, 'Revelation, Creation and Law', p. 277.

[7]    Torrance, *Juridical Law*, p. xi.

[8]    See J. Locke, *Of Civil Government*, II. xi, 134. For all this, see Torrance, *Juridical Laws*, pp. 6ff.

[9]    Torrance, *Juridical Law*, p. 17.

authority of law.[10] Finally, Torrance understands all this to be compounded by the fact that in Britain such legal positivism is as good as 'built into the constitution itself'. For the reduction of law to legislated contrivance is the essential corollary of the absolute sovereignty of the Commons and the practice of what Lord Hailsham memorably characterized as 'elective dictatorship, absolute in theory, if hitherto tolerable in practice'.[11] So, the diagnosis.

The alternative Torrance advances to all such positivism is, not surprisingly, a thoroughly realist one. Indeed, the aim is nothing less than a 'realist reconstruction of the ontological and epistemological structure of our law' and thereby the establishment of a 'deeper and more dynamic concept of *natural law*'.[12] The proposal trades upon a close analogy – even univocity – between physical laws and juridical laws and so also between the operations of natural science and those of jurisprudence. Fundamentally, legal science must regain its 'objective ground' in that same reality which establishes and sustains all creaturely reality, namely the 'ultimate Truth and Rightness of God Himself'.[13]

I will not here provide a full explication of Torrance's views on the pivotal contributions of Einstein, Polyani, and Clerk Maxwell to developments within the philosophy of natural science in particular and epistemology more generally.[14] For our purposes, we can make do with Torrance's summary of their 'far reaching implications' for all human knowledge. They involve,

> the integration of ontology and epistemology in rigorous fidelity to the fact that empirical and theoretical factors are found already inhering in one another in objective reality. Thus the only acceptable structures of thought are those which arise in our minds under the compulsion of the objective structures of the field into which we are inquiring, unencumbered by *a priori* assumptions or antecedently reached or formalised conceptions. We work only with appropriate concepts that are formed on the ground of actual knowledge and in accordance with what is prescribed by the nature of the given realities ... In this way we replace a dualist frame of thought with a unitary basis on which there arises a

---

[10]    Torrance, *Juridical Law*, p. 20. He has arguments from Hayek's *Law, Legislation and Liberty* in view here.

[11]    Lord Hailsham, *Elective Dictatorship*, The Richard Dimbleby Lecture 1976 (London: BBC Publications, 1976), p. 5. Cited by Torrance, *Juridical Law*, p. 19.

[12]    Torrance, *Juridical Law*, pp. 22, xi; Torrance, 'Revelation, Creation and Law', p. 277: 'This surely calls for a basic change in jurisprudence, and in the relation of statute law to common law, in which we recover a realist instead of positivist understanding of law, and its practice in the courts.'

[13]    Torrance, *Juridical Law*, p. x.

[14]    On this see *inter alia*, 'Theological Rationality', in *God and Rationality* (Oxford: Oxford University Press, 1971), pp. 3–28, 'The Concept of Order in Theology and Science', in *The Christian Frame of Mind* (Edinburgh: Hansel Press, 1985), pp. 16–28, and *Divine and Contingent Order* (Oxford: Oxford University Press, 1981).

polarity of ontic and noetic structures in which empirical and theoretical factors while distinguished remain integrated.[15]

In short, the intelligibility and order of things comes into our purview together with the things themselves, and we are thereby made subject to the 'compelling claims of the reality being investigated'.[16] The struggle for knowledge, as Polyani styles it, is a struggle 'to submit to reality'.[17] This means whatever concepts or 'laws' we formulate about the orders of things are fully contingent upon the realities they indicate: knowledge is provisional, always laid open to revision by the field of reality which governs it. This limits the degree to which truth claims can be formalized into systems of logical certainty since their truth lies in the 'real structures' of the world.[18] But more than this, Torrance is deeply convinced that reality itself as a whole is a *contingent order*, which is to say 'not self-sufficient or ultimately self-explaining but … given a rationality and reliability in its orderliness dependent on and reflecting God's own eternal rationality and reliability'.[19] Whatever orderliness we may discover in the nature of things has its sufficient reason and final basis only in God.[20]

Now what of law in light of all this? Torrance avers that 'in legal as in natural science our task is to detect and elicit the hidden patterns of order which we acknowledge to have normative force over our behaviour and to give them coherent and consistent formulation in a way that is invariant with respect to our many individual differences'.[21] Thus, 'laws, properly regarded, are discovered, not contrived'; positive lawmaking arises from recognition of the 'basic patterns intrinsic to the given realities in the fields of moral and legal experience' in order to be able to 'articulate and make public the hidden regulative principles' that give shape to the human obligation to '*behave* strictly in accordance with the

---

[15] Torrance, *Juridical Law*, pp. 24–5.

[16] Torrance, 'Revelation, Creation and Law', p. 278.

[17] Michael Polyani, *Personal Knowledge* (Chicago: University of Chicago Press, 1958), p. 63. Cf. Torrance, *Juridical Law*, p. 4.

[18] Torrance, 'Revelation, Creation and Law', p. 276. In relation to this point, Torrance consistently invokes Einstein's paper on 'Geometry and Experience' in *Ideas and Opinions* (New York: Souvenir Press, 1973): 'as far as the propositions of mathematics refer to reality, they are not certain; and as far as they are certain, they do not refer to reality'.

[19] Torrance, 'Revelation, Creation and Law', p. 274; cf. p. 276; Cf. also *Juridical Law*, pp. 36–7.

[20] 'In the last resort meaning and truth in natural and moral and legal science depend on an epistemic correlation between [wisdom and knowledge]. Behind that correlation is the intersection of symmetries between an ultimate ground of order and an immanent ground of order, or between divine order and contingent order.' – Torrance, 'Revelation, Creation and Law', p. 281. Cf. also *Juridical Law*, pp. 36–7, 52–3.

[21] Torrance, *Juridical Law*, p. 29. Cf. pp. 38–9.

nature of things'.[22] All aspects of the practice of law, no less than other fields of human endeavour, are subject to 'the compelling claims and regulating standards of a transcendent rational order', exposed to 'commanding intelligibility of the universe' and called upon to respond 'to the imperious constraint of a single transcendent reality which we cannot rationally or morally resist'.[23] This requires us to accede that laws 'have an open structure and thus have their truth and rightness not in themselves or in their systematic coherence and formalization, but in their informal non-logical reference to objective reality beyond themselves'.[24] And, Torrance argues, just as the physical cosmos finds its sufficient cause only in God, so too does moral-legal reality. Of this he writes,

> The contingent nature of the order embedded in the ontological structure of interpersonal human relations, within the wider realm of contingent order or empirical reality, points all human law-making beyond itself to a normative source and self-sufficient ground in Almighty God. It is through controlling reference to divine justice as the universal Constant that the contingent intelligibility presupposed by juridical law invites confidence and trust in its integrity, consistency and reliability. Without that final Constant there would be no universal standard of justice in the world and everything would be engulfed in relativism, so that there would be no real ground for objectivity in the making of law or for impartiality in the practice and interpretation of law.[25]

In short, Torrance argues that only acknowledgment of the *uncontingent* reality of divine justice can finally underwrite and sustain a humane 'system of law which is itself subject to the justice it intends to promote and which thereby acknowledges its own limitations in defining justice'.[26]

As these remarks make plain, Torrance sets his account of law firmly within the scope of a doctrine of creation, and elements of this doctrine provide the relevant dogmatic basis for his realist and revisionist proposal. Indeed, in the Warburton lecture Torrance develops the motif of contingent rational order explicitly from patristic accounts of creation and the relation between uncreated and created light.[27] Both the intrinsic incompleteness and ordering of the created world belong to 'our ultimate beliefs, apart from which there can be no rational inquiry'.[28] In fact, Torrance ascribes the very possibility of modern science to the capacity of a Christian doctrine of creation to secure and sustain 'confidence in

---

[22]  Torrance, *Juridical Law*, pp. 26, 28.

[23]  Torrance, 'Revelation, Creation and Law', pp. 280–81.

[24]  Torrance, 'Revelation, Creation and Law', p. 282.

[25]  Torrance, *Juridical Law*, p. 53.

[26]  Torrance, *Juridical Law*, p. 66.

[27]  Torrance, 'Revelation, Creation and Law', pp. 273–5, 282.

[28]  Those of Basil, and John Philoponos in particular – Torrance, 'Revelation, Creation and Law', p. 274.

the rational integrity and authentic reliability of the empirical world'.[29] As has been noted, the same holds good in the sphere of law where the dual affirmation of a divinely contingent order and intrinsic intelligibility to the realities of human right and obligation enjoins a necessary 'confidence and trust' in law's 'integrity, consistency and reliability'.

Torrance's depiction of the nature of creation – as contingent and ordered – remains highly formal. Yet, the proposal implies both the possibility and necessity of producing a more doctrinally substantial detailing of something like the 'orders of creation' – which is to say a detailed depiction of those 'ontological structures of interpersonal human relations' which positive law seeks to articulate and to which it is responsible for their truth and right. The obvious rubric to put upon such an undertaking is, of course, natural law. However it might be styled, the burden of this thinking on Torrance's view is the 'supreme meta-juridical task' of 'testing the bearing of … laws, rules and interpretations upon sheer justice'.[30] This task would never be accomplished fully or settled because of the relentless dynamism, 'depth and range of intelligibility that characterize contingent order'. Torrance imagines such top-tier jurisprudential reflection continuously driving critical and creative reform within positive law for the sake of a better and more humane iteration of human right and obligation. As he concludes, '[o]nly if juridical law is regarded as no more than a human attempt to express and serve the will of God, will it be promulgated, taught and practiced in a way appropriate to the human children of God'.[31]

The force of Torrance's argument is largely borne by the strong analogy (almost to the point of identity) between moral-legal reality and natural-physical reality and the corresponding similarities in the forms of their respective sciences. If this holds, then the proposal to recover the ontological realism of jurisprudence emerges, perhaps surprisingly, as a *progressive* rather than reactionary one, and the perdurance of positivism in law is cast as an anachronism reflecting legal science's continued allegiance to early modern scientific paradigms long since surpassed within the physical sciences themselves. Moreover, the proposal embeds at the heart of legal science a self-critical principle whose mainspring is not ideological suspicion but scientific commitment to the principle of *Nullius in Verba* – the relentless pursuit of an ever better grasp of the nature of human right and obligation solely on the basis of the 'intrinsic intelligibility' of these realities themselves.[32]

---

[29]   Torrance, *Juridical Law*, p. 28. Cf. 'The Concept of Order in Theology and Science', pp. 23–4. It does so against its historic depreciation by 'ancient science and the long tradition of Augustinian culture' even as it resists any metaphysical subjugation of nature to 'arbitrary necessities and timeless patterns'.

[30]   Torrance, *Juridical Law*, p. 65.

[31]   Torrance, *Juridical Law*, p. 67.

[32]   *Nullius in Verba* is the slogan of the Royal Society: 'On the word of no one!' – See Torrance, 'Revelation, Creation and Law', p. 278.

When Torrance speaks of the dynamism of this view of 'natural law' he has these leading features of his account in mind.

While it is true that the doctrine of creation provides the explicit dogmatic location for this account of law, the argument is theologically minimalist. Torrance elects not to bring any of the fulsome dogmatic resources of his trinitarian theology to bear upon the question of law. Neither does he draw the question into the arena of the doctrines of grace and salvation. Rather, he relies upon the barest affirmations of divine creation *ex nihilo* to establish his two realist claims of the open contingency and intelligibility of moral-legal order. Contingency needs only a countervailing transcendence to secure it, something of course for which the cipher 'God' will do quite nicely. But the matter of intrinsic order requires more than this. Here Torrance must go on to specify that legal order is a function of the 'commanding Word or Logos' of God.[33] In the texts we have been considering, he goes no further, content to hold the question of law within a discussion of the 'social transcendental' supplied by the doctrine of the presence of the Logos within creation.[34]

Elsewhere, however, he offers further comment, expressing his full agreement with Polkinghorne that,

> behind the intelligibility of the universe, its openness to the investigation of science, there lies the fact of the Word of God. The Word is God's agent in creation, impressing his rationality upon the world. That same Word is also the light of men, giving us thereby access to the rationality that is in the world.[35]

But Torrance must also admit that the Word is also the architect of another kind of order about which Christians are greatly concerned, namely the 'order of redeeming Love' disclosed in the Incarnation. And this is no idle admission. For, in the end, the hope of the renewal of legal science would seem to turn upon it, since it is only when,

> [the] order that impregnates nature and pervades the whole universe is correlated with the Word of God incarnate in Jesus Christ that it becomes articulate beyond what it is capable of in itself, and as such becomes not only a sounding board, as it were, for the message of the Truth and Love of God in Jesus Christ, but

---

[33]   Torrance, 'Revelation, Creation and Law', p. 275.

[34]   A similar approach is advocated by Dan Hardy in his essay 'Created and Redeemed Sociality', in *God's Ways with the World: Thinking and Practicing Christian Faith* (Edinburgh: T&T Clark, 1996), p. 202f.

[35]   Cited by Torrance, 'The Concept of Order in Theology and Science', p. 26. The remark is drawn from John Polkinghorne, *The Way the World Is. The Christian Perspective of a Scientist* (1983).

the means whereby that message may be received, understood and actualised in human life and civilisation as perhaps never before.[36]

These remarks point well past the unfolding of an account of the 'orders of creation' and indicate that Torrance intimates that the question of law as created reality is finally and fundamentally, like all creaturely reality, decisively impinged upon by the 'order of redemption' because the 'commanding Word or Logos' at issue is not simply the principle of creation's intelligibility, but more fundamentally, the divine agent of its salvation.

## Paul Lehmann – Human Law in the Context of the Gospel

In a sense Paul Lehmann's approach to the question of law begins precisely where Torrance's account leaves off. Indeed, he develops his account of law in relation to a particular problem, and that problem is in fact Torrance's solution, namely, theological recourse to a variation of the notion of natural law. Lehmann stands firmly within a trajectory of those twentieth Protestant theologians for whom the crisis of confidence in the coherence of law amidst the trials of their time could only be adequately met by establishing law upon the revelation of God in Christ.[37] In this they overlept even the Reformers themselves who, when it came to matters of state, social ethics and the *res publica*, suffered what Lehmann considers a loss of theological nerve and left largely undisturbed patterns of argument from natural law.[38] As he describes it, 'almost immediately after the Reformers had made their attempt at a theology adequate for a gospel of forgiveness' the focus of the problems of ethics and law was 'returned to the point from which they had deflected it'.[39] The effect was to keep questions in these fields – including the

---

[36]    Torrance, 'The Concept of Order in Theology and Science', pp. 26–7.

[37]    The leading figures are the likes of Barth, Bonhoeffer, Ernst Wolf, Visser t'Hooft, et al. On this, see Pannenberg, 'On the Theology of Law', pp. 24, 36–8.

[38]    Paul L. Lehmann, *Ethics in a Christian Context* (New York: Harper & Row, 1963), p. 78, n. 2. See J.T. McNeil, 'Natural Law in the Teaching of the Reformers', *Journal of Religion* 26:3 (1946): 168–82. More recently, this continuity has been emphasized by Stephen Grabhill, *Rediscovering the Natural Law in Reformed Theological Ethics* (Grand Rapids: Eerdmans, 2006) and in two related essays by David Vandrunen, 'The Context of Natural Law: John Calvin's Doctrine of the Two Kingdoms', *Journal of Church and State* 46 (2004): 503–25, and 'The Two Kingdoms Doctrine and the Relationship of Church and State in the Early Reformed Tradition', *Journal of Church and State* 49 (2007): 743–63.

[39]    Paul L. Lehmann, 'Towards a Protestant Analysis of the Ethical Problem', in *Journal of Religion* 24:1 (1944): 1–3, a judgement frequently echoed in later writings. In this he follows Troeltsch's historical account – see his *The Social Teaching of the Christian Churches*, 2 Volumes, trans. O. Wyon (Louisville: Westminster/John Knox, 1992), 494f, 528f, 602f, 673f, 999f. Cf. also Lehmann, 'Law', pp. 205–7 and 'Law as a Function of Forgiveness', pp. 109–10.

question of the basis of juridical law – firmly within the ambit of the doctrines of creation and providence, abstracted (or insulated) largely from the central dogmas of emerging Protestant faith. In short, on such matters as these Lehmann contends that 'Protestant theology has never sufficiently regarded the world in the light of the victory of Christ'.[40]

Lehmann's own work in theological ethics has as its overarching aim to regard the world strictly in light of this divine victory won in Christ for the sake of wayward humanity. What Torrance was content to denote simply as the '*Logos of God*' must, in Lehmann's view, be much more precisely specified as the very 'presence and formative power of Jesus Christ in this world'.[41] Torrance's leading motifs of divine sovereignty and the intrinsic and intelligible ordering of things are thus to be christologically inflected. The crucial point of dogmatic orientation for Lehmann is not so much creation and the transcendence of the Creator, as it is redemption and the lordship of the Saviour. In ethics generally, and so too as regards the question of law, the approach must be thoroughly christological. Where it is not, Lehmann muses, Christian inquiry inevitably gets snagged in a dilemma between 'a capricious doctrinal selectivity, on the one hand, and the abandonment of its theological character, on the other'.[42]

In this, Lehmann shows his close fidelity to impulses from the fragmentary ethic authored by his friend Dietrich Bonhoeffer.[43] Lehmann sees himself standing in the trajectory that carried Bonhoeffer's own thinking from 'the response to the Lordship of Christ in the church to the response to the Lordship of Christ in and over the world' and whose upshot was to see to it that in his late *Ethics* and papers from prison the world was considered with increasing clarity 'as the sphere of the *regnum Christi*'.[44] In the relevant programmatic portion of his own *Ethics in a Christian Context*, Lehmann asserts that the significance of the *regnum Christi* for the question of law is best grasped by focusing upon two christological motifs: the 'threefold office of Christ' and the identification of Christ as the 'Second Adam'.[45]

Lehmann's interest in the threefold office of Christ is itself centred, as one might anticipate, upon the royal office: Christ's kingship is the motif that most expresses the effectiveness and scope of his saving work; it indicates that the order of salvation is the context and foundation of the ethical question of human right

---

[40]   Lehmann, *Ethics*, p. 115.

[41]   Lehmann, *Christologie und Politik*, p. 8.

[42]   Lehmann, *Ethics*, p. 105.

[43]   Lehmann, *Christologie und Politik*, p. 14.

[44]   Paul L. Lehmann, 'Faith and Worldliness in Bonhoeffer's Thought', in P. Vorkink II ed., *Bonhoeffer in a World Come of Age* (Philadelphia: Fortress, 1968), p. 38 and then at that same place citing E. Bethge, *Bonhoeffer* [German text], pp. 805–6. On this, see Bonhoeffer's MS 'Christ, Reality and the Good' with its polemic against 'thinking in two spheres' in *Ethics*, pp. 47ff.

[45]   Lehmann, *Ethics*, p. 105. Trinity and Second Advent are more tersely handled in the section which follows.

and obligation.[46] By drawing attention to the 'the political character of what God is doing in the world', Christ's regal function clarifies for faith the 'environment and direction' of all human activity, including lawmaking.[47] Unless one is willing to delimit the Pantocrator to being 'governor of a clearly limited province' like the church, this doctrine requires theologians to acknowledge the decisive importance of Christ 'not only for those who recognize him but for the whole world'.[48] As Lehmann explains,

> the recovery of the doctrine of the threefold office of Christ safeguards ... against the peril of a double standard. The christological focus and foundation of behavior mean that believer and unbeliever are both alike in the same ethical situation. Both believer and unbeliever belong to Christ. Both believer and unbeliever are promised in him the secret and the power of maturity. Both believer and unbeliever are being confronted, in the environment being shaped by Christ's royal and redemptive activity, by the decision to accept or to reject the conditions of a new humanity on Christ's terms, not their own. The difference is that for believers, as members of the *koinonia*, the kingship of Christ is revealed; in the world (that is, among unbelievers) it is hidden.[49]

One significant effect of specifying the nature of present divine sovereignty as the lordship of the risen and ascended Christ is to make plain that from the perspective of Christian faith, 'all [persons] are involved in the situation defined by the gospel'.[50]

The second leading christological doctrine for Lehmann is that of Jesus Christ as the Second Adam.[51] The function of this motif is twofold. First, by focusing the question of humanity upon the eschatological humanity of Jesus, it removes

---

[46]    Lehmann, *Ethics*, p. 115; Cf. Calvin, *Institutes*, II, 15f. On the resurgent importance of the royal office of Christ in Protestant theology during the first half of the twentieth century see W.A. Visser t'Hooft, *The Kingship of Christ: An Interpretation of Recent European Theology* (London: SCM, 1948). Lehmann himself may well have heard the Stone Lectures of 1947 upon which this text is based.

[47]    Lehmann, *Ethics*, p. 116.

[48]    See W.A. Visser t'Hooft, *The Kingship of Christ,* p. 18. Visser t'Hooft notes that Schleiermacher could delimit the exercise of Christ's royal office to the church: 'Christ commands only the forces of the church' – *The Christian Faith*, (§105). For an account of Turretin and Rutherford as earlier examples of this countervailing tendency within Reformed theology which strongly distinguish the *regnum Christi* into a 'twofold kingdom' of the 'natural or essential' and the 'meditorial and economical' corresponding strictly to the distinction between the work of creation and that of reconciliation, see Vandrunen, 'The Two Kingdom's Doctrine', pp. 749ff.

[49]    Lehmann, *Ethics in a Christian Context*, pp. 116–17.

[50]    Lehmann, 'Law as a Function of Forgiveness', p. 105.

[51]    On this, influentially for Lehmann, see Karl Barth, *Christ and Adam: Man and Humanty in Romans 5*, trans. T.A. Smail (New York: Harper & Bros., 1956).

the 'last possibility of a surreptitious resort to [general] anthropology in Christian ethical reflection'.[52] Second, and positively, theological ethics is hereby afforded a material focus, since the new humanity constitutes both 'the subject and the aim or goal of ethical action'. Human acts and institutions (including law) are strictly speaking not significant in themselves but as 'pointers to or bearers of the new humanity which in Christ has become a fact in the world and in which, in consequence of what Christ is and is doing in the world, we participate'.[53] As Lehmann goes on to explain,

> The immediate and direct theological presuppositions of Christian ethics have to do with the context and actuality of the new humanity in Christ, not with humanity in general, humanity apart from Christ. It follows from this shift of concern that Christian thinking about ethics finds it beside the point to take up the question of the nature of an act and of the relation between the nature of an act and the nature of the good. Such an analysis may supply behavior with rational clarification and guidance but says nothing whatsoever about its Christian character. The Christian character of behaviour is defined not by the principal parts of an act, but by the functional significance of action in the context of the divine economy and of the actuality of the new humanity. Thus behavior, as Christianity understands it, is not qualitatively but symbolically significant ... behavior is ethically defined not by perfections but by parabolic power.[54]

And since the Second Adam and in him the new humanity originate as the object of the eternal election of God, this electing action 'gives foundational priority to freedom over order, purpose over policy, future over past, and destiny over devices', and ensures that the 'new order of humanity, in which and by which the Christian lives', takes formative priority and gives rise to 'its own way of looking at things and its own way of living out what it sees'.[55]

So, what do Christians see when they look in their distinctive way upon the phenomenon of human law? How does juridical law appear when considered within a human situation acknowledged to be 'determined and understood only on the basis of the Word of God' thus understood?[56] Just what might we take to be law's 'functional significance ... in the context of the divine economy and of the

[52] Lehmann, *Ethics in a Christian Context*, p. 120.
[53] Lehmann, *Ethics in a Christian Context*, p. 119.
[54] Lehmann, *Ethics in a Christian Context*, pp. 121–2.
[55] Lehmann, *The Transfiguration of Politics*, p. 241; *Ethics in a Christian Context*, p. 123.
[56] Lehmann, *Christologie und Politik*, p. 7. My translation. This of course restates Barth's view that 'the dogmatics of the Christian Church, and basically the Christian doctrine of God, is ethics. ... It is the *answer* – this must be our starting point.' – Barth, *CD* II/2, p. 515.

actuality of the new humanity'? What account of the basis of human law can be won on the explicitly christological grounds advanced here?[57]

Law, says Lehmann, is the 'principle and operation of order in the world', and precisely as such raises a particular problem within Christian theology. The problem is this – how does such worldly order relate to the purposes and acts of God? The basic theological question about law thus runs: 'In a world whose creator and redeemer is God, is law a self-evident expression of God's will and purpose or is law instrumental to another and different or higher expression of God's will and purpose?'[58] As we've already noted, the gospel of the reconciliation of all things to God in Christ provides just such a different and supervening divine purpose. The gospel comes upon the world not merely as affirmation or supplement, but rather Lehmann suggests, as *catalyst* and as such issues in a fundamental re-ordering of things: not the correction or completion of the existing orders, but their fundamental 'transvaluation' is at hand.[59] So, we are not surprised to find him proposing to 'finish what the Reformers started' by advancing a view of law as essentially instrumental to reconciliation. Law, he says, is properly acknowledged to be 'a function of forgiveness' – which is to say, it is the means by which 'justice becomes the concrete occasion and context of reconciliation' between persons.[60] In other places Lehmann expresses this same basic idea of law as a serviceable means to the gospel's humanizing ends by characterizing it as the 'nexus of human reciprocity', as that discourse which 'defines and directs the operation of human gratitude in society', and as the flesh and blood shape love concretely takes if it is to avoid abstraction or mere sentimentality.[61]

---

[57]  Lehmann addresses these questions in several important essays, as well as concisely and maturely in his *The Transfiguration of Politics*. In addition to the discussion *inter alia* in his *Ethics in a Christian Context*, the following are significant: 'Law', *A Handbook of Christian Theology*, eds. M. Halverston and A.C. Cohen (New York: Living Age Books, 1958), pp. 203–7; 'Law as a Function of Forgiveness', *Oklahoma Law Review* 12:1 (1959): 102–12; 'A Christian Alternative to Natural Law', *Die moderne Demokratie und ihr Recht: Festschrift für Gerhard Leibholz zum 65. Geburtstag*, eds. K.D. Bracher et al. (Tübingen: J.C.B. Mohr Siebeck, 1966), pp. 517–49; and 'The Metaphorical Reciprocity Between Theology and Law', *Journal of Law and Religion* 3:1 (1985): 179–92. Paul L. Lehmann, *The Transfiguration of Politics* (New York: Harper & Row, 1975). A German edition, with preface by the author, appeared a decade later under the title, *Christologie and Politik: Eine theologische Hermeneutik des Politischen* (Göttingen: Vaderhoeck & Ruprecht, 1987). The central section on law is found pp. 250ff. of the English text. Lehmann refers to his work in 'A Christian Alternative to Natural Law', remarking that 'in retrospect, this essay seems a kind of first try at an indication of the correspondence between the biblical and the human meaning of politics' (p. 342, n. 27).

[58]  Lehmann, 'Law', p. 204.

[59]  Lehmann, 'A Christian Alternative', p. 533.

[60]  Lehmann, 'Law as a Function', pp. 110, 112.

[61]  Lehmann, *The Transfiguration of Politics*, p. 250; 'Law as a Function', p. 111.

For Lehmann, the truth about law's evangelical instrumentality becomes most clear when law's indicative function is brought to the fore. Of this he writes,

> Human relations always veer toward the boundary on which the issue of the human or the inhumanity of man to man must be fought through, and the direction of God's activity must be sighted again. Law has the function of *exposing this boundary* and in that sense is instrumental to the divine activity. This is the ethical significance of law, and in so far as a given law cannot be shown to perform *this* function, it violates Christian ethics and thus also the Christian understanding of law.[62]

Or again, while no law 'can be the norm or criterion of action in accordance with the will of God', for their relation is precisely the reverse, law does lend order to 'human relations by exposing crucial danger spots affecting human relations and also indicates the direction of humanization'.[63] Remarks like these indicate that Lehmann conceives of human law in terms akin to those of the tripartite 'uses of the law' within traditional Protestant doctrine. Lehmann's modification to this scheme, however, is to stress that when law is firmly set within the covenant of grace, its functions are more permissive than prescriptive, more indicative than imperative and so basically catalytic to the experiment of living faithfully before God. Within this formative context – the context of which Christ's reign and the pressing reality of the new humanity are constitutive – law's service is ever to 'bend the things which have been towards the things which are to come'[64] by offering concrete, if provisional indications of the forms of human right and obligations which bespeak it.

On the view Lehmann advances, neither legal positivism nor legal pluralism are inimical to the proper function of law. For all positive legal regimes are 'functions of a sovereignty in action, fashioning by providential governance and experimentation, the conditions, sustaining and correcting ... a community requisite for the humanization of human life'.[65] If in a world made and actively governed by God with the aim of 'giving human shape to human life, *law is the behavioral function of providence*',[66] then Christians should expect the formation and revision of human law to have and to continue to unfold under what Lehmann later called the 'providential-eschatological pressure of reality upon human affairs'.[67]

---

[62] Lehmann, *Ethics in a Christian Context*, p. 147.

[63] Lehmann, *Ethics in a Christian Context*, pp. 146–7.

[64] Lehmann, 'A Christian Alternative', p. 535. On these themes see 'Law as a Function', pp. 106–7, and most fully Lehmann, *The Decalogue and a Human Future* (Grand Rapids: Eerdmans, 1995), pp. 13ff.

[65] Lehmann, 'A Christian Alternative', pp. 540–41.

[66] Lehmann, 'A Christian Alternative', p. 541.

[67] Lehmann, *The Transfiguration of Politics*, p. 237.

Note well that Lehmann sees the substance of God's providential *gubernatio* in terms of the *regnum Christi*, hence 'providential-*eschatological*' pressure.

Lehmann stresses that while recognition of this is a 'datum of the knowledge of faith', its 'functional reality is independent of such recognition'.[68] There is no need for the plurality of positive legal schemes to be either rejected or 'subsumed under the inferences drawn by reason from a single confessional or rational faith' finally because, as Lehmann concludes,

> In a world, in which Jesus of Nazareth has restored, by the full dimensions of his presence and activity, all created things to their proper subsistence and centered all created things upon the priority and possibilities of human fulfilment, there is an order of things and times which sustains and effects a continuing reciprocity between responsible life and human life. This order bears the secret of a sovereignty which, as Augustine observed, is 'hidden from us, but thoroughly known to Himself; which same order of times, however He does not serve as subject to it, but Himself rules as lord and appoints as governor'. In such a world, *law,* understood … as *primus usus legis*, means the primary order in which man's behavior is set, and by which his behavior is corrected and sustained … . Law is a *function*, not a *principle* of order.[69]

The principle of order is the constancy of God's salutary reign in and through Christ; it is the function of human law to serve the humanizing purposes of this reign – whether by design or despite itself – in the time between the times.

For Lehmann, the issue around which everything turns as regards the matter of law is the nature and purpose of divine agency. As he puts it explicitly in connection with the matter of law:

> Is God upholding the world by changing it; or is God changing the world by upholding it? If God is doing the second, then the given patterns and structures are the fundamental supports indispensable to having any world at all; then order has taken priority over freedom and law over justice. … But if God is doing the first, then the concrete realities are those *not yet given* patterns and structures that are displacing patterns and structures that have been taken for granted; then freedom is the presupposition and condition of order, and justice is the foundation and criterion of law.[70]

As we've seen, strongly oriented as he is by the eschatological heart of the second article of the creed, Lehmann himself takes the latter view. Lehmann's approach to the question of human law within Christian theology is thus a strongly *teleological*

---

[68]   Lehmann, 'A Christian Alternative', p. 541.

[69]   Lehmann, 'A Christian Alternative', p. 541, citing Augustine *City of God*, V.9.33 and XIX, 24.

[70]   Lehmann, *The Transfiguration of Politics*, p. 263.

one. Characterizing law's service – its *usus* or instrumentality – within and under the present reign of Christ becomes the decisive task. The hidden reality and ubiquity of this reign encompasses all actual human lawmaking, subjecting it ever to its formative 'providential-eschatological pressure'. Within the reality of this regime, the leading puzzle is less 'whence comes law?' as 'what is law good for *here and now*? The specific description given of the *here and now* turns out to make all the difference.

## Some Conclusions and Questions

Both Torrance and Lehmann give accounts of the nature of human law which underwrite its immense human significance by anchoring law in that which is most real, even as they relativize actual human legal achievements by stressing their contingency either upon the intrinsic created orders of human obligation (Torrance), or the impinging order or evangelical love and reconciliation (Lehmann). Both these Protestant theologians argue for a realist view of law capable of enjoining permanent and salutary criticism of extant legal regimes. What this realism affords is a finally transcendent referent for law, something which proves decisive for both authors. While for Torrance this transcendence is a function of law's contingency upon the intrinsic order of created reality and, finally of created reality itself upon the will of its Creator, for Lehmann, law's transcendent referent is the effective eschatological reality of Christ's royal office. Correspondingly, the mainsprings of criticism and reform of law are markedly different: on Torrance's view, legal criticism is an iteration of the common scientific discipline of informal (that is, non-logical) falsification; on Lehmann's telling, such criticism arises from present discernment of the incompatibility of the present order with the promise and patterns of the coming Kingdom.

Both authors also hope for an understanding of law that recognizes and even aggravates its humanizing power and prospect. Torrance intimates, as we've noted, that recovered appreciation for the objectivity and intelligible order of the field of legal reality ought to have humanizing consequences, because it holds the promise of moving human life more clearly with, rather than across, the 'grain of the universe'. Such a hope, of course, trades upon affirmation of the anthropic benevolence of reality, that is, upon the affirmation of creation's abiding goodness. Among the strengths of Torrance's proposal are its apologetic power as a 'middle discourse' which taps the cultural prestige and intellectual *gravitas* of the natural sciences for the sake of a juridical law, as he says, capable of being 'promulgated, taught and practiced in a way appropriate to the human children of God'. Yet, I must admit to an evangelical hesitation before an account of human law which, in its strict recourse to creation, seems to concur with Thomas' stated view that 'the New Law had nothing to add as regards external action'.[71]

---

[71]    *Summa Theologia*, IIa, Q.108, art. 2.

In Lehmann's case the humanistic promise of law lies in the fact that under the present reign of Christ, law itself finds fitting service in the 'hammering out' of the new humanity made possible by the forgiveness of sins. The peculiar strength of what Lehmann proposes lies in its greater dogmatic density, its patent entanglement with themes at the heart of the Christian gospel, and perhaps also its capacity – because of its focus upon law's function rather than its essence or origin – to cope with the challenge put to legal science by historicism.[72] His approach decisively shifts the question of human law out of the 'first article', wagering instead that,

> the general power of the Spirit provides the kind of theological and ethical substance and sobriety which instrinsically links the divine economy with human maturity and puts believers and unbelievers upon a common level of integrity about what the struggle for human maturity involves, and upon a common level of imaginative discernment about what the secret of maturity is.[73]

While important questions can and should be put to Lehmann's account – regarding, for instance, the legitimacy of this pneumatological wager as well as the univocity of Christ's *lordship* across the boundary of church and *saeculum* – there is a peculiarly evangelical attraction to a view of law which, by virtue of being set firmly within the outworking of the covenant of grace, ensures that the legal principle of '*suum cuique*' receives a revolutionary specification. For, seen Christianly, what we each deserve is not finally established by natural but rather by profoundly *unnatural right*, since by grace human beings are always those who 'bear a righteousness not their own' (Phil. 3:9).[74]

---

[72]   Cf. Pannenberg, 'On the Theology of Law', p. 24f.

[73]   Lehmann, *Ethics in a Christian Context*, pp. 158–9.

[74]   On this theme, see K. Tanner, 'Justification and Justice in a Theology of Grace', *Theology Today* 55:4 (2004): 510–23, esp. 522–3.

## Chapter 6

# The Advantages and Limits of Irregular and Regular Dogmatics – Political Responsibility According to Lehmann and Barth

## A Discussion Pertinent to the Notification to Jon Sobrino

David E. Demson

### Introduction

Revisiting Paul Lehmann's 1975 book *The Transfiguration of Politics* today, I recall a distinction Karl Barth drew in the first volume of his *Church Dogmatics* (1932) between irregular and regular dogmatics.[1] The purpose of the two is different and, correspondingly, each has its own particular limit and advantage. These become clear, I will try to demonstrate, when the discussion of politics in a work of irregular dogmatics such as Lehmann's *Transfiguration* is compared with a discussion of politics in a work of regular dogmatics such as Barth's *Church Dogmatics*.

What is the difference between the two kinds of dogmatics? Before recounting what Barth says about the difference, it is worthwhile to recall what he says about dogma, since that term is not common, in its positive sense, in the English speaking world. Dogma is the agreement of Church proclamation with the revelation attested in Holy Scripture.[2] Dogma is not the truth of revelation (which is a Person), but rather an act of obedience demanded of his community by the Person of revelation. Dogma is an eschatological occurrence; that is, only when the Word of God commandeers Church proclamation does a harmony occur between the two. Dogmatics as a discipline, then, does *not* establish the correspondence between Church proclamation and the revelation attested in Scripture, but rather constantly enquires about this correspondence.

There is a regular dogmatics and an irregular dogmatics. Regular dogmatics, according to Barth, is the enquiry about the correspondence between Church proclamation and the revelation attested in Scripture which aims at the completeness required for good theological instruction. It aims to impress upon the instructed

---

[1]   Paul Lehmann, *The Transfiguration of Politics* (New York: Harper & Row, 1975).

[2]   Karl Barth, *Church Dogmatics* I/1, trans. G.W. Bromiley and T.F. Torrance (Edinburgh: T&T Clark, 1975), p. 265.

'how one question breaks up into many questions and how in every respect and from every possible standpoint all these many questions are in fact open and inter-related'.[3] Regular dogmatics covers all the themes that are present in the biblical witness, which is its concrete criterion, with an eye to the orientation of Church proclamation to these themes; e.g., with an eye to the actual and possible difficulties and contradictions that one will find in every individual question within the history of dogmatics and with constant attention to the task of clarifying the distinctiveness of dogmatics' path of knowledge.

What is irregular dogmatics? Its aim is not comprehensiveness. It does not aim at instruction about the inter-relatedness of every individual theological question. For specific historical reasons it focuses on a specific theme. It usually elides the distinction between dogmatics and proclamation. Its choice of partners in discussion is often quite free and the distinctive character of its path of knowledge is often only implicit. Irregular dogmatics is 'fragmentary' dogmatics.[4] In saying this Barth does not intend to slight irregular dogmatics. He reminds his reader that before there was regular dogmatics there was irregular dogmatics, which always had its own necessity and possibility. In fact, irregular dogmatics has been the rule in every age of the Church and has always been the origin of regular dogmatics. Barth is clear that neither form should be overestimated or disparaged in terms of the other. At best, liveliness and discipline are present in both.

Barth does speak of a limitation of irregular dogmatics: its significance for the Church is tested by regular dogmatics which asks whether its deliberations can enter into the instruction of the Church. Yet the question of the agreement between Church proclamation and the revelation attested in Scripture may be put more seriously and fruitfully by irregular dogmatics; regular dogmatics will necessarily test the irregular for its universal teachability in the Church, but it is not thereby to be regarded as better dogmatics.

## Lehmann's Irregular Account of the *Parousia* of Jesus Christ

In the preface to *The Transfiguration of Politics* Lehmann announces that 'The pages that follow will seek to show that the pertinence of Jesus Christ to an age of revolution is *the power of his presence* to shape the passion for humanization that generates revolution, and thus to preserve revolution from its own undoing.'[5] Some pages later he elaborates, 'The Christ story is the story of the presence and power of Jesus of Nazareth in and over the ambiguity of human affairs ... he involves us in the struggle for a new and human future. The way leads from a politics of confrontation to a politics of transfiguration and the transfiguration of politics'.[6]

---

[3]  Barth, *CD* I/1, p. 276.
[4]  Ibid., p. 277.
[5]  Lehmann, *The Transfiguration of Politics*, p. xiii.
[6]  Ibid., p. 20.

In these sentences the reader is alerted to the particular nuance of the book: the identification of Christ's presence here and now with the Transfiguration.

Lehmann never defaults on the declaration that Jesus Christ was present there and then at Easter as the inaugurator of the new age and shall be its perfector in his Final Coming. His innovation is that Jesus Christ's presence here and now is not identified with the coming of the Holy Spirit (indeed the Spirit is rarely mentioned in the book), but rather with Jesus' transfiguration on the mountain. He, who was transfigured there and then and was subsequently raised from the dead, lives here and now as the transfigured one who is transfiguring human affairs here and now. These are the terms in which Lehmann speaks of the intersection of divine and human politics. And the implication drawn is that since Jesus, as a transfiguring presence, is the imminence of radical change, revolutionary human politics stands nearer divine politics than the human politics that largely binds itself to the stabilities of experience.

Since Lehmann's account of Jesus of Nazareth's presence here and now is formulated in terms of his Transfiguration rather than in terms of his coming again in the Holy Spirit, some attention to Lehmann's exposition of the Transfiguration narratives is requisite. (He relies mainly on Matt. 17:1–8, but also includes comments upon passages of the Markan and Lukan narratives.)

What occurs in the Transfiguration? Lehmann's answer to this question is given in the heading he assigns to his exposition of Matt. 17, 'Jesus Transfigured: Breaking In and Breaking Up the Establishment'.[7] He comments that the account of the Transfiguration takes care to make clear that it is attesting an *objective* act; an objective act of God, in which there occurs the indication of radical change, 'a foretaste of the long-promised and long-expected new world to come'.[8] 'Indication' does not mean merely a possibility. Christ's coming – here unveiled in its enactment – is the reality by which human affairs and agents are being shaped according to their divine purpose. Such shaping is not divine determin*ism*. God, whose acts are always determined by his act of self-sacrifice on the cross, determines human beings for the activity of human love. Or, in Lehmann's characteristic way of speaking, in Christ's coming and power humans are given the objective space for the freedom which it takes to make and keep human life human. What is going on in the Transfiguration is 'the pressure of the end-time upon times rapidly coming to an end'. The event of the Transfiguration both (1) signals the revolutionary character of the new world Jesus Christ is shaping and in which we human beings live and (2) assigns us the task of corresponding or fitting ourselves to this new world.

Lehmann is aware that the Church in its history has been inattentive to the event of the Transfiguration as the basis for the description of the presence of Jesus Christ here and now in distinction from his presence then and there in his first coming again (as described in the Easter narratives) and in distinction from his final coming (yet to be enacted). In doing so, Lehmann contends, it has missed

---

[7]    Ibid., p. 80.

[8]    Ibid.

noticing the correspondence between the politics of God and revolutions in human political affairs. On the other hand, the Church has rarely been uninterested in the human and historical reality of Jesus' Messiahship. If the character of Jesus' Messiahship can be shown to be summed up in the Transfiguration narrative, then the inattentiveness of Christians to the Transfiguration can be turned.

The Transfiguration of Jesus occurs on his journey to Jerusalem, which culminates in his crucifixion. In the narrative of the journey the tension mounts – time is running out; the time is at hand:

> The question of the Establishment is up for overturn in a radical shift of perspective and direction, and a consequent revision of priorities about 'who's who' and 'what's what'. The question 'Whose world is this and by whose and what authority?' is heading for a countdown and liftoff in a blinding light of shattering presence and power after which the world will never be the same again. A transfiguration – in this case, *the* Transfiguration – has happened! And neither history, nor nature, society nor culture, nor [the human being] will be experienced as before, for they will not *be* as before. In the Transfiguration of Jesus of Nazareth, the Christ, the politics of God has transfigured the politics of [humankind] … . In that light, the mystery and meaning of the ultimate presence and power by which reality *is*, and is defined and directed, are unveiled and concealed in the hiddenness and openness of a human person whose presence and power has occurred. The Maker, Sustainer, Reconciler, Redeemer … of *all* things … has come awesomely and transformingly near the turmoil and travail of the human story… . [9]

God's drawing near releases in his human presence the power of a liberating and fulfilling lifestyle for 'the whole human running race'.

The correspondence between God's politics and human revolutionary politics Lehmann espies in the two formative motifs of the Transfiguration narrative: the power theme and the presence theme. Elijah represents the power theme; his presence indicates that the fulfilment of all things is at hand. Yet there is a reversal in expectations with Jesus' identification of Elijah with John the Baptist. For John was killed, as so too will Jesus be killed. The fulfilment will be accomplished by one who is killed by the Establishment, which thereby manifests that its day and way of power are over, even as Jesus' death forms the ground of the new world, in which his day and way of power are vindicated. The presence theme, instanced by Jesus' glorification, makes clear that Jesus is greater than Moses and Elijah; greater than the written law and greater than the not yet fulfilled promise. It is he who presides over the new world, and not by a *force humaines*. Elijah and Moses too (according to a then current tradition) did not die, but Jesus, having challenged the Establishment, did die and was raised from the dead. In him, the power of the old world (death) is *passé*.

---

[9]    Ibid., p. 83.

A further point pertains to both themes. Moses and Elijah, as the representatives of the law and the prophets, witness to the righteousness of God. The righteousness of God is not a norm in the Old Testament, but rather God's presence in action in the midst of his people. Jesus, as one greater than Moses and Elijah, is the righteousness of God to which they point.

Lehmann does not intend to make a simple identification of the Transfiguration with human revolutionary activity. There is a correspondence insofar as both God's politics and revolutionary human politics intend the breaking up of the Establishment. But God's political activity among us is *also* the transfiguration of revolutionary human politics. The opening phrase of the pericope in Matt. 17, 'six days later', locates the Transfiguration as occurring during the Festival of Tabernacles. The rites of the seventh day of the Festival were intended to arouse the hopes of a national liberation ingredient in the inauguration of the new age. It was a festival celebrated by the people in Jerusalem. 'Why did Jesus go up the mountain instead of the city to celebrate the Feast?'[10] Lehmann suggests that it was because the Zealots would have been about their revolutionary activity there. Not that Jesus would have been entirely unsympathetic with the Zealots' aspirations, but rather because there existed in Zealotism a confusion between God's revolutionary initiative, which Jesus was to enact, with a human grounded revolutionary initiative. That is not to say that God's revolutionary activity did not include a paradigmatic political Christ. Following upon the announcement and injunction from the cloud, 'This is my Son, my beloved, on whom my favour rests; listen to him' is Jesus' injunction to his disciples: 'Stand up: do not be afraid'. The battle with the Establishment is being joined. '[But] there is a difference between the seizure of power by force in order to establish a new order and the unyielding pressure upon established power, already under judgment for its default of order, in response to the power already ordering all things in a new and humanizing way.'[11] This is not to gainsay that Jesus was a radical revolutionary. Those who walk in his path will be, in their political activity, revolutionary. By doing what? By taking care to '"listen to him, my Son, my Beloved, on whom my favour rests" … who in their presence … was transfigured'.[12]

The time between the inauguration of the new age (Easter) and its completion (the final coming of Jesus Christ) is the time of the here and now transfiguring activity of him who was on the mountain then and there transfigured. Lehmann does not speak of this time as the time of the activity of the Holy Spirit. What concrete advantage and limit obtain in this irregular dogmatics of the *parousia* of Jesus Christ will be indicated in the section below entitled 'Barth on Revolt'. Before we arrive there, we will first observe how 'the time between' – our time here and now – is characterized in the regular dogmatics of Karl Barth. And, finally, we will

---

10    Ibid., p. 89.
11    Ibid., p. 91.
12    Ibid., p. 93.

observe the implications for human political activities each of these theologians draw from their respective accounts of the *parousia* of Jesus Christ.

## Barth's Regular Account of the *Parousia* of Jesus Christ

On Barth's reading, the particular force of the New Testament accounts of the *parousia* of Jesus Christ is that by his coming again Jesus – while retaining his own form, i.e., that of a man of a particular time and place – finds a form among us and in us. What Jesus had done for all humans and the whole created order in his life and death, he puts into effect in his coming again. The fact of that yesterday becomes the factor of here and today. 'The New Testament knows of only one coming again of Jesus Christ... Everything depends, of course, upon our seeing and understanding that one event in all its forms'.[13] It occurs to the apostles in its primal and basic form, i.e., in Jesus coming to them palpably, visibly, audibly from the dead; it occurs to the community after the Easter event in the form of the impartation of the Spirit. It shall take place in a definitive form at the coming of Jesus as the goal of the Church, the world and each individual. 'In all these forms it is one event.'[14]

The Easter event is the first (and basic) form of the *parousia* of Jesus Christ. In its content it is identical with the second and third forms of the event. None of the three forms may be regarded as the only form. Even as we must not reduce the three forms to one, so too, we may not separate them. Indeed, the second and third forms are clearly intimated in the primal form.[15] The three forms are to be conceived in terms of a *perichoresis*: Each contains and anticipates or recapitulates the other two without any of them losing their individuality: first, in his coming from the dead Jesus is already engaged in the pouring out of the Holy Spirit and in raising the dead; second, the outpouring of the Holy Spirit takes place in the power of his resurrection from the dead, yet is also already his knocking at our door as the one who is definitively coming; third, his final coming is the completion of what he has begun in his resurrection and continues in the outpouring of the Holy Spirit.

In his life and death Jesus Christ accomplished the once-and-for-all alteration in the situation between God and humans. What had there and then been accomplished is by his resurrection 'thrust before every human and thus made a factor in the existence of the world and every human, so that account has necessarily to be taken of its presence and efficacy'.[16] The resurrection of Jesus Christ is God's pronouncement of his great Yes to the human creature and the world, and the Yes spoken in the Holy Spirit and to be spoken in the final mode of Jesus' coming

---

[13]   Karl Barth, *Church Dogmatics* IV/3, trans. G.W. Bromiley and T.F. Torrance (Edinburgh: T&T Clark, 1961) p. 293.

[14]   Ibid.

[15]   Ibid., p. 294.

[16]   Ibid., p. 297.

again consist in confirmations of this Yes. All humans may appeal to this Yes and cleave to it 'as an implicate of their own existence'.[17]

In Jesus' resurrection from the dead God's Yes was, primally and basically, pronounced to our sphere. That is, something happened to the world. 'The world is not the same as before'.[18] This pronouncing is powerful; it incorporates into itself, which is to say that the world has been given a new form. The human's reconciled (i.e., justified, sanctified and called) being is conferred upon, or appropriated to, the human by Christ's resurrection. The human could more easily divest itself of its being than of this conferral upon it. The changes in human attitudes, speech and thoughts that follow from this conferral can only be confirmations of it. From this event the world and the human creature can move forward only in the direction indicated by that event, for every power which stands against it is at root already defeated and the effective presence (which is the meaning of *parousia*) of Jesus Christ has penetrated the whole cosmos and every human. In affirming the reality of this direction, Barth has to confront the question of 'the almost complete invisibility of this definite direction'.[19]

Barth begins dealing with this question by speaking about the particular character of the event of Jesus' resurrection. Although Jesus is the one who came before, his risen life is not simply the extension of his Bethlehem to Golgotha existence. In coming again he comes from death and the dead. If the creature is to have life from beyond death it can only be new life from God and with God. It can only be the eternal life which is given after the manner of God's own life. In Jesus' resurrection from the dead, the frontier between life and death has been crossed in the reverse direction. The radically new thing in the coming again of the man Jesus was not a prolongation of his existence, but the appearing of his terminated existence in its participation in the sovereign life of God, in its endowment with eternity. Now his temporal life shone as eternal life. There appeared in Jesus Christ, in his resurrection from the dead, the life of all creation and all humans already made eternal and lived with and for God. The future determined for the world (in and with reconciliation) became its true and concrete present. Death is now behind and existence with and for God is before. The news of the presence of this future, of this today of the last hour, is the Easter message.

Yet how is it possible that the world's future already made present in that event should not engulf the world at once? The goal is reached only in Jesus Christ, whereas for the rest it can only be a goal that is distant in virtue of the frontier of death between him and the rest. World occurrence seems to go on as if nothing had happened; as if Christ were not risen. At this point Barth does not speak of the insufficiency of the event of Jesus' resurrection. Rather, he says that the power of this event,

---

[17]   Ibid., p. 298.

[18]   Ibid.

[19]   Ibid., p. 307.

transcends its spatial and temporal limits. It must work itself out in another [mode of the] event filling and governing all times and places. As the power of this [first mode of the] event it anticipates that other, all embracing and conclusive [mode of the] event. It makes and characterises Easter Day as the day of proclamation and ... the commencement of the day of all days, of the last day, of the day of the final return of Jesus Christ.[20]

'Why has the self-revelation of Jesus Christ in the world and our lives taken place only at that point? ... How could it commence there without at once reaching its goal everywhere and perfectly?'[21] Barth maintains that the New Testament yields indications of an answer to this altogether appropriate question. These indications are attestations that God wills that his creatures exercise real agency. God by the activity of *his* agency has accomplished the reconciliation of the world to himself in the life and death of Jesus Christ. Now Jesus Christ is striding from the commencement of his revelation of that reconciliation to its goal. As he strides, he involves us human creatures in the work of confirming and attesting his striding through our history, a striding which constitutes the reality of our history and provides the space and time for our present participation and agency in that reality. Jesus Christ is striding through the world which in him is reconciled to God, but is far from redeemed. Evil, wickedness and death are still the way of Adamic flesh, which therein still exists in a sea of suffering. Jesus calls us to struggle against these powers, even despite the fact that we humans carry out such resistance under the burden of our own errors and wickedness. Yet the work of these powers and the weakness of our resistance against them, faith is assured, are only the epiphenomenon of the reality of reconciliation already accomplished, which in Jesus Christ is on the way to its full revelation. Our resistance to the powers is clouded and partial, but we press on in the knowledge that we are in the company of him who is the effective contender against the powers on his way to the goal.

Jesus Christ is the effective contender against the powers of evil. He wills to have the time and space between the commencement and goal of his revelatory work in which to enact his combat among us and in this combat to reveal to us who he is and who we are. And he wills this time for us, a time during which he wills to enlist us in his struggle as his witnesses in our words, attitudes and actions. He wills us not merely to observe (in faith) his work, but to be active and free agents in its declaration. The dynamics of his coming again, his movement from commencement to goal, determines the direction of what takes place in our sphere. Indeed, his coming again 'maintains and even creates the time and place and opportunity' for the free activity of the human.[22]

In this time between there are both non-Christians and Christians. What does this time mean for non-Christians? Jesus Christ has died and risen for them too; his

20   Ibid., p. 324.
21   Ibid.
22   Ibid., p. 333.

Word comes to them too. The direction Jesus gives to time is a direction for them too. They are ignorant of all this. Yet his coming again also precedes and follows them too. He is not conditioned by their ignorance, but rather he conditions and arrests it. He consistently calls them into freedom. He is their hope, too.

The Christian is different. The Christian looks back in the gratitude of faith to the first coming again of Jesus Christ and forward to the final coming in the hope that overcomes fear. The powerful direction Jesus Christ gives to our time and place is the Christian's power, the power of the new creation, the power of love. Yet, we ought not think of the Christian's situation as simply the obverse of the non-Christian's. For one thing, Christians are often also non-Christian. But more importantly, the Christian never renounces solidarity with non-Christians. They are our brothers and sisters reconciled to God. Can Christians follow Christ's direction and forget those who don't? Are we unaffected by their misery? or by their bondage? Can we who know the comfort of the knowledge of Jesus Christ enjoy that comfort and be unconcerned about the comfortless? No. The Christian enacts the apprehension that Jesus Christ is also (and perhaps primarily) the hope of the ungodly. In so enacting this apprehension, the Christian is enacting also the Christian's own hope, since the Christian so often regresses into the situation of the non-Christian.

In sum, the Christian is the person who knows Jesus Christ. Christians owe their knowledge of Jesus Christ to the Easter event and ever 'look back' to it to know him. They see in this commencement the goal, which means they cannot 'look back' without 'looking forward' to the final revelation of Jesus Christ. Thus, 'they exist in a great tension which does not exclude but relativises, critically reduces and purifies all little tensions … '. The Christian is always under the pressure of this tension. 'There is … no moratorium … of the Gospel and its command.'[23] Barth does not indicate by 'all little tensions' merely the tensions of private life. God has said his Yes to the world in the vindication of his Son and his No to the passing world judged and dispatched in the crucifixion of his Son. So the Christian is a public person. The Christian is here and now called to declare to the reconciled public world God's Yes pronounced to it in Jesus Christ and also God's No pronounced upon the passing world in Jesus Christ.

Finally, Barth turns to the topic announced in the title of the section in the *Church Dogmatics* we have been following, 'The Promise of the Spirit'. It has sometimes been said that Jesus Christ impels us humans from the event of his resurrection and therein orients us to his future coming; in the meantime his *parousia* is suspended. On this supposition, Jesus Christ does *not* himself speak in this time between; rather, his representative, the Christian or, perhaps, the Church speaks in his place. Barth is quick to put paid to this supposition. Even as Jesus spoke in his resurrection and shall speak in his final coming, so he speaks now and here in the time between. He is present as the active Subject of his Word. Barth has already at least implied this when he spoke of Jesus striding from the commencement of his

---

23   Ibid., p. 343.

Self-revelation to its goal. Not even temporarily does he let himself be absorbed by the Christian or by the Church. He remains the Presider. The Christian and the non-Christian are confronted by him who comes again here and now. In his 'today' of Easter and of the final day he encounters us in our today. This coming again is his coming in the promise of the Spirit. In this mode of his coming again – today to us – he is present as the one who promises and is promised.

The promise of the Spirit means for Christians that Jesus promises them his final coming (the perfection of revelation and thus of the world and them in it). In so doing he also promises his presence and help on the way to the goal; i.e., in the Spirit he promises to accompany them, to illuminate the path to the goal and to impart the power to them by which they can walk the path. The promise of the Spirit means for non-Christians that the Spirit is promised to them. He is not yet alive in them; they have not yet received the Spirit. But 'since Jesus Christ has risen for [the non-Christian], his power, that of the Holy Spirit, is already on the way to [the non-Christian], and on the point of reaching him, of indwelling him, of giving him the promise, causing him to participate in its lights and powers and gifts, of radically refashioning and continually refashioning his existence' and overthrowing his ignorance.[24]

Jesus' coming again now is, evidently, distinct from its other two modes. He does not come now in the mode in which he was manifested to the disciples, nor in the mode in which he shall be finally manifested to all flesh. Yet the mode in which he is here and now present and manifest to us is the *power* of his coming again in the first mode. Barth makes three points about the second mode of Jesus' *parousia:* first, in this form 'it is no less genuinely His own direct and personal coming ... than was His coming there and then to His disciples in the Easter event, or than will be one day His coming in its final and conclusive form ... .';[25] second, the middle form of his coming again is the coming of the same Jesus Christ who came again then at Easter and who comes now (perichoretically) in the Holy Spirit; third, the coming again of Jesus Christ in the impartation of the Holy Spirit is no less glorious than it was in his first coming again and shall be in his final coming again. In this mode he no less reveals the reconciliation of God and humans wrought in him than in the other two modes. Our present is not tragic. 'How can we help being merry even here and today? ... in the one hope in Jesus Christ our time is given us only for eternity and eternity only for our time.'[26]

Yet Barth admits that the riddle – 'Why must there be this intervening time?' – has not finally receded. His earlier reply, 'it is a time in which we may enact our freedom', is not deep enough. The deeper answer is: the coming again of Jesus Christ in this middle mode has its own specific glory. This does not mean that one is to ignore the dark side of this riddle, that in this mode Jesus Christ is dealing with a world which, while reconciled, is still wrapped in thick darkness.

[24]   Ibid., p. 355.
[25]   Ibid., p. 356.
[26]   Ibid., p. 360.

Yet all the more we are not to ignore the fact that in this mode God's faithfulness encounters us in its power already in the fulfilment of the penultimate promise in which Jesus Christ is with us here and now. There is a luminous side of the riddle of our existence in transition from the passing world to the new world: the fact that Jesus Christ himself is in this transition, as its reality. If our day is a day in which all sin, in which the earth is covered with suffering, in which death ends life and demons resist – this is not decisive. The decisive thing is that today is a day of his coming again. We are his contemporaries and witnesses of his action. He is the neighbour of every other human. 'He does not do what He does without us, nor we without Him. Our action is ours, yet directed by Him.'[27] We take part in his *parousia* and in this way we humans are linked indissolubly with one another. And the Christian does well to remember that the principal concern of the history of Jesus' coming again, which fills our time, is with non-Christians. Their existence is a reminder of the darkness which resists him. It is for their sake that the history of Jesus' coming again must go forward. Their transition from ignorance to knowledge, from unbelief to faith, from bondage to freedom, is the temporal goal of his *parousia* in its middle form. He is the non-Christian's hope particularly.

The Christian, for his part, listens to the Word spoken by Christ in His coming again today, receives his enlistment in Christ's cause and becomes a responsible agent in his cause instead of a mere object of his cause. He repeats what he hears in his attitudes, acts and words. He does not merely belong to Jesus Christ, as all do, but acknowledges that Jesus Christ's activity is the meaning of his work, and Jesus' fight against the powers is the cause to which he dedicates himself. The Christian is aware of the godlessness and brotherlessness around him and especially in him. But in the acknowledgement that Jesus Christ is effecting the transition from the passing world to the new world he can believe and declare, 'If God is for us, who can be against us?' (Rom. 8:31). From the very first moment of his enlistment, his life is one long calling upon God. And 'he calls upon God representatively for those who do not yet do so, or do not seem to do so'.[28]

## Lehmann on Revolution

Lehmann's irregular account of the *parousia* of Jesus Christ, with its particular concentration upon the Transfiguration, issues in an account of responsible human activity – particularly in its political aspects – as revolutionary activity. Revolution 'has displaced war, and functions as a "kind of economy of history" (Rosenstock-Huessy)… [and the revolutionary] creed now is: justice, human rights, the liberation of all mankind, and power to the people!'[29] While Lehmann heeds this analysis, he believes that for the sake of grasping the possibility of a genuine humanization

---

[27]  Ibid., p. 363.
[28]  Ibid., p. 367.
[29]  Lehmann, *The Transfiguration of Politics*, p. 104.

in revolutionary activity, 'revolutions are best and rightly understood as signs of transfiguration ... they make room for a *novus ordo saeculorum* in a God-man world'.[30] By 'signs' Lehmann does not mean merely tendencies to be observed, but also invitations to be accepted, invitations to participate in what God is doing in the world. 'Current revolutionary experience signals the righteousness of God in action, freeing human beings for being human in [the world] and in the world to come.'[31]

Lehmann specifies 'current revolutionary experience' under three headings: the movement against colonialist imperialism, the movement against imperialist colonialism, and the movement against racism. Each of these movements reflects the light of the Transfiguration in that they expose what is passing away and illuminate how room is being made for the joining of power to genuine purpose. The respective locales of these movements to which Lehmann attends are East Asia, Latin America and the United States.

The communist revolution in China brought to an end what had been establishment centres of power. What is crucial in the aftermath of that 'ending' is that revolutionary passion and purpose be transfigured, so that revolution is liberated from itself for itself, i.e., for the humanization of the human.[32] The Cuban revolution 'is a sign of transfiguration. In and through it, a human future has broken in upon a moribund past, fresh possibilities of freedom and justice, of hope and fulfillment, have become imminent exactly where old and dehumanizing patterns and practices of human existence had played themselves out'.[33] In 'a world under the dynamics of messianic politics, the Chinese and Cuban Revolutions are the bearers ... of new and humanizing possibilities, breaking in upon old and dehumanizing ones, possibilities for freedom and justice, for power at the disposal of truth, and for suffering as the prelude to the healing of enmity by reconciliation. As such, they are signs of transfiguration.[34]

The Black Revolution in the United States differs from the Chinese and Latin American Revolutions. The latter are movements against deprivation, while the former is a movement against de-identification, i.e., against preferential valuation in inter-group relations.[35] Martin Luther King Jr. is the figure many regarded as the primary leader of the Black Revolution in the United States. As a Christian he believed that as Jesus Christ abolished the wall of partition between Jew and Gentile, so too Jesus Christ is breaking down the wall of partition between black and white. Thus, King advocated conformity to the non-violent revolutionary activity of Christ. And on that ground his leadership was contested within the black community. While the use of violence in revolutionary activity is an issue

---

30   Ibid., p. 101.
31   Ibid., p. 109.
32   Ibid., p. 125.
33   Ibid., p. 140.
34   Ibid., p. 142.
35   Ibid., pp. 163–4.

raised also by the Chinese and Latin American revolutions, Lehmann attends to it at greatest length in his discussion of the Black revolution in the United States.

If revolution is the sign of the transfiguring light of Jesus Christ in the world, then Lehmann will not think through the question of violence in revolution in terms of moral distinctions – e.g., in terms of such distinctions as 'ends and means' – but rather in terms of the Transfiguration. Such thinking begins with the biblical acknowledgement that death is the power of the passing world (Rom. 5:14). In such a world violence undergoes a double transfiguration.

> At the level of revolutionary politics, violence is unveiled not as the endemic nemesis of revolution, but as a sign that politics has arrived at an apocalyptic moment of truth and point of no return. At the level of biblical politics, violence as the *ultima ratio* of a fallen [passing] world, in which civilization rests upon a primal crime, is exposed as the *ultima ratio* of a world already lost, in the act of being displaced by a new and human world already on the way. In short, the apocalyptic significance of violence is the talisman of its transfiguration.[36]

The new age is pressing in on the old. The messianic secret of historical reality is nearing the point of 'being let out of the bag'. That secret is that Jesus Christ is presiding over this reality, bringing to naught what is, in order to bring from naught what shall be. God is changing things according to his purpose. Violence is the sign of a transfiguration already underway.[37] It is unavoidable. *God* brings what is to naught. At the same time, *human* violence is never justifiable.

What is violence? It is 'the violation of the humanity of my neighbour, by whatever means – military, psychological, moral, medical, institutional, religious'. It is not simply killing somebody. 'Violence is what I do to my neighbour insofar as my involvements make it impossible for him to be a human being.'[38] We all live violently. What humanly can be opposed and is to be opposed is the justification of violence.

How is the Christian both a revolutionary and an opponent of the justification of violence? By discerning the transfiguration Christ effects in the relation between power and violence. Conceived in terms of apocalyptic, 'violence is a sign of the imminent breaking in of divine judgment upon the established order of power and life that has been weighed in the balance and found wanting'.[39] Violence is the handwriting on the wall. The inbreaking of the new human political order is indeed a divine judgement on the old. 'The new [human political] order, however, is not on that account justified ... Nothing and no one are justified in themselves.'[40] God alone sets things right. It is he who shatters the vicious circle of the necessity of violence and he who disallows its justification.

---

[36] Ibid., pp. 262–3.
[37] Ibid., p. 263.
[38] Ibid., p. 265.
[39] Ibid., p. 296.
[40] Ibid., pp. 266–7.

Lehmann speaks of the revolutionary lifestyle of the Christian. In what does this revolutionary lifestyle consist? In opposing the Establishment, the Christian, who by his calling is a revolutionary, knows that his activity has about it the *risk* of violence. But he will not make violence into a policy or programme.[41] The integrity of his stance, where maintained, will preserve revolutionary passion and promise from revolutionary fate, the fate in which 'revolutions devour their own children'. The refusal to make violence into a policy or programme 'unveils the possibility and power of a biblical life style as the secret of a revolutionary commitment and achievement. When this happens ... the happening called revolution is undergoing a transfiguration of its own'.[42]

Lehmann characterizes the Transfiguration as the middle mode of the *parousia* of Jesus Christ. 'Biblical politics identify transfiguration as the happening according to which the providential-eschatological pressure of reality upon human affairs gives political shape to a divinely appointed new and freeing and fulfilling human order.'[43] In this section we have glimpsed Lehmann's thinking through of this characterization of the *parousia*: 'As signs of transfiguration, revolutions herald a long overdue revision of political priorities that can no longer be deferred.'[44] Lehmann goes on to say that if the temptation to convert violence from a risk into a policy is resisted, then revolutionary activity as a sign of transfiguration will have been confirmed – in a transfiguration of revolution itself.


## Barth on Revolt

Where Lehmann in his irregular dogmatics speaks of revolution, Barth in his regular dogmatics speaks of revolt. We have now to observe how Barth thinks through his regular account of the *parousia* of Jesus Christ in terms of responsible human political activity.

In the time between the first and final modes of his coming again, Jesus Christ in the Holy Spirit gives direction, and empowerment in that direction, to the human creature. Although, according to Barth's reading of the New Testament, this powerful direction is the objective reality of this time, it absurdly meets with resistance. The human creature ever wills to be without a lord, to have no lord over itself. Since the direction of the Lord constitutes creaturely reality, the human creature posits itself in contradiction to reality and, thereby, in contradiction to itself. In the face of this absurdity, Christians are called by Jesus Christ in the Holy Spirit to a specific revolt. They are aware, of course, of other revolts. They, too (like others), can revolt against that which takes away or restricts their freedom. They can revolt against oppressive conditions, against being made to do what they

---

[41]    Ibid., p. 267.
[42]    Ibid., p. 269.
[43]    Ibid., p. 271.
[44]    Ibid.

do not wish to do. Supremely, they may revolt against tyrants.[45] Yet as Christians they cannot primarily fight for their own freedom. Such is not 'the good fight of faith' (1 Tim. 6:12).

'The good fight of faith' in dogmatic terms is the enactment by the Christian of a correspondence to what Jesus Christ is doing as he strides from the commencement to the goal of his Self-revelation. And this striding may be characterized as that of a 'Warrior' as long as the attacked enemy is understood not to be other human beings, but rather the lordless powers. What are these lordless powers? They are originally the forces of creaturely possibilities and capacities; they are good. However, where the human creature decides to have no lord other than itself, these powers escape him. 'They become spirits with a life and activity of their own, lordless indwelling forces' and act 'as absolutes outside him, behind him, over him and against him, according to the law by which they rose'.[46] Indeed, they now rule the human creature, and in ruling act against what is genuinely human. '[I]n consequence of man's emancipation of himself from God these abilities emancipate themselves from man and they acquire the character of entities with some kind of existence and dominion of their own, [even if] only a pseudo-objective reality and efficacy can be possessed by them and ascribed to them.'[47] They have power and lordship only by virtue of the human creature's refusal of its relationship to God. And while the human creature cannot free itself from their rule, it can be liberated from their rule and even be implicated as an agent in the struggle against their rule.

These powers are, indeed, 'powerful', possessing all the force of the ruthless lie. 'They are the motors of society … [embedded in the human creature's] conventions, customs, habits, traditions and institutions; the hidden wirepullers in the human's … enterprises, movements, achievements and revolutions'.[48] They are of such force that only in the final form of Jesus Christ's *parousia* will they be finally abolished (1 Cor. 15:24). If in Jesus' first coming again they were de-demonized by the promise of their abolition to come, in the transition from his first to his final coming, he continually acts against them and enlists us in the revolt against them.

The first lordless power which Barth identifies is political potentatism. 'If power breaks loose from law' and the one who governs, who should be concerned with the order of freedom, 'chooses to value and love as such his sovereignty and dominion, his power and force over others, if he undertakes to establish and exercise these things for their own sake … demonism in politics arises'.[49] Indeed, such a lordless ruler himself falls into the service of sheer power. Law is made to subserve his power, rather than being a safeguard for human life by establishing measures of freedom and peace. The state, then, no longer serves the governed;

---

[45]   Karl Barth, *The Christian Life: Church Dogmatics IV/4, Lecture Fragments*, trans. G.W. Bromiley (Grand Rapids: Eerdmans, 1981), p. 207.

[46]   Ibid., p. 214.

[47]   Ibid., p. 215.

[48]   Ibid., p. 216.

[49]   Ibid., p. 220.

rather the governed serve the state. 'The demonism of politics consists in the idea of "empire" which is always inhuman as such.'[50]

For a description of 'empire' or political potentatism Barth turns to Hobbes' *Leviathan*. Leviathan

> is the epitome of the rise and existence, ... the essence and reality of the all-wise, all-knowing, all-powerful and, in its way, all-good ... state as the only earthly potentate and sovereign with one or more heads (and preferably with only one). In the hopeless fear of the war of all against all that would be the result of the individual possession and exercise of power, people have handed over and entrusted to it all their political, social, economic, intellectual and even moral and religious freedoms, possibilities and rights. By their consent, not actually given but to be supposed *a priori*, Leviathan is safeguarded against every possible protest; he therefore rules in their place and over them, teaching, instructing, directing, using and expending them according to his own incontestable good pleasure. They are not his meaning and purpose; he is theirs ... their life can be no more than a functioning in his honour and service.[51]

In sum, Leviathan is a God-man. While the depiction of Leviathan is political potentatism in its absolute form, Barth attends to it, since we need to acknowledge that no state is immune from tendencies towards it and these tendencies are evil and harmful enough.

Before turning to Barth's account of revolt against the lordless powers, ideology as a lordless power should briefly receive attention. The human being has the ability to formulate concepts. What occurs when a human being decides to have no lord but itself? It comes about that his own conceptual schema gains a normativity, and often (more intensively) an absolute normativity. He no longer wishes to enquire about such a conceptual schema, but thinks only from it. As this occurs, his control over it recedes, and the schema controls him. It is 'the guiding star of his actions'.[52] Parroting replaces thought. When such schemata rise up as social ideologies, they become their most powerful, as *one* schema is proposed or enforced as the regulator or dictator in relation to all others. The *apotheosis* of such a schema is typically carried out in terms of slogans, which do not instruct but intend to exert pressure in one direction: 'workers of the world unite'; 'the American way of life'; 'equal rights'.

In rendering his account of the second mode of the *parousia* of Jesus Christ, Barth speaks of Jesus Christ promising to his community his presence and help on his way to the goal. He promises to illuminate to it the path to the goal and impart to its members the power to walk that path. At the conclusion of his account of the *parousia* Barth speaks of Jesus' fight against the lordless powers as the cause to which the Christian dedicates himself. And in *The Christian Life*, the heading originally

---

[50]   Ibid.

[51]   Ibid., pp. 220–21.

[52]   Ibid., p. 225.

proposed for the section we have been surveying runs: Christians 'revolt against all the oppression and suppression of humans by the lordship of the lordless powers'.[53] Having surveyed a portion of this section, which originally was to fall under this heading, we turn to Barth's description of Christian activity in the face of the lordless powers – what Barth denominates 'The Struggle for Human Righteousness'.

Christians are summoned by God's command to revolt, to enter into a conflict that involves them in effort, danger and distress. While this is a human activity, it is commanded by the Word of God and is therefore not a revolt undertaken on the basis of human initiative. The human activity commanded is correspondence to the revolt in which Jesus Christ is engaged. Christians may have to renounce other kinds of revolt or to see to it that their importance is relativized. The preparation for the revolt to which Christians are summoned includes a leaving behind of revolts of the more personal kind by integrating them into the activity of the revolt which is commanded of them, by letting that revolt change and sanctify the more personal ones. (If we know that this change is never pure, we must not use this point as a means of obscuring what is commanded of the Christian.)

The revolt is never a revolt directed against other humans. Christians revolt and fight for all humans. 'Their cause ... is the cause of humans precisely because it is the cause of God. Thinking, speaking, and acting in a friend-foe relationship, that is, in favour of some people and to the detriment of others, can never be their purpose.'[54] They revolt against that which oppresses all humans. Desiring to have no lord but itself, each human creature, together with all other humans, has come to belong to alien powers. The *parousia* of Jesus Christ effectively reveals that the human does not rightly belong to alien powers, but rather 'belongs to God and is the creature of God as God is the God of the human creature ... . [The *parousia* is] the declaration of ... divine righteousness as the basis and guarantee of human righteousness.'[55] When the human desires to be lordless, it falls prey to the absolutization of a power which comes to control it. Since these 'absolutes' are multitudinous, each human serving a different absolute or absolutes, humans live against one another. They cannot live rightly with one another or at peace with one another. Christians 'cannot acquiesce ... in this dominant disorder'.[56] They recognize in Christ's coming again that this is the world that is passing away. Although it is Christ who effects its passing away, they are commanded themselves to resist this 'passing away world' – to revolt against it. 'The decisive action of their revolt ... is their calling upon God.' They call upon Jesus Christ to come again – this is what is commanded of them. They call upon God to impart 'the universal and definitive revelation of [his] righteousness which judges and establishes humanity ... [and to institute] his perfect lordship in human relations and interconnections'.[57] Christians

---

[53]   Ibid., p. 205.
[54]   Ibid., pp. 210–11.
[55]   Ibid., p. 211.
[56]   Ibid., p. 212.
[57]   Ibid.

have this freedom and, when they use it, it is their demanded revolt. But while Barth describes 'calling upon God' as the primary and basic form of revolt, he does not propose it as comprehensive. 'Invocation of God ... obedient human action in this vertical direction, implies (as the same obedient human action) the horizontal of a corresponding human, and therefore provisional, attitude and mode of conduct in the sphere of the freedom which, as they pray [for Christ's coming again], is already given to them here and now on this side of the fulfillment of the prayer.'[58] Or, again, calling upon God, Christians are in turn called, directed and empowered by God to enact their revolt here and now against the powers of the passing world. Or, again, in response to Christians calling upon Christ to come again, he comes in the power of his revolt and directs and empowers the Christian's provisional revolt here and now. He enables Christians to see and grasp 'the possibilities which are provisionally present ... not for divine but for human righteousness ... [and enables them] to actualize these within the limits of their weak ability and above all their continually errant and perverted will'.[59] In the midst of this time between Christ's first and final coming, what kind of calling upon God would it be, Barth asks, if Christians in calling upon God were not motivated therein to do resolutely what they can here and now on this side of the final coming, looking towards it, not trying to do what only God can begin and finish, but rather rising up to fight for human righteousness in the midst of the lordless powers' opposition to it? Where calling upon God is a living event impelled by the hope of Christ's coming again, little hopes are nourished, and free and responsible advocacy for human right, human freedom and human peace will occur.

## The Advantages and Limits of Irregular and Regular Dogmatics

The task of irregular dogmatics is to think through some *particular* and pressing issue which has arisen for the mission of the Church and Christian vocation. The occasion of Lehmann's enquiry in *Transfiguration* is current political revolutions. His grasp of both the phenomena and literature of revolution is impressive. The dogmatic task which he undertakes is to enquire into the Church's proclamation and the Christian's vocation in relation to current political revolutions. Or, in his own terms, where do the politics of God intersect human politics? And his broad reply (which is followed by more specific commentary) is that they intersect in the presence and power of Jesus Christ as he presides over human affairs. A regular dogmatics at this point would enquire about the *parousia* of Jesus Christ in its fulness. An irregular dogmatics aims at maintaining a concentrated focus. So rather than dealing at length with Jesus' resurrection from the dead, his final coming again, and his coming again here and now in the Holy Spirit, Lehmann concentrates on a portent of the *parousia*: Jesus' transfiguration on the

---

58    Ibid., pp. 212–13.
59    Ibid., p. 213.

mountain, which, in Lehmann's reading, is the 'Breaking In and Breaking Up of the Establishment'.[60] In Jesus Christ God is bringing to naught the things that are, in order to bring from naught the things that shall be. And the human political struggle against the Establishment is a sign of what God is doing in the world. Lehmann describes, then, a correspondence between a portent of the *parousia* of Jesus Christ and human political revolutionary activity. It is important to notice that Lehmann indicates a *correspondence* between God's politics and human political revolutionary activity, not an identity.

The recognition of this correspondence is ingredient in Christian vocation. Christians are comrades of the revolutionaries. The Christian lifestyle is a revolutionary lifestyle. The Christian's particular vocation within political revolution is to revolutionize (or humanize) human political revolutions – by silence and by waiting. By 'silence' Lehmann means that the Christian will not attempt to justify revolutionary activity. Self-justification is the characteristic of the Establishment (i.e., of the passing away world). By 'waiting' Lehmann indicates a constraint on revolutionary political activity, but a constraint that is divinely revolutionary: 'Owe no one anything, except to love one another' (Rom. 13:8). If one is to resist the governing authorities, it can only be on the ground that one's debt to the neighbour outweighs one's debt to the governing authorities. Or, if one resists the governing authorities, it must be done out of love for the neighbour. But what constitutes 'love for the neighbour' is an unknown. So, too, the power to love the neighbour does not inhere the human being. The knowledge of what love of the neighbour is in the concrete situation and the power to enact that love come only from the direction and power of Christ's transfigured and transfiguring presence. The Christian waits upon his presence and power in and among the tensions of revolutionary activity. While Christ's direction and power are only known in the midst of concrete situations, a certain axiom of that direction can be derived from the character of the past activity of him who is Lord and Presider: violence as an ingredient in human planning and policy is ruled out. Of course, where revolutionary pressure is exerted against the Establishment, violence is always a risk.

In this irregular dogmatics, what enables Lehmann to make human political revolutionary activity the point of departure? God in Christ is changing history. (This is the talisman of the Transfiguration.) Human political revolutions in history are signs of what God is doing in human affairs. The irregular dogmatics of Lehmann achieves what irregular dogmatics at its maximum can achieve: a high degree of concreteness. From the perspective of Jesus Christ's transfigured and transfiguring presence and power, Lehmann can analyse and analogize the East Asian Revolution, the Latin American Revolution and the Black Revolution in the United States. In doing so, he supplies the Christian community the possibility of proclaiming with nearly maximum concreteness the Christian's contemporary

---

[60]    Lehmann, *The Transfiguration of Politics*, p. 80.

political responsibility. That is the advantage of his irregular dogmatics. Its limit can be indicated by reviewing the regular dogmatics of his contemporary, Karl Barth.

The aim of Barth's regular dogmatics is not to concentrate on some particular and pressing problem that has arisen for the Church's proclamation (or mission). Its aim is completeness, but not a mere intellectual completeness (or *gnosis*). The integrity of the Church's proclamation (or mission) depends upon its recognition that it is responsible to all the themes of the biblical witness. On the face of it, there appear many difficulties and contradictions among these themes as they have been taken up in the witness of the Church. Regular dogmatics enquires about these difficulties and contradictions and attempts to bring to clarity their genuine inter-relationships. This enquiry is always to be executed in the faith that God himself is light and enlightens.

Christian political responsibility is itself one of the themes of Scripture (e.g., Rom. 13). But in the sections of the *Church Dogmatics* reviewed above, Barth does not begin there. He begins with the *parousia* of Jesus Christ in its fullness. Jesus in his life and death has worked the work of the reconciliation of all flesh with God.[61] In his *parousia* this reconciliation is radiated to the whole cosmos and to each individual. All are included in it. His *parousia* is the revelation and presence of Jesus Christ and what he has done. He commences his Self-revelation in his resurrection from the dead, and shall complete it in his final coming. Here and now he is striding among us from his first coming again to his final coming again. He strides among us in the mode of the Holy Spirit. He strides among us as a Warrior and the Promiser. As a Warrior, he fights against the lordless powers who, while defeated at the cross, are still, in their absurdity, at work. As the Promiser he promises Christians direction in their struggle (which he commands) against the lordless powers and power for their struggle. He promises non-Christians that he will deliver them, too, from bondage to the lordless powers. The most critical task for Christians is to attest this promise to their non-Christian brothers and sisters. Christians live, then, by the promise of Christ's direction and help here and now as well as by the promise of their ultimate deliverance into eternal life.

Christ as the Warrior commands his people to join his revolt against the lordless powers. Two points are to be noted: first, the opponent according to this regular dogmatics is the lordless powers, rather than the Establishment; however, revolt against the lordless powers includes the revolt against potentatism and ideologies; second, Barth employs 'revolt' rather than 'revolution' since the latter principally emphasizes 'change' while the former emphasizes 'active aggression against'. The assurance of Christians of the efficacy of their revolt comes with their knowledge that their revolt is grounded in Christ's own revolt against the lordless powers; that he commands them to take part in the revolt he is enacting. Barth's emphasis is on obedience to Christ's command to revolt when he speaks about the Christian's political responsibility. Christ defines the revolt against the

---

[61]   So *Church Dogmatics* IV/1 – IV/3, trans. G.W. Bromiley and T.F. Torrance (Edinburgh: T&T Clark, 1956–62).

powers in his enactment of it. When Barth speaks of revolt, he distinguishes it from human revolutionary activity. The latter involves acting for oneself and one's group in order to overcome oppressive conditions of life. The revolt against the lordless powers relativizes political revolutionary activity and integrates it into itself in a changed form. Barth does not then indicate that the ongoing movement of human affairs yields up signs of God's work. Christ is bringing in a new world. This is revealed to us only by Christ's revelation of himself in his eschatological activity for us. For the faith that lives from this revelation there are signs in history of God's work.

The advantage of this regular dogmatic account of Christian political responsibility lies in its greater intricacy. This is a consequence of its much greater attention to a full account of the *parousia* of Jesus Christ, which grounds Barth's account of Christian political responsibility. Jesus in the middle form of his *parousia* is contending against the lordless powers and enlists the Christian in his (Christ's own) warfare. The lordless powers – in their multitudinousness – are at work at all places and with all flesh here and now. No human or human group or all humanity is any match for them. The good fight is a wider and deeper matter than opposition to empire or potentatism. This wider perspective arises from the fact that regular dogmatics is everywhere involved with all the biblical themes and therein with the multitude of lordless powers.

A limitation of this regular dogmatics is exposed by its comparison with Lehmann's work. Lehmann's irregular dogmatics achieves a considerably greater degree of concreteness in his thinking through of the mission of the Church today and for the Christian's political vocation today than is possible for regular dogmatics. His freely chosen dialogue partners are the twentieth-century revolutionaries of East Asia, Latin America and Black North America. These are not the dialogue partners of a regular dogmatics!

* * *

During the question period after Lehmann had delivered one of his Cousland Lectures at Emmanuel College in the University of Toronto in 1977, a member of the audience asked: 'Professor Lehmann, how do we know you are doing theology?' *Paulus Magnus* replied: 'Do you describe a theologian as someone who never emerges from the safe precincts of his study?'

# 'Where Have We Been? Where Are We Going?' – Paul Ramsey, Paul Lehmann, and Karl Barth's Doctrine of God

James F. Cubie

## Introduction – Ramsey vs. Lehmann

It might seem that we have here a minor chapter in the modern history of American, theological ethics. But that would be wrong. The confrontation between Paul Ramsey and Paul Lehmann should be understood as the first in a series of chapters – yet to be written – which attempt to draw Christian ethics back into relationship with the concerns of theologians working on the doctrine of God. There is a simple way to portray this new relationship: we cannot know what to do unless we know who God is and what God does. Both Lehmann and Ramsey understood this, and found impetus in Karl Barth's doctrine of God for their ethical projects. Each would finally take Barth's discussion in very different directions, and neither had what might be called a more systematic understanding of the development and continuities in Barth's doctrine. So it may be that in their confrontation we only have a preface. But it is a preface which merits our attention, and which has largely been passed over in the debates and directions pursued in theological ethics since the 1960s.[1]

The nature of God's presence lay at the heart of the dispute between Paul Ramsey and Paul Lehmann. Lehmann and Ramsey's procedures – their styles of argumentation, and what they omit or emphasize as worthy of discussion – point to a striking difference in how they understood God as the One who, in Barth's words, loves in freedom. Barth's understanding of eschatology struck very different roots in each author. Lehmann appears to have taken it over much more thoroughly than Ramsey. That Ramsey might be wary of talk about God's in-breaking kingdom, is obvious in light of the concerns expressed in *Basic Christian Ethics* about the general tendencies of then-current Protestant ethical thought.[2]

---

[1]  Exceptions to this arrive on the scene in the early 1990s – an ethicist, Nigel Biggar, *The Hastening the Waits: Karl Barth's Ethics* (Oxford: Clarendon Press, 1993) and a systematic theologian, John Webster, *Barth's Ethics of Reconciliation* (Cambridge: Cambridge University Press, 1995).

[2]  *Basic Christian Ethics* (Louisville: Westminster/John Knox Press, 1993), p. 192.

Ramsey's re-introduction of the virtues in that same work[3] reveals his concern to move ethical discernment in a more prudential direction.

Lehmann's interest, from first to last, was in the 'thoroughgoing' aspect of Barth's construal of eschatology. Lehmann understands God's in-breaking kingdom to move us away from what he calls 'preceptual understanding', to an ever-renewed attempt to discern what God is doing in the world 'to make and to keep human life human'. Ramsey's interest – perhaps taken over from H. Richard and Reinhold Niebuhr – takes up the more 'consistent' aspect of Barth's eschatology: God is not an object in the world, but has graciously bound himself to us in an ongoing, covenantal history of veiling and unveiling. Any attempt to describe God's 'activity' without consideration of the manner in which God is for us takes away from a prudential account that might better shape our lives. For Ramsey, the chief risk Lehmann ran was that of being too easily blown about by every wind (Eph. 4.13–15). Lehmann's thought does appear to be almost entirely 'apocalyptic', so much so that the pretensions of ethical systems in the face of God's free activity must be met with the full force of prophetic witness to God as the Sovereign of all life and thought. Ramsey's thought is, to put it simplistically, more 'deuteronomic': God graciously gives humanity revealed and natural law, and these indicators of his will offer the only still points in the storm of competing idols.

It is important at the outset to note two things. First, Barth's doctrine of God is not the only live option for theological ethicists. His doctrine just happens to be at the heart of the dispute between these two theologians. By suggesting that their debate represents the first chapter, or preface, of a book yet to be written, I do not mean to suggest that all the following chapters should have Barth as the chief protagonist. In fact, the conversation this paper might initiate would be much more fruitful if theological ethicists and systematic theologians, working in other confessional districts, were to attempt similar projects. Second, as I alluded to earlier, neither Ramsey nor Lehmann were privy to more recent developments in scholarship on Barth's doctrine of God. They cannot be faulted for failing to delay the debate they had; hence, some modesty is in order when evaluating their use of Barth. I will address this point at the end of the chapter, so as not to unduly prejudice our reading of these authors, and will suggest how developments since this debate might influence how ethicists can interact with Barth's doctrine of God.

The aim of this chapter, then, is twofold. First I offer a close reading in turn of Ramsey's critique of Lehmann's *Ethics in a Christian Context* and the *Ethics* itself with Ramsey's objections in mind, to see if he has made a charitable and accurate reading; in both sections I will attempt to inhabit the concerns of each author, exegete their critiques where necessary, and save my own reflections for the conclusion. I then go on to indicate how each used Barth at key points in their argumentation, noting the aspects of his theology onto which they latched so as to strengthen their respective projects. This allows me to point a way forward for those who wish to interact with Barth's doctrine of God when

---

[3]    Ibid., pp. 191–233.

doing theological ethics. The result of my analysis should support the claim that Lehmann's *Ethics* represents a 'promising *problematique*' for the future of Protestant theological ethics.[4]

## Paul Ramsey's Critique of *Ethics in a Christian Context*

Ramsey's first moves in his debate with Paul Lehmann are unambiguous: 'Paul Lehmann makes the exception the rule. It will be seen that he is a thoroughgoing proponent of *act-agapism*'; Ramsey borrows this latter term from William Frankena, and means by it the 'boundless freedom of atomistic individualism that hides behind the terminology of Christian ethics'.[5] As a counterbalance, Ramsey puts forward a form of 'rule-agapism' as a means of reining in the destructive wills of individuals run rampant. The driving force behind Ramsey's inquiry is a threefold question: 'What does Christian theology imply for the doing of Christian ethics, for the methods of ethics and the meaning of the Christian life?'[6] Before turning to these, Lehmann's missteps must be pointed out.

Ramsey takes special exception to a word Lehmann uses, namely *contextual*. The sudden introduction of this term, a 'non-biblical, non-theological word should be disturbing to anyone concerned with Christian ethics. It forms no ethical trinity [along with "Trinitarian" and "eschatological" – the other two bases Lehmann establishes for his ethic] ... yet it is used today as if it did'.[7] What frustrates Ramsey generally about the way ethics was done in his time achieves a kind of pure form in Lehmann's *Ethics*. Further, Ramsey laments that 'church pronouncements' have 'ceased to be formative of human life.[8] And this lament – coupled with his diagnosis of what he simply calls 'today' – seem to point to an 'apologetic' interest: broadly, it would appear to be Ramsey's wish that first-order Christian language continue to have some purchase on public life today. He takes theologians like Lehmann to be responsible for the growing absence of that purchase, precisely because they have refashioned theological discourse by making 'exceptions to be rules'.

Though Lehmann claims to reintroduce the authentic ethical insight of the Reformation, Ramsey says that he simply belongs to the group which,

---

[4]    See Philip G. Ziegler, 'Justification and Justice: the Promising *Problematique* of Protestant Ethics in the Work of Paul L. Lehmann' in *Justification: What's at Stake in the Current Debates*, eds M. Husbands and D.J. Trier (Downers Grove, IL: Intervarsity, 2004), pp. 118–33.

[5]    Paul Ramsey, *Deeds and Rules in Christian Ethics* (New York: Charles Scribner's Sons, 1967), p. 48. Emphasis added.

[6]    Ibid., p. 49.

[7]    Ibid., p. 50.

[8]    Ibid., p. 50. For later developments on this theme, see Ramsey, *Who speaks for the Church? a critique of the 1966 Geneva Conference on Church and Society* (Nashville, New York: Abingdon Press, 1967).

has revived less of it, and after the recent decades of an increasingly Christ-less religiousness in the church, it was predictable that celebrated theologians would begin their futile search for a religion-less Christianity to proclaim it in a secular world that is supposed to have 'come of age'. Lehmann may yield too much to this Bonhoefferish mood.[9]

Though the fragments of Bonhoeffer's late work may be lurking in the back of Ramsey's mind as progenitors of what he calls 'atomistic individualism', it is finally Lehmann's own emphasis on the *theological* context of decision making onto which Ramsey wants to fasten before he begins his formal critique:

> [W]e may be able to learn from Lehmann whether a full-bodied understanding of the Christian life can be recovered, or even articulated, simply by dwelling upon the immediate encounter of today's world with the *theological ultimates* ingredient to the Christian context, without a significant Christian *ethical analysis* and guidance fully elaborated in between.[10]

While Ramsey will accept (in a qualified sense) Lehmann's characterization of the theological landscape in which we live, he wants an additional prudential account – an 'ethical analysis' – that goes further toward a more specific interpretation of the moment. But, if this fairly characterizes Ramsey's analysis, he must admit to being a situationist of some stripe, since he also wants to address specific decisions confronting believing individuals, to present a full theological description of the moment, and to maintain that whatever decision is reached must be guided by a set of criteria. In this very broad sense, Ramsey and Lehmann are on the same page, and thus keep away from any detailed and systematic interrelation of doctrines as an enterprise not directly related to their questions.

Ramsey attempts to summarize Lehmann's theological description of the ethical landscape in four propositions: First, Christian ethics is 'the ethics of the *koinonia*'. Second, this ethics 'calls for the obedience to what God is doing in the world'. Third, this ethics 'means response to what God is doing to keep human life *human*'. And fourth, this ethics is 'Christological, or the ethics of messianism'.[11] Though Ramsey's critique of Lehmann includes other matters, we pass over these because they neither bear directly on Lehmann's reading of Barth nor substantially affect the critique he develops in his treatment of these four themes.

---

[9]    Ibid., p. 50. See p. xxiv, in Ramsey's *Basic Christian Ethics*, which he calls an essay in Christocentric ethics of the Reformation.

[10]   Ibid., p. 51.

[11]   Ibid., p. 51.

*Koinonia Ethics*

Under the heading 'Koinonia Ethics', Ramsey discusses Lehmann's emphasis upon the believer *as a member of Christ's church*, and charges that Lehmann unjustly minimizes the individual character of the Christian existence. Under Lehmann's scheme the questions, 'what *ought* or *should* I do, what am I *required* to do, or what is *good* for me to do',[12] fundamentally countermand the discipline of Christian ethics. This, for Ramsey, is a crucial semantic error that permeates the rest of Lehmann's construal of the Christian life: once Lehmann uses language poorly, poor practice must ensue.[13] In fact, Lehmann's language about 'koinonia ethics' is so messianic that there appears to be no distinction between what God and the church are doing. As Ramsey says, 'there is no such thing as Christian ethics if God's action in laying His gracious claim upon human life and effectuating it in and through the *koinonia* is the same as all the ethical decisions and acts that take place in the church'.[14]

According to Ramsey, Lehmann's 'messianism' springs from being 'obsessed' with removing moralism from Christian ethics – the notion that ethicists should, in any way, prescribe behaviour, is completely removed from the 'proper business' of Christian ethicists. Ramsey admits that Lehmann is partially right to glimpse this special pitfall of Christian ethics; but he thinks Lehmann takes this insight too far. Lehmann's emphasis on the descriptive force of Christian ethics, and the 'dialectical relation between the hidden and the empirical' reality of the church, is finally meant to asphyxiate the implications of belonging to a church. Once we encourage people to 'Get out into the world to see what God is doing in it', we should not be surprised if the identity and character-forming activity of worship and church participation find themselves in second place.

Ramsey, cognisant of Lehmann's dependence on Barth, next attempts to read the latter against the former. If his characterization of Lehmann's construal of the church – whether visible or invisible – is correct, then Ramsey thinks Lehmann has broken one of Barth's hermeneutical rules: 'As Barth says, "The being of the community is a predicate of His being"; He is not a predicate of the being of the community, of the church, or the *koinonia*.'[15] As proof that Lehmann has hurled himself into a sandstorm of dialectical verbiage while discussing a concept as

---

[12]   Ibid., p. 53.

[13]   See *The Essential Paul Ramsey: A Collection*, eds W. Werpehowski and S.D. Crocco (New Haven: Yale University Press, 1994), esp. 'The Case for Making "Just War" Possible', pp. 68–83 written in 1968, though this concern with language extended back to his first work, in 1950: see *Basic Chrisitian Ethics*, p. xxiv.

[14]   Ibid., p. 53.

[15]   Ibid., p. 55.

important as the Church, Ramsey simply cites Lehmann's dictum: "'Where the church is, there is Jesus Christ" (ECC 53).'[16]

For Ramsey, Barth's understanding of the twofold love-commandment under the aspect of *agape*, as exercised by the church, should push strongly against Lehmann's supposed reversal of these priorities. Thus, through the indeterminacy of Lehmann's *koinonia* ethic, which attempts to broaden the activity of God as supremely Subject, God's agapic act is, ironically, narrowed to an almost indistinguishable point. Because Lehmann only wishes to give *indications* of God's activity, the specific requirements of the Christian life are muted, and therefore anything and everything can be considered the act of the *koinonia*.

Ramsey's final objection to Lehmann's reading of Barth, in this section, is that Lehmann, though he wishes to be bold in laying waste to the preceptual pretensions of ethicists who deny the presence of God in human affairs, *in fact* has been too timid, and not followed Barth closely enough. Lehmann really wants to do dogmatics as an elaboration of God's permissive will, and not ethics as rigorous analysis of humanity's faithful response: 'In Barth there is no less ethics than dogmatics; no less elaboration of the ethical claim than there is articulation of the context … . The last word in that Barthian refrain is an imperative word!'[17] Ramsey here simply registers the commonplace that every volume of the *Church Dogmatics* ends with a section on ethics – the imperative always follows (relatively) close on the heels of the indicative. Lehmann's overweening interest in the indicative leads him to 'secular expressions to illuminate the meaning of the *koinonia*',[18] such as psychological language fashioned for notions of self-realization and self-acceptance.

*'What God is Doing'*

Next, Ramsey examines Lehmann's *Ethics* under the title 'What God is Doing'. This is a section in which explicit recourse to Barth is not made, but which builds on criticisms of Lehmann's problematic reading of the same, and which points to similar problems identified in the third and fourth sections. Ramsey is specifically concerned with Lehmann's contention that God is a 'politician'. He sees what Lehmann is driving at, but prefers the term 'statesman', which he thinks expresses more precisely what Lehmann means:

> It is appropriate to Lehmann's meaning, but not an apt denotation of the full truth, to say that God is a 'politician' (ECC 83) – for Lehmann's God is something of an opportunist, more than He is a statesman. There can be no 'preceptual apprehension of the will of God', he writes, not because of the complexity of

the human situations in which our apprehensions take place but because of 'the complexity of the will of God itself'. The point is made simply by iteration and reiteration: 'The will of God cannot be generalized' (ECC 77). A being of whom such a statement can be made scarcely deserves even the name of 'politician', since a politician more often shapes human life by precepts, by having a will from which the community he governs can take normative direction.[19]

Ramsey's issue with Lehmann is, again, semantic, in the deep sense of the word: Lehmann is simply using words inappropriately, and therefore risking the integrity of Christian ethics as a discipline. Even if Lehmann wishes to understand God as Subject under the heading 'politician', he does so without rudimentary attention to definitional parameters. But Ramsey, nevertheless, opts for terminology similar to Lehmann's, and thus turns to an explanation of how God's will operates 'in a general way':

> If God can bind Himself in steadfast faithfulness to the particular, He can bind Himself in steadfast faithfulness in a general way … . Lehmann derogates upon the freedom of God to bind the world to Himself in a general way, or in one or some ways rather than others, and thereby to claim certain – and not a variety of – responses from disciples of Christ and members of His *koinonia*.[20]

Ramsey, next, fastens onto Lehmann's account of the political activity of God as doing 'what it takes to make and to keep human life human'. This way of construing God's presence is not detailed enough; Ramsey wants to know what Lehmann means by the word 'human'. He suspects any such definition would compromise Lehmann's project by means of 'a normative [definition] implying imperatives and precepts'.[21] This supposed mania for eschewing precepts and imperatives – and for giving maximal freedom to God's activity – results in simply positing a God who is no different from 'this world of rapid change' and although in Barth there remains the possibility 'of entirely novel, free acts of God, there is a shape to the gospel of God and a shape to His action that enables us to reflect upon it for our knowledge into God and for our knowledge into the shape of Christian moral action'.[22]

### 'Keeping Human Life Human'

And yet, in the third theme of Lehmann's theology, 'keeping human life human (mature)', Ramsey claims to find an indication of what Lehmann means by 'human'. The fruit of divine activity is 'human maturity' and the 'wholeness' of

---

[19]  Ibid., p. 58.
[20]  Ibid., p. 58.
[21]  Ibid., p. 59.
[22]  Ibid., p. 60.

every person in the new creation of Christ. Yet Ramsey notes that for Lehmann neither of these has to do with morality, for 'Christian ethics is oriented toward revelation rather than toward "morality" ... (ECC 54)'. Christian faith gives birth to a mature life, and morality is simply a by-product of this maturity. This, for Ramsey, is another cardinal sin against language, because Lehmann seems to have created a distinction without a difference. Ramsey looks to Barth to make his point: 'Either [Lehmann] makes here a merely verbal distinction between "ethics" and "morality"; or else he does not quite believe, with Barth, that Dogmatics is Ethics and for this reason he allows revelation and morality (or ethics) to fall apart.'[23] Ramsey thinks Lehmann has taken an aspect of Barth's thought – one part of the dialectic – and run with it, pushing God's aseity, freedom, and sovereignty to near incredulity, such that those whom God brings into covenant appear at best incidental and, at worst, superfluous and hopelessly inept:

> '[T]here is none good but one, that is God', Karl Barth remarks that to 'receive this truth is not to reject and abandon the question of *the goodness of human action. It is only with this truth that we take it up*'. It is true that under the doctrine of God – where Lehmann says Barth 'located' ethics, neglecting the rest (ECC 271) – Karl Barth gives extended analysis simply of the proposition that 'there is no good which is not obedience to God's command'. This is the source and extent of Lehmann's ethics of 'freedom in obedience'. However, Karl Barth's undertaking for the entirety of Christian ethics requires another statement: '*there must be seen and demonstrated the fact and extent of the existence of good human action* under the lordship and efficacy of the divine command'.[24]

If this characterization of Lehmann's reading of Barth is correct, then it shows the gap between 'the nature of action and the nature of the good'[25] which Lehmann either seemingly ignores, inadvertently minimizes, or wilfully neglects. And '[s]uch a Christian ethics is, indeed, dynamically "on the move" and "more informal" ... and reflection about the moral life is more undisciplined'.[26] Because Lehmann lingers a little too long in one part of the doctrine of God, Ramsey thinks a vacuum is created into which categories other than those provided by Christians ethics push: '[T]he development of a Christian ethics is frustrated by his readiness to turn elsewhere for the meaning of maturity.'[27] Ramsey muses rhetorically at Lehmann's recourse to the 'philosophy of self-realization' and 'a liberal dosage of Freudianism' – 'Why is it more "mature" for a person to develop organically in

---

[23]   Ibid., p. 61.

[24]   Ibid., p. 62, emphasis original.

[25]   Ibid., p. 63.

[26]   Ibid.

[27]   Ibid., p. 66.

interpersonal relationships than for his maturity to be determined by wholly other claims, commands, obligations, imperatives, and by what's right?'[28]

*'Christocentric Ethics'*

Ramsey concludes with a section entitled 'Christocentric ethics' in which he maintains that Lehmann has failed to construct a properly Christocentric theological anthropology, and therefore unthinkingly offers secular anthropological insights ultimately destructive for ethics. It is here that Lehmann's 'messianism' gets him in the same kind of trouble as before, and 'a secular theory of contextualism comes to fill the vacuum'.[29] Barth makes no such mistake, but 'secures by unhesitatingly basing a large part of his ethics on a carefully worked-out theological anthropology'.[30] Ramsey wishes to contrast, as strongly as possible, how Barth and Lehmann handle the exceptional case, and does not think it a fair reading of Barth to maintain that 'Christianity specializes in the exception'. Lehmann has mistakenly understood Barth to include ethics only under the doctrine of God, and not under the doctrine of humanity:

> The fact is that there is an ethical articulation of *every* doctrine in Barth's *Dogmatics*; and that our knowledge *into God*, *into man*, and *into ethics* are all fully explored and fully Christocentric. Anthropology is no further removed from Christology than theology is, or for that matter ethics with its statements about actions and abstentions ... .[31]

Ramsey then returns to a point he made previously: in order for Lehmann to realize his project, he needs 'that part of Barth's dogmatic ethics where he seems only to locate ethics within the doctrine of God. For here the freedom and uniqueness of the Divine command and claim are emphasized'.[32] But this is to miss Barth's emphasis on 'what is entailed for man in God's binding Himself to the world and the world to Himself' – in fact, Barth's sections on 'special ethics' can be 'quite specific'.[33] Before Barth surrounds and locates an 'exception', it is understood to be 'steadfastly preserved in its nature as an exception by its environment in Christian ethical analysis'.[34] Ramsey thinks Lehmann specializes too much, and by apologetic sleight of hand sets the 'Christian conscience free from a good deal that is necessary if there is to be any such thing as Christian ethics'.[35] Lehmann's

---

28    Ibid.
29    Ibid., p. 69.
30    Ibid.
31    Ibid., p. 70.
32    Ibid.
33    Ibid., p. 71.
34    Ibid.
35    Ibid., p. 73.

ethics, therefore, are 'characteristically American', and he had done nothing more than fashion a theology for the 'Committees on Christian Social Concerns'.[36]

## Paul Lehmann – The Apocalypse Begins at God's Church

In what follows, I will discuss Lehmann's *Ethics* in three parts, each of which is intended as a response to Ramsey's critique. The first part does not have to do directly with Lehmann's use of Barth, but concerns Lehmann's understanding of the *koinonia* as 'the context of ethical reflection'. In the second part, Lehmann's discussion of 'what God is doing in the world' – a commonplace of Lehmann's thought – is shown to be inaugurated by appeal to Barth's early work in the *Romerbrief*. In the third part, I draw attention to Lehmann's own summary of his engagement with 'philosophical ethics' (prosecuted for a little over 100 pages) by means of insights drawn directly from Barth's doctrine of God. These three sections constitute a response to Ramsey, and together serve to 'point a way forward' for those who see in Barth's doctrine of God a tool with which to test critically current modes of theological ethics.

*Koinonia Ethics*

> If a shepherd has a hundred sheep, and one of them has gone astray, does he not leave the ninety-nine on the mountains and go in search of the one that went astray? And if he finds it, truly I tell you, he rejoices over it more than over the ninety-nine that never went astray. (Matt. 18.12b–13)

Though Lehmann's interest is, in part, to criticize individualism, his *Ethics* could charitably be read along the lines presented in the above parable. Lehmann mentions this parable – along with that of the lost coin and the prodigal – as classic instances of the thrust toward the individual that has defined some forms of Christianity.[37] If it can accurately – but, finally, only suggestively – be said that the Parable of the Lost Sheep is also at the heart of the Reformers' understanding of justification, then perhaps Lehmann's investigations in *Ethics* can be seen as much more consonant with their thought than Ramsey gives him credit for.

Before turning to the notion of an *ecclesiola in ecclesia*, Lehmann lays a foundation first in Christ's work as attested in scripture, and then in the church as (in a qualified sense) the continuation of that work.[38] Here there is no excess

---

[36]   Ibid.

[37]   Paul Lehmann *Ethics in a Christian Context* (New York: Harper and Row, 1963), p. 57.

[38]   Indeed, in his response to Ramsey's critique – *Theology Today*, 22: 1 (April 1965), pp. 120–25 – Lehmann draws special attention to the fact that Ramsey has missed the ecclesial starting point that he himself emphasized. See p. 121.

verbiage, but an informed exegesis, followed by a concise judgement: '[S]o marked is the proleptic sense of reality in the New Testament that the "inheritance of Christ" is viewed not only as a transforming membership in a brotherhood which is to be but also as the fruit and function of the Spirit's operation here and now.'[39] Lehmann cites Romans 8.23 and 2 Corinthians 1.21–2 and 5.5 as the basis for these claims. If Ramsey wished to critique Lehmann's understanding of *koinonia* more thoroughly he would need to do so by the kind of appeal to Scripture that Lehmann undertakes.[40] These verses lack Ramsey's 'prudential account', yet Paul, not lacking for paper, trusted that the communities to which he sent his letters would be guided by the Spirit and by Paul's basic indications of the maturity consequent upon Christ's work. I suggest that like Paul, Lehmann is properly limiting himself and trusting in the work of God who is present in his Spirit. He might counter that Ramsey's critique, ironically, creates its own vacuum by introducing rules and 'ethical analysis' divorced from a robust understanding of God's apocalyptic presence. The vacuum Ramsey creates comes about (at least partially) by the omission of Scripture in his critique of Lehmann – Barth's understanding of the Bible as the strange, new world that completely re-describes, and claims, the earth as God's own, appears to have no purchase on Ramsey's thinking at this point.

Though Lehmann may wish to engage (in Barth's words) 'other lights and words', and in doing so criticize, modify or 'annex' them, it is clear that the directing light and word for the Christian is to be found in the proclamation of the church:

> Just as there is no Messiah without his people, so there is no real presence of Jesus in history without or apart from the true people of God which as the work of the Holy Spirit is always at the same time a spiritual and visible reality. It is this reality of the *koinonia*, whatever the word for it may be, which denotes the concrete result of God's specifically purposed activity in the world in Jesus Christ. We might, therefore, say that Christian ethics is *koinonia ethics*. This means that it is from, and in, the *koinonia* that we get the answer to the question: What am I, as a believer in Jesus Christ and a member of his church, to do?[41]

The presence of Jesus Christ in the world, then, is to be found amongst his 'true people', and their work is the work of the Holy Spirit. This work is nothing less than a 'concrete result' to which God will attend and accomplish. It is 'specifically purposed', but it is within the context of the *koinonia* that it is worked out; there

---

[39]   Ibid., p. 46. See also: 'Indeed, it is the *koinonia* context and character of Christian ethics that give ethical sense and substance to the seeking and doing of God's will. For in the *koinonia*, and owing to the *koinonia*, man is concretely and inescapably involved in what God is doing in the world.' Ibid., p. 80.

[40]   Lehman, in *Ethics in A Christian Context*, p. 27. In footnote 1, which begins on p. 26 he faults Ramsey's *Basic Christian Ethics* with ignoring 'the hermeneutical problem'.

[41]   Ibid., p. 47.

need be no checklist a congregation may use as a means of following Paul's instructions. Paul does not wish them to follow him. His desire – and Lehmann follows him in this – is that all good things be attributed to their Author.

All of this 'specifically purposed activity' has a simple but definite form, namely 'in Jesus Christ'. Perhaps Lehmann could have brought out a more detailed reading of Barth's Christocentric understanding of revelation at this point. But Lehmann affirms that the church – just as Jesus, the God-human – is not a static reality: '[T]he church, the fellowship which is the body of Christ, the *koinonia*, is the *fellowship-creating reality* of Christ's presence in the world.'[42] Because the church, and its mission, is God's work, it is not to understand itself as primarily a keeping-of-the-keys operation. The Church must be ready for reform by God's own hand, and not sacrifice the work of God's Spirit for the tempting apparition of outward stability. This reform does not necessarily proceed along clear, simple, or even general lines: 'The secret is that the Gentiles are fellow heirs and members of the same body and that the church is the instrument through which the complex wisdom of God is made known.'[43] This is not complexity as obfuscation via prophetic utterance, but complexity as mystery and discernment. As stewards of this mystery (1 Cor. 4.1–5), and as those charged to discern the spirits (1 Jn. 4.1–6),[44] the church can expect a difficult, complex job; the stakes are high, and the church has to do with the living God, whose concerns are quite other than the successful maintenance of a virtue-forming institution.

Once Lehmann has established this base, he moves not to maintain God's capricious freedom, but to expound more fully the basic confession that 'Jesus Christ is Lord'. He does this by elaborating on what he means by the 'complex wisdom of God':

> This means that ... believer and unbeliever are fellow heirs – not primarily as Jews and Gentiles, or merely as human beings, but as human beings who as members of a 'third race' are proleptic of the transformation and fulfillment of all human beings in the new humanity of which Christ, the head of the body, is also the second Adam, the first fruit.[45]

Though Lehmann clearly maintains that whatever the Church accomplishes is truly the work of the Holy Spirit, he just as clearly does not wish to maintain the kind of strict, one-to-one correspondence with which Ramsey charges him. For Christ is the head of the body, the captain of the 'third race'. Concerning

[42] Ibid., p. 49.

[43] Ibid.

[44] Something Christopher L. Morse of Union Theological Seminary, New York – one of Lehmann's doctoral students – undertook without fear or favour in his *Not Every Spirit: A Dogmatics of Christian Disbelief* (Valley Forge, PA. : Trinity Press, 1994).

[45] Ibid., p. 51.

Ignatius' famous dictum – 'where Jesus Christ is, there is the Catholic Church' – Lehmann writes,

> ... as soon as one begins to put the matter the other way around, namely, 'where the Catholic Church is, there is Jesus Christ', one has not only begun to distort what the Bible, moreover, and the Apostles say that the Church is ... one has also lost the sense for the ethical reality of the *koinonia* in the world.[46]

Without maintenance of the properly ordered, dialectical tension Lehmann identifies, the church can quickly become an all-too-human bureaucracy; it can think itself identical with the work of Christ (and then be truly guilty of a messianism); or it can simply become a group of activists only peripherally interested in the true worship of God. Through identifying and maintaining this tension, Lehmann establishes the kind of ecclesiology – properly ordered with Christ as its head – which provides the *koinonia*, not with a vacuum, but with an understanding of the complex task of discerning God's activity in the world. The church is in the world, and Christ is Lord over both – Lehmann only means this much when he establishes God's freedom in relation to the church and humanity.

*What God is Doing in the World*

Lehmann bases his treatment of 'what God is doing in the world' upon moves Barth makes early in his authorship. For instance, he cites Barth's contention from the second Romans commentary that wide reading of secular literature – especially newspapers – is necessary for anyone who wishes to understand the message of Paul. From this Lehmann concludes that 'certainly a perceptive reading of the Bible requires also a reading of the papers'.[47] Given this, Lehmann makes clear – using the same section of Barth's *Romerbrief* – that 'the Christian life is lived not only in the church but also in the world; and whatever God is doing in and through the *koinonia*, he is doing also in the world', or as Barth himself wrote, 'if our thinking is not to be pseudo-thinking, we must think about life; for such a thinking is a thinking about God. And if we are to think about life, we must penetrate its hidden corners, and steadily refuse to treat anything – however trivial or disgusting it may seem to be – as irrelevant'.[48] If this is so, we cannot think we know too easily what the 'will of God' is; for God has to do with the whole earth, and clichés never get us to a real answer to the ethical question.[49] Lehmann contends that the 'ethically sensitive' person will know the following: First, that

---

[46]   Ibid., p. 53. Much of what Lehmann says in his treatment of the church which precedes these remarks is developed by reflection on sources other than Barth.

[47]   Ibid., p. 74.

[48]   Ibid., p. 75 and Karl Barth, *The Epistle to the Romans*, trans. E.C. Hoskyns (Oxford: Oxford University Press, 1933), pp. 424–5.

[49]   Lehmann, *Ethics in a Christian Context*, p. 75.

the simple admonition to 'do God's will' is so remote from how lives are lived out that such admonishment inevitably collapses into 'frivolous platitude'; and second, that even when one is prepared to acknowledge one must do the will of God the 'troublesome perplexity' is not thereby removed, namely, just 'what is the will of God which he admits he is to do'?[50] This, then, would be the nub of Lehmann's response to Ramsey: God is personal and specific, through and through, and in no way bound to us 'generally':

> There is no formal principle of Christian behaviour because Christian behaviour cannot be generalized. And Christian behaviour cannot be generalized because the will of God cannot be generalized ..... And even if such generalized persuasion of the will of God were given propositional formulation for the purposes of ethical counsel and guidance, the result would be a maxim or precept, good for edifying repetition but devoid of behavioural precision.[51]

*The Insufficiency of Philosophical Ethics*

In the section entitled the 'insufficiency of philosophical ethics', Lehmann returns to Barth – and especially to his doctrine of God – in order to explain the importance of including 'ethics under the doctrine of God'.[52] Barth includes ethics under the doctrine of God – and not, like Thomas, under the doctrine of humanity – because he wants to move the locus of Christian inquiry in 'philosophical ethics' to 'God's self-revelation in Christ':

> Barth attempts to explore the problem of ethics in the light of the sovereign freedom of the God who has revealed himself in Jesus Christ. 'Ethics', he declares, 'belongs to the doctrine of God because *God is claiming man for himself thereby originally mak[ing] himself responsible for man.*'[53]

Lehmann has, at this point of crucial summary, endorsed a properly Christocentric theological anthropology; he has identified, and approved, nothing other than an encapsulation of Barth's theological anthropology – God claims humanity for himself in Christ, and this is humanity's fundamental determination. The God who reveals himself in Jesus Christ not only questions the sufficiency of attempting an ethics divorced from this revelation, but brings our ethical discernment and activity into his own gracious, 'claiming' activity. 'Self-determination', or 'the individual character of a believer's existence', names positions radically incompatible with Christian ethics, because it cannot concede that '"man makes

---

[50]    Ibid., p. 76.

[51]    Ibid., p. 77.

[52]    Ibid., p. 271.

[53]    Ibid., pp. 271–2; the citation is from Karl Barth, *Kirchliche Dogmatik* II/2, p. 564, in Lehmann's own translation.

ethics" ... . For Christian ethics, "God makes ethics", that is, God initiates and establishes the humanity of man. As Barth says, "Precisely because the divine election is ultimately the determination of man, the question arises concerning the self-determination of man in the light of his determination by God"'.[54] For both Lehmann and Barth, ethics can only be considered on the basis of this (incipient) theological anthropology, and only in this way can a consideration of the freight that 'philosophical ethics' brings be engaged with integrity.

## Conclusion

> It was no light task gradually to put right these not underserved misunderstandings, including my own misunderstandings on which much that I said at that time rested, and to guide theology out of the suspicion under which it had fallen of being only 'theology of crisis'. It could not actually be the 'theology of crisis' for more than a moment. And that it could be it only for a moment showed that the basic, eschatological application on which it rested was too strong and arbitrary and independent like all reactions. It was necessary and right in face of the Immanentism of the preceding period to think with new seriousness about God's futurity. But it was neither right nor necessary to do this in such a way that this one matter was put at the head of all Christian teaching, just as the previous epoch had wanted to make what they claimed to be the knowledge of God's presence the chief point in Christian doctrine. Such interesting concentrations in theology must be completely avoided if we are not to come in some way under the domination of compelling ideas, which we can enjoy ourselves and with which we can for a while give pleasure to others, yet of which sooner or later we will inevitably tire, because what is merely interesting always becomes tedious in the course of time. The doctrine of the living God will not tolerate any such concentrations. [55]

The merits and defects of Lehmann's and Ramsey's appropriation of Barth, are represented in miniature in this excerpt from *Church Dogmatics* II/1. Barth expresses here some regret over the dominant emphases of the 'theology of crisis' in a manner which might qualify the ways in which both Lehmann and Ramsey sought to use elements in Barth's doctrine of God. It would seem that this excerpt is especially fitted for Lehmann's project, which emphasized God's in-breaking, apocalyptic activity, perhaps at the expense of a more prudential account of the regularity of God's relation to us. But it could equally apply to Ramsey's tendency

[54]   Ibid., p. 274; citation from Barth, *KD.* II/2, p. 566.
[55]   Karl Barth, *Church Dogmatics II/1: The Doctrine of God*, eds G.W. Bromiley and T.F. Torrance, trans. T.H.L. Parker et al. (Edinburgh: T&T Clark, 1964), p. 636.

to reduce the Gospel to *agape* extended to the neighbour.[56] There is a sense in which each author concentrated his protest against a tendency in then-current thought: Ramsey, against a situationism that developed from simplified readings of Barth, Brunner and Bonhoeffer, and which found popular expression in Joseph Fletcher's *Situation Ethics*;[57] Lehmann, against legalism, which he took over from concerns central to Barth's re-description of philosophical ethics within the doctrine of God, as a means to combat easy moralism, whether in the pastorate or the academy.[58]

Though Ramsey's contribution to theological ethics, in the later part of the twentieth century is without question one of the most substantial on offer, it has to be said that his reading of Lehmann's *Ethics* is largely a polemical one, determined in advance by concerns extrinsic to Lehmann's project. This is not to say his critique is uncharitable: if Ramsey did not think Lehmann worthy of such extended engagement, he would hardly have expended as much effort on him. The volume in which Ramsey's critique appears, *Deed and Rules in Christian Ethics*, is concerned with the problems raised by the situation ethics of the time, and Lehmann appears therein as an instance of the problem Ramsey wants to address. *Deeds* should be read in conjunction with the volume Ramsey edited with Gene Outka one year later, *Norm and Context in Christian Ethics*.[59] Both works respond to an incipient situation ethic by fashioning a more 'steadfast' form of agape.[60]

Ramsey's deep concerns with how Lehmann uses language are not out of place, but they cannot go all the way down. The language of the Bible, in its attempt to bespeak the eschatological reality it describes, is bound to mirror that mystery, and therefore necessarily to break down at certain points. Some of Lehmann's

---

[56] See D. Stephen Long, *Tragedy, Tradition, Transformism: the Ethics of Paul Ramsey* (Boulder, CO: Westview, 1993), p. 1. While I agree with Long's characterization of Ramsey's reduction, I must respectfully disagree with his assessment that Ramsey's project underwrote an 'ontology of tragedy'. Ramsey's practice of intellectual engagement – which had, as Long notes, a kind of pastoral focus to it – simply pushes too strongly against such a reduction of his ethical project. Ramsey would hardly have engaged as many partners, and done as much casuistry, if he thought there was nothing but tragedy around every turn. Certainly he wrote because he thought his writing might change the course of events.

[57] Joseph Fletcher, *Situation Ethics: The New Morality* (Philadelphia: Westminster, 1966). I am indebted to Long, *Tragedy*, pp. 104–6, for drawing these connections between Barth, Brunner and Bonhoeffer, and Fletcher.

[58] It is precisely this that Nancy Duff, in her incisive and forceful *Humanization and the Politics of God: The Koinonia Ethics of Paul Lehmann* (Grand Rapids, MI: Eerdmans, 1992), pp. 65–6, draws attention to in another context. Ramsey has overlooked an incipient, and sometimes full-blown 'ethical absolutism' which stretches back to Plato and which has encouraged a serious misinterpretation of the Gospel throughout the Church's history.

[59] *Norm and Context in Christian Ethics*, eds G. Outka and P. Ramsey (New York: Scribner, 1968).

[60] See Long, *Tragedy*, pp. 105–6. Joseph Fletcher communicated to Ramsey in a letter that he saw this incipient ethic in Ramsey's *Basic Christian Ethics*. In his reply to Fletcher, Ramsey wrote, 'I have come to see that *agape* can also be steadfast'.

tendency to hyperbole can be considered a faithful witness to this. But some – and perhaps much – of this tendency cannot. Ramsey's critique will remain something of an acid test for those who want to go forward with Lehmann. Lehmann often draws broad, powerful distinctions that illuminate the landscape of a particular issue, and offer a kind of refreshing insight into the activity of the living God. But these distinctions do, sometimes, raise the question of clarity. The charge that Lehmann belongs with all those who wish to make 'exceptions to be rules' seems to miss Lehmann's thoroughly ecclesial starting point – one which is intended precisely as a means to test the spirits, and to testify to God's specifically purposed activity in the world. If Lehmann has 'made the exception the rule', he has done so at the foot of the Master. It was hardly a piece of 'atomistic individualism' when the Shepherd sought out the lost sheep.

A very brief word, then, about a way forward. Two aspects of Barth's doctrine of God – related but distinguishable – are important: the theme of Divine simplicity, and the corresponding lack of a 'substance ontology'.[61] Both have significant ramifications for how one thinks about the continuity of the ethical agent. If there is to be fruitful confrontation with other tendencies in modern Christian ethics, such as those which emphasize the acquisition of virtues as a means of fashioning agents who meet difficulties consistently, then Barth's construal of sanctification, as it is rooted in his doctrine of God, with special reference to the possibility of progress in the Christian life, will be especially important to elaborate and put into conversation with such tendencies.[62]

To illustrate, briefly, what is as stake in Barth's account of sanctification, it is important to understand that Barth does not think God has a 'substance' He shares with us, which then grows 'inside' us, either deifying or sanctifying us into perfection. Since Barth's account of Divine simplicity ('there is no substance or essence in God') challenges this model of growth, and therefore calls into question the extent to which grace can be thought of as a substantive ontological power which shapes virtues in the agent, it is possible to see in Barth's account of sanctification a more realistic account progress in the Christian life. In place

---

[61] I am indebted to the exhaustive labours of Bruce McCormack for these basic insights into the development of Barth's doctrine of God. See McCormack, 'Barth's grundsatzlicher Chalcedonismus?' *Zeitschrift für dialektische Theologie*, 18.2 (2002): 138–73 for the refinement of Barth's doctrine of God from *CD* II to *CD* IV.

[62] Karl Barth, *Church Dogmatics* IV/2. *The Doctrine of Reconciliation*, trans. G.W. Bromiley (Edinburgh: T&T Clark, 1958), §66. See also McCormack's 'Afterword' to the 2001 Kampen conference on Barth's doctrine of sanctification in *Zeitschrift für dialektische Theologie* 18.3 (2002), pp. 369, 371, 374. See esp. p. 372: 'Thomas presupposes a substantialist ontology which enables him to think of grace as a power which can be "infused" into the "essence" of the soul, issuing in virtues which flow into the power of the soul (S.T. 1a2ae. 110, art. 4) … But Barth has swept aside all substantialist ontologies of this kind with his doctrine of election. For him, any talk of an "in us" would have to refer to the empirical self and it alone, since that which is truly "essential" to the human is not found "in us" but in the divine act of relating to us in the covenant of grace.'

of the traditional, substance ontology, there stands a more relational, existential and personal model – one which, no doubt, would have been useful to both Ramsey and Lehmann, because it gives priority to God's commands, and to his objective, in-breaking presence which confronts and disrupts, but also sustains and makes whole.[63]

[63]    This paper was first written for Dr Nancy Duff's 'Types of Christian Ethics' seminar at Princeton Theological Seminary, Spring, 2006. I am grateful for her comments, suggestions and encouragement. It was presented again in Dr Jeffrey Stout's 'Religion and Critical Thought Workshop' at Princeton University in the Fall, 2007 semester. For his comments and suggestions, and for those of my colleagues in the workshop, I am deeply grateful.

# PART III

# Chapter 8
# The Living Word in the Living World – Lehmann for Preachers

Sally Ann Brown

Imagine the painter at his work: brushes in hand, he leans toward his canvas and, with deft strokes, sets out near its centre a simple, striking motif. This figure will anchor the work, influencing the whole. The canvas is vast; it will occupy the artist not for mere days or even weeks, but for years. Sometimes he may leave it untouched for long periods, but at intervals he will return. Gripped by personal passion or the urgency of world events, he often works feverishly, introducing unexpected colours or techniques. At other times he may sketch only the barest outline of a concept too crucial to lay aside, yet not fully developed. Years later, observers will find themselves standing before a work clearly unfinished, the artist's brush left aside as if he had been suddenly called away. Yet, seen whole, the canvas pulses with a vibrant dynamism, its splashes of colour and bold lines alive with possibilities not yet disclosed.

As I consider the theological life-project of Paul Lehmann, it is this image that comes most readily to mind. Certainly Lehmann's style of expression, frustrating to readers who prefer their theology packaged systematically, suggests the passion and urgency of the artist and prophet rather than the orderliness of the systematician. Nancy J. Duff, one of Lehmann's chief interpreters, readily admits that Lehmann 'tends not to give precise definitions' and describes Lehmann's style as 'dynamic and explosive'. Critics, she observes, accuse Lehmann of 'preferring the flair of a well-turned phrase' to clear exposition.[1] Yet I would venture that preachers, on the whole, find Lehmann's style far less problematic than many other readers. Maybe it is simply that preachers know another preacher when they hear one and, sympathetic to the difficulties of communicating the mysteries of faith, are inclined to grant him a hearing. But I suspect it is more than that. When Lehmann lures his readers into a web of meaning and makes them work to find their way around, or when he coins a phrase, and instead of defining it, turns it loose and asks us to learn what it means by watching how it works, preachers sense they are on familiar ground. Beside the fact that these strategies are uncannily Gospel-like,

---

[1]  Nancy J. Duff, *Humanization and the Politics of God: the Koinonia Ethics of Paul Lehmann* (Grand Rapids: Eerdmans, 1992), pp. 3, 4. I am indebted throughout this essay to my colleague, Nancy Duff, for her helpful insights along the way as I sought to grasp the import of Lehmann's central concepts for critical reflection on the theology and practice of preaching.

every preacher knows the terrain Lehmann is trying to negotiate: they, too, have laboured amid the fragile structures of language to point to realities that do not stand still, but pulse with life, movement, and astounding possibility. What some critics dismiss as sloppiness or conceptual instability in Lehmann's prose may strike preachers as the adaptation of rhetoric to its subject matter: at stake here is news that bursts the constraints of everyday language.

What I propose to do in these pages is to explore what new light Lehmann's approach to theology and ethics can shed on the work preachers do. I want to do that by considering three prominent convictions – or, better, paradigmatic concepts – that lie at the core of Lehmann's theological project, and then explore the implications of these paradigms in relation to three critical questions about preaching.

I have yet to meet any preacher who, in his or her most honest moments, does not question what in the world it is that he or she is up to in the pulpit. I do not have in mind here the vocational self-doubt that plagues us all, and which, for preachers, comes out in nightmares about lost sermon notes or showing up in church distinctly under-dressed (or not dressed at all). Nor do I mean those late-night ruminations about whether we might have been as good, or better, at pasturing sheep as pastoring congregations; or whether a comfortable career in finance might have worked out just as well. What I have in mind here are serious questions – theological questions – about the nature of the act of preaching as an act. What is going on in preaching as a theological event? What is happening, theologically speaking, when we preach? What should be going on hermeneutically? That is, how can preachers best negotiate the distance between biblical text and present human context? What ought to go on rhetorically – or, in other words, how can we best express the Gospel news? Homiletical literature today offers an array of possibilities: preaching sounds like promise, like prophecy, like story, like testimony. How does the nature of the Gospel itself shape the rhetoric of the sermon?

Often, it is only in the safe company of other preachers that many of us who preach allow these critically important questions to surface. My conviction is that Paul Lehmann is not only safe company, but potentially enormously illuminating company, in which to entertain these questions.

Lehmann certainly valued preaching highly, and he himself preached throughout his career. Notably, he opens his first book-length work, published in 1940, *Forgiveness: Decisive Issue in Protestant Thought*, with a critical assessment of the state of preaching in North America in the first half of the twentieth century, contrasting 'textual literalism' with 'topical liberalism' – a discussion to which we will have occasion to return later. Undoubtedly, the close connection between preaching and what it takes to equip Christian communities to think and act ethically was never far from his mind.

The three theological paradigms in Lehmann's thought that I want to draw into relationship with preaching emerge in Lehmann's first three major works, *Forgiveness: Decisive Issue in Protestant Thought* (1940), *Ethics in a Christian Context* (1963), and *The Transfiguration of Politics* (1975). The first of these paradigms, sketched in *Forgiveness* and more fully developed nearly twenty years later in *Ethics*, is Lehmann's conviction that a dynamic interplay of divine and human action conditions every situation. This theological motif, the dialectical interplay of '*the ways* of God and *the ways* of men', Lehmann contends, is thoroughly characteristic of the Reformed theological tradition, comprises the dialectical root of Protestant theology, and is one of its most distinctive contributions to theology as a whole.[2]

In *Ethics*, Lehmann elaborates this first paradigm and builds upon its foundation a second: a 'parabolic' strategy for reading Scripture as the basis for establishing the relationship between biblical texts and concrete, present human situations. Parabolic hermeneutics foregrounds the juxtaposition of divine and human action in both Scripture and human situations. These first two paradigms provide, in turn, the basis for a third, anticipated in *Ethics* but worked out explicitly in *The Transfiguration of Politics* – the practice of 'transfigural' re-imagination of the dynamics and possibilities of action in human situations. Transfigural imagination re-envisages concrete situations according to the criterion of God's true intention for humanity, revealed in Jesus Christ. This new, truly human future claims and overtakes every present situation, coming towards us as the new humanity in Jesus Christ. In the last part of this chapter, I will explore ways that these three paradigms – the dynamic interplay of divine and human action, parabolic hermeneutics, and transfigural imagination – recalibrate our answers to homiletical queries about the theological nature of the preaching, about hermeneutics, and about the rhetoric of Gospel proclamation.

## The Dynamic Interplay of Divine and Human Action

In his first book-length work, *Forgiveness: Decisive Issue in Protestant Thought* (1940), Lehmann focuses on the doctrine of forgiveness. His real quarry, however, is what he sees as a problematic imbalance in both of the two dominant theological projects influencing North American theology at the time, the liberal tradition as it had come to expression in the work of Albrecht Ritschl and the new, 'dialectical' theology taking centre stage in the then-unfolding work of Karl Barth.

Comparing Ritschl's approach to the doctrine of forgiveness with Barth's, Lehmann trains his lens on the way each theologian characterizes the interplay of divine and human action in the doctrine of forgiveness. In this regard, he finds the two theologians guilty of opposite errors. Ritschl, Lehmann charges, over-identifies humanity and divinity, with the result that he underemphasizes the necessity and priority of divine action in human forgiveness. In fact, Lehmann contends, Ritschl's doctrine of forgiveness amounts to a kind of

---

[2]   Paul Lehmann, *Ethics in a Christian Context* (Harper and Row, Publishers, 1963), p. 90.

'self-forgiveness'.[3] Yet Barth's approach falls into the opposite error. So concerned is Barth to preserve the priority and sovereignty of divine agency that the human consequences of forgiveness – especially the consequences for human relational action – get almost no attention whatever. True, says Lehmann, human beings can only hear and respond with repentance and obedience as they are continuously and graciously enabled to hear and respond by God. Yet, any truly dialectical theology must, in Lehmann's judgement, give an account of the real-time-and-space human difference that divine action makes for human action.[4] Barth, who had once spoken of his as a theology 'between' the times was in danger, quipped Lehmann, of writing instead a theology that hovered 'above' the times.[5]

Although Lehmann had access only to Barth's earlier works, and the weakness of Barth's theological anthropology with respect to forgiveness was later redressed, Lehmann's fundamental point about the dialectical nature of theology continues to be important for contemporary theology. Theology abandons part of its task when it fails to give an account of the material, experiential difference that the gracious acts of God make in human lives. As Lehmann puts it, 'Creation means not only that the reality of man and the world is a fundamentally derived reality but also that wherever else God and man may have relations with each other, they must and do have them in the world, our world'.[6] Theology is accountable to show the new possibilities that divine forgiveness opens up in 'the world of time, things, and men' (to borrow, as does Lehmann, Barth's own phrase).[7]

On one crucial point, though, Lehmann agrees with Barth. Divine action must be privileged as the pre-condition of any human experience of forgiveness. But it is Ritschl, Lehmann points out, who keeps faith with the Protestant tradition on the human side of forgiveness, stressing the this-worldly, new reality that obtains in the forgiven community. A truly dialectical theology of forgiveness will include an account of *both* divine action and new possibilities for human experience, so that 'the full priority of Christ and the full personal activity of the individual are both maintained'.[8]

This motif of the dynamic interplay of divine and human action in human situations is one that Lehmann carries forward into all of his subsequent work. In *Ethics*, Lehmann's stress on the dialectical interplay of '*the ways* of God and *the ways* of men', between divine and human action, remains firmly in place; but as Lehmann turns his attention to the subject of Christian ethics, he puts the formal motif established in *Forgiveness* 'into motion', so to speak.[9]

---

[3]    Paul Lehmann, *Forgiveness: Decisive Issue in Protestant Thought* (New York: Harper and Brothers, 1940), pp. 81, 99.
[4]    Ibid., pp. 184–5.
[5]    Ibid., p. 178.
[6]    Ibid., p. 176.
[7]    Ibid., pp. 165, 176.
[8]    Ibid., p. 78.
[9]    *Ethics in a Christian Context*, p. 90.

Lehmann's emphasis on context rather than precept, rule or virtue made his Christian ethics startling in the 1960s. Yet it is all-important to understand what defines 'context' for Lehmann. The context, or contextuality, of human ethics, is determined by the fact that every human situation is defined, or bracketed, by the fact of God's ongoing 'humanizing' activity. This makes every human situation a dynamic theatre of action, the arena where the constant interplay of divine and human action is played out. It is this dynamic interrelationship of divine and human action that crucially defines the *context* for Christian ethical discernment and action for Lehmann.

The nature of God's context- and situation-defining activity – 'what God is doing in the world' – is God's constant, ongoing strategic redemptive action 'to make and to keep human life human'.[10] To the consternation of many of Lehmann's interpreters, precisely what it means for human life to be 'made truly human' is one of the many concepts that Lehmann seems reluctant to define outright and prefers to establish inductively. Humanly speaking, he describes the goal of Christian ethical life as 'maturity', which he defines in purely anthropological terms as the capacity for each individual to be 'himself in togetherness, and in togetherness each to be himself'.[11] *Theologically*, however, mature humanity is 'the humanity with which Christ identified himself in his incarnation, which Christ restored through his humiliation, and which Christ glorifies in his resurrection and ascended body and through the *koinonia* which is his body in the world'.[12] Lehmann makes it clear that the aim and measure of truly mature humanity, then, is Jesus Christ, the firstborn of God's new creation.

God's ongoing work in the world 'to make and to keep human life human' Lehmann calls God's 'politics'. Drawing on Aristotle and citing the biblical narrative of God's formation of the people of Israel, Lehmann defines politics as people-forming activity: '[W]e may say that politics is activity, and reflection upon activity, which aims at and analyzes what it takes to make and to keep human life *human* in the world.'[13] Divine 'politics' is what God is doing in human situations to form humanity in the direction of greater conformity to the new humanity that has already come to be in Jesus Christ.

What is at stake for Christians ethically, says Lehmann, is to discern how God is at work in concrete and *particular* human situations, 'making and keeping human life human' so they may contribute, creatively and constructively, to that humanizing action. The kind of ethical discernment that recognizes God's humanizing work requires a particular kind of community – one that relies on the resources of Scripture and the practices of faithful worship. It is such a Christian community, which Lehmann calls the *koinonia*, that is best equipped to undertake these judgements. Crucially important to appropriate Christian discernment is

[10] Ibid., p. 99.
[11] Ibid., p. 55.
[12] Ibid.
[13] Ibid., p. 85.

Lehmann's foundational principle that every situation must be understood as, by definition, the arena of divine redemptive (humanizing) activity. In other words, *koinonia* ethics is Christian discernment that proceeds with the understanding that the range of possibilities for constructive human living is opened up and undergirded by a prior and ongoing reality, 'the concrete, personal, and purposeful activity of God'.[14]

This sense of situations as theatres of action, constantly under construction as they are shaped by the lively interplay between God's possibility-shaping activity and human action, makes Christian ethics 'more dynamic, more on the move, and more informal' than an ethics of precept and principle can imagine.[15] Human situations are not static; they are dynamic arenas of God's people-forming ('political') activity. Situations are in flux because God is at work in them, changing them. For Lehmann, both an ethics based on applying absolute rules and an ethics of relativist expediency are excluded because neither takes seriously enough the dynamic nature of human situations, constantly being reshaped by God's humanizing work. This dynamism and flux both complicates and liberates Christian ethical discernment and action, for what lies before us in any situation is 'the possibility of ever fresh and experimental responses to the dynamics and the humanizing character of the divine activity in the world'.[16]

It is crucial that the same stress on the priority of divine action in human situations that Lehmann establishes in *Forgiveness* not be lost sight of in reading *Ethics*. This point, made clear in the following passage, remains crucial in Lehmann's thought, although it is often missed by critics who mistakenly categorize Lehmann as a 'situation' ethicist:

> The complexity of the actual human situation with which a *koinonia* ethics tries seriously to deal, is always compounded of an intricate network of circumstance and human interrelationship *bracketed by the dynamics of God's political activity on the one hand and God's forgiveness on the other.*[17]

For Lehmann, the possibilities, the concrete patterns, and the consequences of human action in any given setting are conditioned by prior and ongoing divine action. This activity is of two kinds; it includes both God's 'political' activity in the world 'to make and to keep human life human' and God's activity of forgiveness.[18]

If we take seriously Lehmann's stress on the dynamic interplay of divine and human action in all situations as the pre-condition for all ethical discernment, this requires for many of us no minor adjustment to our thinking, not only about ethics, but about the nature of the world in which we live. Asserting that God is already

---

14   Ibid., p. 14.
15   Ibid., pp. 99, 122.
16   Ibid.
17   Ibid., p. 141.
18   Ibid., pp. 99, 105.

'politically' at work in every human situation to make and keep human life truly human both stabilizes and destabilizes our sense of the world with which we have to do. It is, on one hand, a world held and upheld by the creative presence and power of God; and yet, on the other, it is a world in which situations are dynamic, fraught with risk and possibility, ever in flux. It takes keen alertness, flexibility, humility, and courage to participate in any given time or place in what God is doing to move human being (and beings) toward fuller humanity.

Lehmann would insist that understanding situations in this way does not in any sense constitute a radical departure in Reformed theology; in fact, in his view, what he is doing is simply taking with full seriousness a fundamental impulse in Protestant theology since the Reformation – namely, attending to present and continuous divine activity, moving the world toward its truly human future, already initiated in the risen Christ. This reframing of human action within the theatre of divine action, for Lehmann, constitutes one of Reformed theology's most distinctive and significant contributions, one that we neglect at our peril. He writes:

> The Protestant Reformation introduced into the Western cultural tradition a liberating grasp of the *ways of God* with men and thus also the possibility of ever fresh and experimental responses to the *dynamics* and the humanizing character of the *divine activity* in the world.[19]

The God of Reformed theology is a God who has acted, acts now, and will act in the future to bring all things to completion in Jesus Christ. God is constantly laying redemptive claim to human beings and human situations in order to conform humanity to its future wholeness according to the pattern of Christ; and this is true everywhere 'in the world of time and space and things', as Lehmann likes to say. The implications for our understanding of Christian ethical discernment and action are challenging and liberating – as are the implications for our understanding and practice of preaching.

*The Dynamics of Divine and Human Action and the Nature of Preaching*

Lehmann's fundamental insight that there is a constant, dynamic interplay of divine and human action in all human situations bears directly on the question at the heart of homiletical theology and theory: Theologically speaking, what is the nature of preaching? In a sense, understanding every situation, including the situation of the congregation settling in to listen to the sermon on Sunday morning, as a dynamic arena in which God is at work to 'make and keep human life truly human' both simplifies and complicates our theological understanding of what is at stake in that preaching moment. On one hand, if Lehmann is right that God is already at work in every human situation to make and keep human life human, then we can take comfort in the fact that God's humanizing activity goes on in every congregation

---

[19]    Ibid., p. 14, emphasis added.

long before we preachers arrive. In other words, simply by virtue of its character as 'situated' action, preaching is 'bracketed' and conditioned by God's ongoing 'political' activity to make and keep human life human. We step in as co-actors in an ongoing, divinely-initiated process in which God is actively conforming all human beings to the maturity of Christ. We preachers participate in a saving work that is already in progress.

In a sense, Lehmann makes the work of preacher both easier and more difficult. Preachers do not have to labour under the misconception that it is up to them to 'bring God into the room', nor do they need to feel it is up to them to convince their congregations that human situations that seem neutral or hostile have religious or ethical potential. It is simply not true (tempting as it may be to preach this sermon) that absolutely *all* hope for redemptive change in the perplexing situations that impinge on our congregations' lives depends on what they do on Monday. Preaching faithfully means disclosing to the best of our ability the humanizing presence and power of God in our congregants' real world, urging them to discover and participate in God's redemptive work. Yet the first and last word is the faithfulness of God.

Recognizing that we step into a matrix already bracketed by God's saving work relieves us to a degree from attempting to sort out which 'part' of preaching is human word and which part divine; the act of preaching is *always* preceded, sustained, and followed by God's action. Yet Lehmann's construal of all human situations as arenas of divine and human action may somewhat occlude a conviction that the Reformed tradition has long affirmed: that preaching is a particular, indispensable form of action. It is God-ordained discourse that is God's instrument for the salvation of those who hear. Romans 5:14–15 asks, 'But how are they to call on one in whom they have not believed? And how are they to believe in one of whom they have never heard? And how are they to hear without someone to proclaim him? And how are they to proclaim him unless they are sent?' (NRSV). Does the fact that God is ever working to draw humanity toward wholeness in all situations constitute a reason to set aside preaching lightly, or to substitute some other kind of action for Gospel proclamation? The Reformed tradition would say 'no'. Nonetheless, Lehmann's insight about the dynamic involvement of God in every situation can make the preacher less anxious. The act of preaching does not take place in a situation devoid of God's power and presence, nor does it in any sense 'bring God' into a room where God was absent.

In another sense, Lehmann's insistence on the genuinely *dialectical* nature of theology, taking with full seriousness both the divine and human side of the activity that makes and keeps human life human, encourages us to take seriously the human necessity and human significance of our preaching. Preaching is preceded and sustained by the political, humanizing action and forgiveness of God; but it remains indispensably instrumental to God's saving work. Divine action opens up and enlarges the possibility of effective human action, but does not *substitute* for it. Preaching certainly cannot accomplish its saving purpose without the prior and sustaining activity of God; yet, at the same time, God *intends* the human action of proclamation and lays claim to human speaking, nothing else, to broadcast the saving Word.

Lehmann infuses Christian ethical discernment and action with both liberating possibility and great risk. Human beings can make choices to act in ways either *more* likely or *less* likely to participate in divine humanizing activity in given situations. Is the same true, then, of preaching? Can preaching sometimes function more faithfully, sometimes less faithfully, in relation to God's activity in a given place and time to make and keep human life human? A first and very general answer would have to be, 'yes'. *How* preaching would be faithful in a given place and time would have to be determined contextually; but preachers can rest assured that the act of preaching, like all human action, is *'bracketed by the dynamics of God's political activity on the one hand and God's forgiveness on the other'*.[20] God's forgiveness – God's will and ability to make the fallen and failing human creature to stand – upholds and restores us and our congregations in the frail, risky event of preaching. Nothing we say or do not say makes God less likely to work in the moment that we preach. Sometimes we come to the pulpit, our arms full of bread for the hungry – but other times we arrive, despite our best efforts, with what looks to us like a handful of crumbs. Nevertheless, we can still trust the God who is ever at work to feed the multitude in every situation.

Two final insights about the nature of preaching emerge from our exploration of Lehmann's first paradigm – the dynamic interplay of divine and human action in every situation. The first has to do with the 'who' of preaching. Discerning and responding to the humanizing work of God is neither the work of isolated individuals nor of experts, but rather the task of the *koinonia* of the church as a whole. So too, discerning and responding to the saving Word is the work of the whole church and not just the preacher. A second insight has to do with the 'what' – the content or purpose – of preaching. At the heart of all Gospel proclamation is the straightforward task of declaring what God has done, is doing, and will do. To put this in Lehmann's terms, this means that preachers need every Lord's Day to stand up amid the concreteness of the situations in which their congregations make decisions, experience conflict, love, and work, and name and claim those concrete human situations as possibility-charged arenas of God's humanizing activity. This is essential work if the women and men, teenagers and children who hear our sermons are going to recognize the workplace, courtroom, home, shopping mall, and classroom, as places in which God precedes, sustains, and follows us in our choosing and acting.

## Lehmann's Parabolic Hermeneutics

Lehmann's commitment to the dynamic interplay of divine and human action in human experience shapes, in turn, a second prominent feature of his work: the parabolic hermeneutic by which he relates biblical text and human situation.

---

[20]  Ibid., p. 141, original emphasis.

Christian ethics, for Lehmann, is a matter of creatively determining appropriate patterns of human action in relationship to 'what God is doing in the world to make and keep human life human'.[21] Discovering what God is already doing to shape human beings more humanly – or, in other words, discerning the pattern of divine 'politics' – requires a close reading of biblical texts drawn into a lively intertextual conversation with contemporary situations.

A discerning reading of biblical texts in relationship to concrete situations depends on a particular community of readers – the *koinonia*. For Lehmann, the *koinonia* is that community which, by faith and disciplined by its engagement with Scripture, discerns what God is doing in situations. As Lehmann states,

> When ethical thinking starts with the *koinonia*, the activity and purposes of God become the concrete context from within which behaviour can be regarded as both guided and shaped. It cannot be too strongly stressed that the contextual character of Christian ethics, as these pages seek to analyze it, is derived from the ethical reality and significance of the Christian *koinonia*.[22]

In their initial responses to *Ethics*, Lehmann's critics often missed this latter point, accusing him of undertaking a purely situational ethics. Yet, if we keep the groundwork laid in *Forgiveness* in mind, as well as the point Lehmann stresses here, there can be no mistaking the nature of the context Lehmann has in mind: It is a context *bracketed and continually shaped by the prior and ongoing activity of God* in pursuit of human wholeness in all its dimensions.

Thus for Lehmann, the starting point for Christian ethics cannot be some abstract set of principles and precepts 'read off' the Bible to undergird a moral calculus, nor can a situation be rightly assessed with a loosely related set of virtues. For distinctively Christian ethics, the starting point is a pointed question: 'What am I, as a believer and a member of the *koinonia*, the community of faith, to do in response to what God is already doing in the world to make and to keep human life human?' The form of the question clearly signals that, however we may ultimately respond to any human situation, we do so knowing we are stepping into a dynamic matrix in which God's activity has preceded ours: God is already creatively at work.

Just as crucial as a discerning community of readers is an appropriate understanding of the way texts function in relationship to concrete situations. The trope that anchors Lehmann's intertextual reading of biblical texts and human situations is neither precept nor rule, but parable. 'Parable, at least in the biblical sense', writes Lehmann, 'has to do with an imaginative juxtaposition of what is incommensurable: namely, the ways of God and the ways of man'.[23]

---

21  Ibid., pp. 99, 105.

22  Ibid.

23  Ibid., p. 87, n. 2.

Lehmann's own readings of biblical texts in relation to situations make it clear that the concept of the 'parabolic' functions in at least three ways in his hermeneutics, and in each case, expresses the juxtaposition of the divine and human activity that constitutes the dynamic matrix of all situations. First, Jesus' parables present the juxtaposition of divine and human activity in condensed, pungent images. Second, Lehmann construes Jesus' actions themselves as enacted, paradigmatic parables of the juxtaposition of divine and human action working within situations to move them toward more genuinely human life. Third, Lehmann describes the creative ethical action of the *koinonia* community, undertaken in response to the parabolic texts of Scriptures, as 'parabolic'. Action that 'plays forward' the parabolically-expressed possibilities for humanization drawn from Scripture becomes a living experiment in what it means to participate in God's humanizing activity in the world. Such risky, parabolically-shaped and parable-like behaviour 'intrinsically connects both "gospel" and "situation"' and becomes the 'parabolic bearer of a new humanity'.[24]

Parabolic hermeneutics, then, is the practice of 'the dynamics of biblical imagination' both in our hermeneutics of Scripture and our hermeneutics of action. Read parabolically, scripture functions disclosively, allowing us to discern the shape of human fulfilment 'already on its way'. We must also undertake a hermeneutics, or interpretation, of the concrete situations in order to participate in what God is doing to make human life truly human.[25] Situations are always 'dynamic', says Lehmann, because God is at work in them; and for this reason, ethical discernment and action is always provisional and experimental. The divinely-generated dynamism of human situations renders static principles insufficient to guide truly Christian behaviour, Lehmann contends. 'For the Christian, the *environment* of decision, not the *rules* of decision, gives to behaviour its ethical significance.'[26] Believers seek to act in ways that serve the humanizing purposes of God, knowing there can be no one 'right answer' within human situations which are always in motion. Taking action is always risky; yet believers dare to act on the basis of a parabolic reading of Scripture and situation, knowing their activity is bracketed by God's humanity-forming actions and God's forgiveness.

Although Lehmann does not elaborate on the trope of narrative, the narrative character of the sweep of biblical witness has a place in his hermeneutics. Parables, he suggests, function within an overarching framework in the Bible, the framework of the biblical story of God's people-forming activity over time. Biblical narrative constellates the array of parabolic actions by which God undertakes to form a people. The Bible tells a story about the ways in which 'the humanity of man is being hammered into being by the political dynamics of the divine activity'.[27] The horizon of meaning in the biblical story, as a whole, is not first and foremost a story

---

24    Ibid., p. 154.
25    Ibid.
26    Ibid., pp. 144, 347.
27    Ibid., p. 99.

of individual salvation, but a story of God's formation of a new humanity, socially and politically, which is the condition and context for individual transformation.

Lehmann's parabolic hermeneutics of biblical text and human situation operates within the arc of eschatological vision. Christian action amid the complexity of human situations is risky and provisional, but it is not rudderless. It is not only bounded by divine action and guided by parabolic readings of Scripture; it is judged by the criterion of Christ's revelation of true humanity, the firstborn of the human future that is already coming toward us. Lehmann's parabolic hermeneutic is not oriented to some idealized, primordial human past, nor is it measured by a philosophical ideal or set of virtues developed independently from the biblical witness. Rather, its measure is the already-dawning 'apocalypse', or coming-towards-us, of full humanity in Jesus Christ. Parabolic images in Scripture, as well as the parabolic actions of Christ and the contemporary *koinonia* reveal a fully human future that 'is already on its way'.[28]

*The Question of Hermeneutics for Preaching – Parabolic, Intertextual Reading of Biblical Text and World*

Lehmann's parabolic hermeneutics opens up rich possibilities for rethinking the hermeneutical moves preachers make in negotiating the territory that connect biblical texts and present human contexts. Lehmann insists that appropriate patterns of action in present situations cannot be 'read off' the pages of the Bible uncritically, nor can those possibilities be 'read off' human situations independent of Scripture. What is crucial, however, is to allow biblical texts to function in a way that opens up the possibilities for faithful action in the real-time situations of our lives.

It is important to recognize that for Lehmann, the proper focus in biblical interpretation is on *patterns of action* both in biblical text and human situations – and more specifically, the *juxtaposition* of divine and human 'humanizing' activity. 'Parabolic' reading of Scripture means approaching a biblical text with an eye to precisely the *situated action*, divine and human, that it expresses. These patterns of action in Scripture become templates, or paradigms, for the 'parabolic' interpretation of the possibilities in concrete human situations. The goal is to discern the presence and direction of divine humanizing activity in the real settings where a congregation lives every day, and to project possible patterns of faithful response in those situations, so that there, too, divine and human 'humanizing' activity is juxtaposed.

Such a parabolic hermeneutic steers us between the twin dangers of preaching that either sacrifices real-time relevance in the name of dogged attention to every detail of the biblical text, or, alternatively, reduces Scripture to folk wisdom in the name of relevance. We noted earlier that Lehmann began his first book, *Forgiveness*, with a critical assessment of the state of preaching in the first half of

---

[28]   Ibid., p. 122.

the twentieth century in North America. What Lehmann was seeing and hearing left him disheartened. A considerable number of preachers, lamented Lehmann in 1940, had fallen captive to one of two tendencies. On one hand, some preachers had succumbed to what he called 'textual literalism'. These preachers had plenty to say about the details of the biblical text, but disappointingly little to say about the consequences of the text's claims for the complex, concrete realities of human experience. Yet other preachers had been seduced, said Lehmann, by 'topical liberalism'. These preachers displayed consummate ability to pick out subjects for Sunday-morning sermonizing that would pique congregational interest, but had only the most tangential relationship to the biblical text. While textual literalism could hardly be accused of being unbiblical, and while topical liberalism had the advantage of guaranteeing listener interest (after all, who is not eager to hear about themselves?), neither, lamented Lehmann, was adequately theological.

What is required is to read Scripture and situations intertextually and parabolically; this opens to preaching a third way. Preachers cannot read Scripture faithfully without reading it intertextually – that is, in relationship with particular, here-and-now human situations. As for relevance, in Christian preaching the only 'relevance' that counts is helping the Christian community bear a witness that is 'relevant' to what God is doing – a witness that can only be guided by Scripture. Discerning how divine and human action are juxtaposed in the world of the Bible and then in the world of our listeners allows us to imagine with them ways to participate in what God has done and is doing to remake human life.

In *The Transfiguration of Politics*, Lehmann seems to point us towards a robustly intertextual attention to situations as well as biblical texts, suggesting that on the basis of the theology of incarnation, situations as well as texts can be indicators of what God is doing in the world: 'A theology of the incarnation affirms that the presence of Jesus of Nazareth in the human story opens up a way of perceiving the world of time and space and things that gives primacy and priority to the human sense and significance of what is going on.[29] Lehmann reasons that incarnation points to the juxtaposition of divine and human agency, not only in the person of Jesus, but in all that has to do with the human, since what is human is now caught up in the moment-to-moment, humanizing work of God. This gives human events new significance. Yet, lest we imagine now that anthropology swallows up all theology, as if every kind of human action now participates in the divine, Lehmann offers a corrective: we must affirm that 'all theology is anthropology *as a reflex of Christology*'.[30] In phrasing reminiscent of 2 Corinthians 5:16 – 'from now on we regard no one from a worldly point of view; though we once regarded Christ in this way, we do so no longer' – Lehmann makes it clear that our knowledge of all that is human is 'the knowledge of human things in Christ'.[31] The criterion and touchstone of a preacher's interpretation of patterns of action in both texts

---

[29] Lehmann, *The Transfiguration of Politics*, p. 230.
[30] Ibid., p. 231.
[31] Ibid.

and situations is always the new humanity revealed in Christ. The hermeneutic that Lehmann offers to preachers is as much apocalyptic as it is parabolic. God's embrace of humanness in Jesus Christ, now coming over the present in the living Lord, has claimed the vectors of human action themselves as avenues for God's activity, often hidden, to make and keep human life human. All preaching ultimately announces the anticipated 'apocalypse' of new creation, God's future for humanity already inaugurated and coming towards us in Jesus Christ. As preachers dare to 'read' human events as disclosive of God's humanizing activity in the world, the criterion of human maturity will always be Jesus the Christ, who in weakness and humility reveals the true humanity of God's new creation.

This means that for preachers, not everything that counts as 'success' in mundane human terms counts as 'success' in light of Christ. What is apparently weak in this world may need to be lifted up as the presence and power of God; what appears to be dazzling may need to be exposed for the false bid for human fulfilment that it truly is. As James F. Kay has suggested, preachers who interpret human experience by the measure of the true humanity coming towards us in the risen Christ will 'read' and describe human experience 'bifocally' or 'stereoscopically', helping their listeners to discern the emergence of God's new creation amid the old.[32]

## Practicing Transfigural Imagination

Lehmann's next book, *The Transfiguration of Politics* (1975) is a complex work. Here, Lehmann-the-artist brings new materials to the canvas. The material fleshing out of Lehmann's formal commitments, a project already begun in *Ethics in a Christian Context*, gets played out in far more detail and specifically in relation to political movements on a large scale. Lehmann draws on the biblical account of the Transfiguration of the Lord in Matthew 17, reading that text intertextually with human situations of social reconstruction, specifically the revolutionary movements of the 1960s. By means of this intertextual reading, Lehmann shows how a parabolic hermeneutic produces, in turn, a 'transfigural', critical re-imagination of the humanizing possibilities that lie within situations of human revolutionary action.

In the Transfiguration, Jesus' relation to both God and humanity, to the historical past, to the present, and to the eschatological future, is constellated in a single, parabolic scene. The event on the mountaintop discloses to the disciples, and to us, the active presence-in-the-present of God's already-begun future for humanity within human history. With characteristic poetic passion, as if trying to gather up the enormity of the moment in a single rush of words, Lehmann writes that, at the Transfiguration,

---

[32]    See James F. Kay, 'The Word of the Cross at the Turn of the Ages', *Interpretation* 53:1 (1999): 44–56.

the mystery and meaning of the ultimate presence and power by which reality *is*, and is defined and directed, are unveiled and concealed in the hiddenness and openness of a human person whose presence and power set the whole off-course world and human story on course again ... .The Maker ... of all things visible and invisible, has come awesomely and transformingly near the turmoil and travail of the human story: its sin and suffering, its exploitation and enmity, its promise and possibility, its forgiveness and fulfillment.[33]

Lehmann takes the measure of the 'human shape of human life' in apocalyptic perspective. The Transfiguration becomes the parabolic lens that enables us to discern 'the steady pressure upon the shape of things to come of the sovereign, freeing, and fulfilling purpose and power of God ... who, in the power of a future that is coming to be, picks up the humanizing pieces of the past and makes a humane and humanizing present'.[34] Humanity's future has not yet fully arrived; but we see in the transfigured Lord that transformed future coming toward us, already overtaking our present by means of God's powerful presence in human situations.

Lehmann focuses, in particular, on the way the Transfiguration reveals the ongoing *political* activity of God. He calls our attention to the fact that, according to Matthew, Jesus takes his disciples to the mountain *instead* of going to the Feast in Jerusalem. In other words, he sidesteps the Jerusalem crowds feverish with Zealot hopes. This parabolic action of Jesus is very telling, Lehmann suggests. Jesus eschews a particular strategy for precipitating change in human affairs. 'There is a difference', he writes, 'between *political messianism* and *messianic politics*'.[35] Social movements that fall prey to the illusions of political messianism see themselves as the divinely-ordained bearers of the human future and so are in peril of failing to perceive the dangers inherent in their own success. If political messianism succeeds in bringing about its vision for the human future by force, it takes on the characteristics of the forms of power it sought to overthrow. The Transfiguration reveals that divine presence and power to bring about a whole human future is not allied with Zealot strategies designed to gain dominance over the oppressor. Instead, the scene on the mountaintop reveals that divine power to make human life more truly free, and therefore more truly human, lies hidden within apparent weakness – within God's apparent absence from the scene where human powers collide.

The Transfiguration parabolically reveals that it is the messianic power of weakness that is making room for God's future. Jesus refuses to precipitate a different future by force or fiat, for that would be no real transformation, only more of the same.

What does the Transfiguration have to do with the here-and-now politics of social change? Lehmann contends that only by reframing socio-political revolution

---

[33]   Lehmann, *The Transfiguration of Politics*, p. 231.
[34]   Ibid.
[35]   Ibid.

within God's *specific* story of a truly human future coming towards us in Jesus Christ, the one who is crucified before he is raised as the firstborn of new humanity, can revolutionary movements be transfigured and saved from the dangers of their own desire for power. Revolutionary movements require a 'saving story' about power if it is to bring about a genuinely human future.[36] The biblical story of human transformation, distilled into the Transfiguration scene, contributes to situations a crucial ingredient: the 'power of weakness' to expose the 'weakness of power'.[37] When human movements for change are joined to the saving story of Jesus, God's transformation of the nature and use of power can press upon the human dynamics of revolution, making a redemptive claim on them, savingly 'transfiguring' their uses of power. Only through this saving story can such movements be prevented from 'devouring their own children', argues Lehmann.[38]

*The Transfiguration of Politics* makes for challenging reading – and yet, to undertake a robust, discerning transfigural 'reimagination' of the dynamics of power in human relations, at whatever level from the personal to the socio-political, is demanding work. Human politics (which in basic terms means the human use of power) pervade our lives; yet the dynamics of power in human situations, and the myriad ways that power can either be constructively used or tragically abused, are often hidden from our view. In a sense, we do not *want* to see what we are doing, or recognize the dangers inherent in having power and using it. Yet attending to this 'subtext' in all the situations of our lives is crucial if we mean to be alert to the ways that God is at work to make and keep human life truly human. The paradox of Jesus Christ's power – the fact that the power of God was disclosed through a first-century Jew, and continues to be disclosed today, as apparent human weakness and folly – stretches our minds; and if our thinking and acting is going to be converted to the ways and purposes of God, the transfiguration of our understanding of power is crucial.

## The Rhetoric of Christian Preaching: Transfigural Re-imagination

Apart from his discussion of the state of North American preaching in the 1930s at the beginning of *Forgiveness*, Lehmann rarely makes explicit references to preaching. Yet here and there, we find allusions that indicate what Lehmann hopes preaching might accomplish. In *Ethics in a Christian Context*, Lehmann defines the 'living word' as 'the verbal expression of the full complexity and totality of the existing, concrete situation', a word 'which makes it possible for human beings to be open *for* one another and *to* one another'.[39] What will be the character of the 'verbal expression' that envisages the trajectory of redemptive action to which a congregation is summoned in any given moment?

---

[36]   Ibid., p. 229.
[37]   Ibid., p. 26.
[38]   Ibid., p. 10.
[39]   *Ethics in a Christian Context*, p. 130.

Lehmann contends that the Transfiguration forces us to contend, in real terms, with the coming-over-the-present of God's future. Certainly, this is the urgent task of preaching, and the source of its relevance. The function of the Christian preacher is to discern how divine 'politics' concretely and savingly reframes human situations. With this in mind, we can project several implications for the rhetoric of Christian preaching.

First, Christian preachers need to say 'what is' before they say 'what ought to be'. Christian preachers announce God's promise, kept and continually being kept, in Jesus Christ. In a Christian understanding of the world all our choosing and acting is undertaken against the backdrop of what God has done, is doing, and will do. Or, to put this in more technical grammatical terms, what we are saying here is that the indicative mood is preeminent and always brackets the imperative ('we must, we ought, and we should'). The grammatical 'mood' of Christian preaching is announcement, not admonishment. If we put the imperative first, we imply that God's new creation is something that 'depends' on the efforts of the Church to construct it. But the truth of the resurrection is that God's new creation is an event already under way in which believers are summoned to participate.

Picking up again on a point made earlier, this means, among other things, that preachers need to name and claim every human situation as the arena where God is *already* savingly at work. For many congregations, this will be news – maybe even a paradigm shift so radical that it will take weeks and months of preaching before it really sinks in. Many congregations have been trained to think of themselves either as a righteous, beleaguered remnant huddled behind stack of Bibles, or an armed-to-the-teeth regiment of God blazing into hostile territory. While there are no doubt occasions when these sorts of images can be illuminating, they are for the most part not helpful; and if they do motivate the congregation at all, they may motivate it in the wrong way and for the wrong reasons.

It is simply not faithful to the witness of Scripture to claim that God is only at work in the church. God is at work everywhere and continuously to subvert all that destroys human life, however hidden this redemptive (or in Lehmann's vocabulary, 'humanizing') activity may be. Thus the transfigural rhetoric of preaching will reframe every present moment as a time and space in which God is already reconstructing human situations according to God's intended future, using a variety of human means.

The language of this reframing may well require daring new images and metaphors. Lehmann suggests that 'divine pressure about the dynamics and the shape of things' will press us toward 'its metaphorical description and communication'.[40] The imaginative transfiguration of human situations by the form of human wholeness revealed in Jesus Christ will require the 'proposal of paradigmatic metaphors, which illuminate and are in turn illuminated by the *kairotic* actions of a revolutionary time', a wager in language that always

---

40   *The Transfiguration of Politics*, p. 234.

'involves risk'.[41]As Lehmann's own work shows, transfigural imagination may require innovative, sometimes explosive speech. Speaking about God's world-disrupting new creation with only the tools of the present order on hand will create ruptures in language and call into play tropes of metaphorical juxtaposition and paradox.

Yet, if the task of the preacher is to reframe for the people in the pews their real, present experience as the arena where God is bringing about new creation, then the language of preaching must be thoroughly local speech. Preachers need to envisage recognizable *local* realities and sketch the outlines of realistic, local acts of daring witness. It will not do to speak in other-worldly terms of new creation if we really believe that God is acting here and now, in this present place and time, and if we want our congregations to be able to believe it too.

Finally, the rhetoric of Christian preaching will include naming what Lehmann calls 'the weakness of power' and 'the power of weakness'.[42] Power – its use and abuse – is a fundamental issue in all human relations, from the bedroom to the boardroom, from the hallways of the local high school to the halls of government. Reimagining the nature of world-changing power in light of God's revelation of true humanity in Christ is crucial subject-matter for preaching.

The saving story of Jesus Christ is a story that undercuts the widespread assumption that it is the power of domination that effects real change. As Lehmann argues throughout *The Transfiguration of Politics*, the Christian story is a story of divine power revealed in weakness. The power of the Crucified – the power of fidelity to the ways of God for the sake of the purposes of God – is power that destabilizes and ultimately overthrows the power of domination, exposing its fragility. As faithful preachers re-imagine the shape of human action amid the pressing political and social problems that bear upon their congregations' life and witness, they will do so in ways that foreground the liberating politics of God among the humble and insignificant whose lives testify to God's fully human future in Jesus Christ.

## Into Deep Waters – Lehmann's Invitation to Preachers

Lehmann himself never returned to dwell at length on the subject that occupies him in the opening pages of his first book – the critical assessment and renewal of preaching. Perhaps, had there been time and energy enough, he would have done so. Yet, those with eyes to see and ears to hear can discern just under the surface of his vigorous theological project an intriguing map of the theological, hermeneutical, and rhetorical terrain that the preacher must negotiate every time she or he composes a sermon. On the other hand, perhaps what Lehmann has

[41]   Ibid., p. 235.
[42]   Ibid., p. 26.

given preachers is not so much a map as it is a nautical chart. Intended or not, Paul Lehmann's theology invites preachers to plunge with new confidence into that exhilarating, turbulent zone where the winds and currents of living Word and living world meet and swirl.

# Chapter 9
# *Koinonia* Ethics and Preaching in South Korea

Eunjoo Mary Kim

## Paul Lehmann and Korean Preaching

It was during my PhD years at Princeton Theological Seminary when I was first introduced to Paul Lehmann, not in a classroom but in the seminary bookstore. A new volume in the new book section drew my attention with its interesting title, *Humanization and the Politics of God: The Koinonia Ethics of Paul Lehmann.*[1] In that book, I was so fascinated by Lehmann's ethical perspective that I subsequently buried myself in his works. In my doctoral dissertation, I was concerned with the renewal of Korean preaching in its theology and method and invited Lehmann as my primary dialogue partner. In Korea, three indigenous religions – Shamanism, Buddhism and Confucianism – had coexisted for more than 1500 years. When Protestant Christianity was introduced to Korea in the late nineteenth century, these indigenous religions greatly influenced the formation of the Christian faith among Korean believers. One of the crucial issues for Korean Christians has always been: how can they live as individual Christians while, at the same time, be members of families and a society in which the Christian ethos and values are not dominant?[2] Lehmann's *koinonia* ethic, inviting believers to God's humanizing activity, gave me insight into a new understanding of preaching and became my theological ground for proposing a new homiletical theory for Korean preaching in my dissertation.[3]

---

[1]    Nancy J. Duff, *Humanization and the Politics of God: The Koinonia Ethics of Paul Lehmann* (Grand Rapids: Eerdmans, 1992).

[2]    Confucianism, which was the state religion when Christianity was introduced to Korea by Western missionaries, is one of the most influential indigenous religions. It has provided Koreans with moral guidelines for how to live as a member of one's family and society. Confucianism has greatly influenced Korean Christianity in its process of inculturation.

[3]    Eunjoo Kim, 'The Preaching of Transfiguration: Theology and Method of Eschatological Preaching from Paul Lehmann's Theological Perspective as an Alternative to Contemporary Korean Preaching', PhD Dissertation (Princeton: Princeton Theological Seminary, 1996).

## South Korea in the Age of Globalization

Ten years after completing my doctoral dissertation, I had the opportunity last autumn to teach at two theological schools in Korea. Through my time there, I was continuously surprised by dramatic changes in every aspect of Korea, resulting from the compelling forces of globalization: excessive individualism and consumerism; the seemingly invincible power of capitalism; rising unemployment and the widening gap between the haves and the have-nots; the direct threat of nuclear weapons by North Korea; serious ecological crises caused by air, soil and water pollution; problems with migrant workers from Asian and African countries, and confusion over national identity and personal values in the midst of a flood of global cultures and commodities.

These conditions are not brand new for Koreans, but ten years ago they were not nearly as serious as today. We, living in the twenty-first century, are experiencing globalization at an unprecedented speed. Today, more than ever, we feel that we are drawn into a network of global relationships, regardless of where we live. The term globalization connotes a broad spectrum of experiences, widely and disparately shared, ranging from consumerism and market forces to cultural diversity, from political and military intervention to environmental issues. The advancement of information technology has accelerated this process, so that today's world is intimately interconnected by the forces of globalization. The problems and issues I observed in Korea we are experiencing all over the world.

As Rosemary Ruether reminds us, it is important to recognize that one of the forceful ideologies behind globalization is neoliberal capitalism, grounded in a 'materialistic utilitarian anthropology',[4] which defines individual human beings as *homo economicus* and *homo consumptor.* According to this ideology, humans are autonomous rational subjects who act solely to maximize their individual self-interest, especially in terms of their economic possessions. They equate maximizing their economic wealth with the ultimate expression of human well-being and happiness. The hypothesis is that the more one has, the better off one is. And as possessions are derived from consumptions, the more one consumes, the better off one is.[5]

In Korea, since the 1990s, the government has deliberately encouraged all areas of society to become more global by opening the door to free market trade and international relations. Toward this end, they provide funds for globalizing institutions and corporations. The idea of 'becoming more global' has become a new ethos that influences the people's mindsets, cultural trends and life values. Obviously, the ideology dominating personal and social life in Korea today is individualistic materialism, which is a byproduct of neo-liberal capitalism.

---

[4]    Rosemary R. Ruether, *Integrating Ecofeminism, Globalization, and World Religions* (Lanham: Rowman & Littlefield, 2005), p. 33.

[5]    Ibid., p. 34.

Individualistic materialism erodes the traditional value of the community life and the virtue of frugality, long honoured in Confucian culture.

By my observation, not only secular society but also Christian communities in Korea have been impacted by the ideology of neoliberal capitalism. Commodity relationships and the market value system, in which people are often judged only by what they can produce or afford, are the driving forces in many churches. Although some churches strive to survive the competitive, dehumanizing commodity culture, an increasing number of Korean churches are co-opted by that culture. They consider their preaching ministry a consumer-oriented business. They regard churchgoers as consumers and adopt market value tactics to achieve growth in church membership. Their main concern is to offer the kind of services that will attract more 'consumers' of religion.

With regard to preaching, sermons often stress materialistic, success-oriented individualism based on the pop-psychology of positive thinking. I recall once visiting a large upper-middle class church in a rich suburban area of Seoul. The preacher, one of the most well-known ministers in Korea, emphasized in his sermon that we could be *more* successful in the world by the grace of Jesus Christ. After the service, I expressed to one of the church staff members, who was also an alumnus of my seminary, my discomfort with the theological direction of the sermon. I wondered why the sermon focused on worldly success for those who seemed to be already successful by those standards, rather than emphasize stewardship or sharing their possessions with the poor. He explained that Sunday sermons strategically stressed popular human wishes and worldly desires in order to attract more people to the church and to increase the amount of offerings, because the church had to maintain its facilities and large staff. He then added that the sermons preached at Wednesday worship, attended by a small group of people, were more faithful to the Christian gospel. After that conversation, I could not help asking myself: What is the Christian church? What does it mean to preach in this age of globalization? These questions lead me to revisit Lehmann's *koinonia* ethic because it is not about morality but about identity.

Once again, I invite him to be my dialogue partner for theological reflection on Korean preaching in the age of globalization. Lehmann's *koinonia* ethic will provide some clues to answer my questions and offer homiletical guidance for contemporary Korean preaching in three aspects: the *koinonia* as the identity of the church; preaching as the politics of God; and preaching toward maturity.

## The *Koinonia* as the Identity of the Church

Although some preaching happens outside the church, usually it is practiced in a particular local church. As Lehmann accurately describes, the true nature of the church is the *koinonia*, i.e., 'the fellowship-creating reality of Christ's presence in the world'.[6] The *koinonia* can be understood by the metaphor of 'the body' – the 'embodiment of Christ' or 'the embodiment of the Spirit' – in which 'each individual functions properly himself [sic] in relation to the whole, and the whole functions properly in so far as each individual is related to it'.[7] Christians are called to live within the *koinonia*, the body of Christ in the world.

Lehmann's concept of the *koinonia* is based on his understanding of human nature as relational and communal. We humans become fully mature in the community of faith. No one can become new as a solitary individual.[8] The new person means more than the individual believer who has been justified and sanctified. In the body of Christ, the individual becomes new through fellowship with others and by expressing his or her newness towards the world as a living parable. In the *koinonia*, each individual member is invited to the fellowship of maturity or 'the new humanity'[9] in love and togetherness. The *koinonia* is neither a hierarchical nor egalitarian community but is grounded in the recognition of the differences among the members. In the *koinonia*, humans can become fully mature by practising 'reciprocal responsibility'.[10]

Hence, Lehmann's *koinonia* ethic is not concerned with the private soul who is lost in individual well-being and piety. Rather, his *koinonia* ethic is concerned with the transformation of the community, in which God's transforming power opens the individual believer to becoming a living parable of God's action or 'a living sign and occasion of what God in Christ is for', that is, 'the bearer of new and fulfilling life'.[11] Our action as a living sign signifies the new age that has been inaugurated by Christ and is a fragmentary 'foretaste' in the world of the fulfilment that is already on its way.[12] Dietrich Bonhoeffer explains the image of a living parable as follows:

> 'You *are* the salt' – not 'you should be the salt'! The disciples are given no choice whether they want to be salt or not. No appeal is made to them to become salt of the earth. Rather they just are salt, whether they want to be or not, by the power of the call which has reached them. You *are* the salt – not, 'you have the salt' … . What is meant is their whole existence, to the extent that it is newly grounded in Christ's call to discipleship … . 'You *are* the light' – again, not: 'you should be the light'! The call itself has made them light. It cannot be any other

---

6    Paul Lehmann, *Ethics in a Christian Context* (New York: Harper & Row, 1963), p. 59.

7    Ibid., p. 62.

8    Ibid., pp. 57–8.

9    Ibid., p. 17.

10    Paul Lehmann, *The Decalogue and a Human Future: The Meaning of the Commandments for Making & Keeping Human Life Human* (Grand Rapids: Eerdmans, 1995), p. 11.

11    Paul Lehmann, 'The Servant Image in Reformed Theology', *Theology Today*, 15:3 (1958), p. 338.

12    Lehmann, *Ethics in a Christian Context*, p. 101.

way. They are a light which is seen ... . He who speaks directly of himself by
saying, 'I am the Light, says directly to his disciples, 'You are the light in your
whole lives, as long as you remain faithful to the call'.[13]

The *koinonia* as the community of the true disciples of Christ is the context in
which the preacher can experience the real presence of Christ, for God works in
the community by revealing God's divine will to the members of the *koinonia* and
makes the wisdom of God known to them. Yet, the *koinonia* is neither identical to
the empirical reality of the visible church nor separable from that church. In other
words, not all visible churches in the world are the contexts for discerning what
God is doing in and for the world. Instead, as Lehmann expresses, the *koinonia*
is, 'the little church within the Church, the leaven in the lump, the remnant in the
midst of the covenant people'.[14] Only those churches that represent the true church
in which Christ is present, can concretely experience the dynamics of divine acts
for reconciliation and transformation.

The true church is called to become 'a revolutionary community',[15] confronting
the *status quo* and co-opting dehumanizing worldly ideologies. As Lehmann
claims, the church is 'not as an institutional or bureaucratic structure', but 'the
visible community, called together in the world, to be the vanguard of the presence
of Christ in his purposed liberation (or, salvation) of all people for full participation
in human fulfillment'.[16]

Lehmann's *koinonia* ethic challenges preachers to ask themselves what kind of
church they envisage as the outcome of their preaching. A true church or a worldly
institution? Furthermore, his *koinonia* ethic suggests that Christian preaching aims
at a church's transformation into the *koinonia*, where new and biblical possibilities
of life occur. Toward this goal, the preacher should help the congregation see
itself, constantly and sincerely, as a reflection of the biblical image of the church.
Sermons preached week after week remind the congregation of who they are and
what their church must be, and make an effort to continuously reform their church
(*ecclesia reformata reformanda*).

## Preaching as the Politics of God

In his books, *Ethics in a Christian Context* and *The Transfiguration of Politics*,
Lehmann interprets the activity of God in the world in terms of politics. Politics in
general means 'the study of the form of political community that is the best of all

---

[13]    Dietrich Bonhoeffer, *Discipleship*, trans. M. Kruske and I. Tödt (Minneapolis:
Fortress, 2001), pp. 111–12.

[14]    Lehmann, *Ethics in a Christian Context*, p. 72.

[15]    Paul Lehmann, *The Transfiguration of Politics* (New York: Harper & Row, 1975),
p. 168.

[16]    Ibid.

forms for a people able to pursue the most ideal mode of life'.[17] The theological definition of politics derived from this general concept, is 'an activity and reflection upon activity, which aims at and analyzes what it takes to make and keep human life human in the world'.[18] For Lehmann, therefore, it is supremely legitimate to express what God is doing in the world as political activity and to see God as a 'politician'.[19] In fact, the Bible uses political images when describing who God is and what God is doing in the world. For example, the Christological title 'Messiah' is a political term. The Messiah, who is 'the anointed of God', is the most crucial political image in the eschatological worldview of the ancient Jewish community.[20]

According to Lehmann, the politics of God corresponds to human politics in that both are concerned with what it takes to make and to keep the whole of human life whole. However, the ideal concept of human politics, says Lehmann, cannot be identified with the reality of the politics of the state. This is because the politics of the state validates power and always justifies itself in the use of its power, whereas the politics of God calls all power into question and has power to transform worldly politics.[21] Lehmann's understanding of the politics of God as the 'transfiguration'[22] of human politics implies that Christian preaching should be a parabolic event of God's politics for radical humanization. Christian preaching should be as political as God's activity witnessed in scripture and in human history. When preaching is limited to individual morality or private success in the world, its message loses revolutionary power, which is the core of the Christian message. However, when preaching is mainly concerned with what God is doing in the world to make and to keep human life human, and when it participates in and serves the politics of God, such preaching participates in the politics of God.

Preaching as the politics of God relativizes the world's reality and interprets the congregation's existential experience of the concrete conditions of their everyday lives by discerning and describing how God is at work for their humanization. How, then, can the preacher discern God's activity in the world? Regarding this question, biblical stories function paradigmatically as clues to an interpretation of God's politics in our time. The creation stories, the history of the people of Israel, and the life, death, and resurrection of Jesus Christ in the Scriptures are genuine

---

[17]   Lehmann, *Ethics in a Christian Context*, p. 83.

[18]   Ibid., p. 85.

[19]   Ibid., p. 83.

[20]   Ibid., pp. 94–5.

[21]   Lehmann, *The Transfiguration of Politics*, p. 52.

[22]   Lehmann uses the term transfiguration to express the eschatological power of the politics of God. According to him, while transformation means a marked shift from the old form of power to the new one, and transvaluation means 'the turning of an accepted value inside out', transfiguration connotes 'a radicalization of transvaluation as transvaluation connotes a radicalization of transformation', which means that transfiguration is the highest in intensity (ibid., pp. 73–6).

parables through which the preacher can discern God's continuing activity of grace in the world in the present and in the future.

When the preacher attempts to discern living parables of God's politics in the world, the *koinonia* is the primary locus where she can find what God is doing to make and to keep human life human in the world. However, God's politics are not limited to the context of the *koinonia*. Lehmann, on the one hand, uses an extreme statement to stress the significant role of the *koinonia* for the politics of God:

> ... there is only one way to 'belong' to what God is doing in the world, to be partakers of it. That way is the way of membership in a social body ... there is no salvation outside the ecclesia, the church. The church is the fellowship of partakers, the body of those who belong to the way of salvation.[23]

On the other hand, Lehmann reminds us of God's freedom to self-manifest to the whole world, stating,

> There is, of course, one marginal possibility which must always also be kept in mind ... . The marginal possibility is that God himself is free to transcend – *ubi et quando visum est Deo* ('where and when it pleaseth him') – what he has done and continues to do in and through the church. God's action and God's freedom are never more plainly misunderstood than by those who suppose that God has acted and does act in a certain way and cannot, therefore, always also act in other ways. Of course, God is bound *to* what he does and has done. But he is not bound *by* what he has done.[24]

God's action and freedom are so mysterious that they go beyond our simple understanding or imagination. Whatever God is doing in and through the *koinonia*, God is doing also in the world; the God of the *koinonia* is also the God of politics and social lives in the whole world. What, then, is the difference between Christians and non-Christians? Lehmann responds that the difference between them is not determined by church membership, for both believers and unbelievers belong to God. The only difference is that for believers, as members of the *koinonia*, the kingship of Christ is revealed, while for unbelievers it remains hidden.[25]

Just as the *koinonia* ethic is open to the world, so should Christian churches be. They should not be closed circles of faith but be open to the wider world, where the ongoing activity of God is often found. The preacher can discern God's politics on a broad scale, both by observing what is happening in other parts of the earth and by seriously engaging in conversation with other religious and non-religious communities. In fact, in response to the question, 'What is God doing in the world

---

23   Paul Lehmann, 'Deliverance and Fulfillment', *Interpretation*, 5:4 (1951), pp. 397–8.
24   Lehmann, *Ethics in a Christian Context*, pp. 72–3.
25   Ibid., p. 117.

to make and to keep human life human?' the preacher often finds the answer outside the Christian community, because the whole world belongs to God.

While the whole world is the locus for God's revelation, it is important to remember that God is especially present at the margins of the world, 'in the least expected place, in the midst of sinners, in the company of the poor, in the deep hiddenness of the cross'.[26] Biblical stories attest that God is present at the margins of society. God stands for individuals and communities who are marginalized from mainstream society because of social status, wealth, health and so on. A reversal of the social order is anticipated and seen as essential to the coming of God's reign. God's incarnation in Jesus of Nazareth affirms that the margins of society are in fact the centre, at the core where the Spirit of God is working on reconciliation and transformation. The awareness that the margins of society are the places where we can discern the presence and activity of God encourages the preacher to look deeper into our world today. In the age of globalization, the important tasks for the preacher are to identify the margins of society globally, as well as locally, and to discern the politics of God in the margins of the global world.

Yet, God's politics involve not only human relationships but also a universal ecological dimension. In his posthumous book, *The Decalogue and a Human Future*, Lehmann claims, with regard to the Third Commandment of the Decalogue, that Christian salvation is cosmic and universal because the nature of a human being and that being's interrelatedness with nature are mutually inclusive. Just as the individual cannot be understood apart from the community, so the community cannot be understood apart from nature.[27] Despite its magnitude, however, the earth suffers because of human irresponsibility. Ecological crises and nuclear weapons of worldwide destruction threaten life and health in ways we cannot imagine. Therefore, humans must be responsible for the 'freedom of nature to be what it was made to be; the environment of humanization'.[28] This cosmic dimension of the politics of God requires that the preacher discern God's politics for the whole of creation, for nature as well as for human beings. Toward this task, the preacher must 'read the times' with sensitivity, to know what God is doing in the world in order to make and to keep human life human. In this effort, all human beings are individually responsible not only for themselves but also for others and for the whole of God's creation.

Preaching as the politics of God is an invitation to the congregation to hear what God is doing in the world to make and keep human life human in the world. Those who understand through the sermons they hear what God is doing in the world can no longer support the politics of the established order. Instead, they live out what they hear, inspired by a desire to take human responsibility for the world. Consequently, preaching as the politics of God transcends the lure of the

---

[26]    Daniel Migliore, *Faith Seeking Understanding: An Introduction to Christian Theology* (Grand Rapids: Eerdmans, 1991), p. 24.

[27]    Lehmann, *The Decalogue and a Human Future*, pp. 145–8.

[28]    Ibid., p. 148.

*impasse* of individualistic reference and becomes itself a fragmentary foretaste of the fulfilment of God's salvific action. Preaching participating in God's politics is itself a living parable of what God is doing in the world to make room for the freedom and fulfilment that human beings assume.

## Preaching Toward Maturity

Lehmann's *koinonia* ethic requires that preaching connect with the ethical dimension of human life. Preaching should respond to the fundamental ethical question of the believers: 'What am I, as a believer in Jesus Christ and as a member of his church, to do?'[29] Here, it is important to distinguish ethics from morality. For Lehmann, while morality is an actual practice of behaviour according to customs, rules and laws, ethics is the reflective consideration of the foundations and principles of behaviour.[30] And Christian ethics aims 'not at morality, but at maturity'.[31]

Lehmann defines maturity (or the new humanity) as 'the integrity in and through interrelatedness which makes it possible for each individual member of an organic whole to be himself in togetherness, and in togetherness each to be himself'.[32] More precisely, maturity means the full or complete development of human beings as individuals and of all beings in their relations with one another. Therefore, according to Lehmann, maturity is 'the fruit of Christian faith', while 'morality is a by-product of maturity',[33] and the ultimate goal of the *koinonia* ethics is to achieve maturity.[34]

How, then, can preaching contribute to the *koinonia* ethics? In other words, how can preaching help the congregation achieve maturity? With regard to this practical question, it is necessary to pay attention to Lehamnn's emphasis on the nurture of apperception. For Lehmann, the term 'apperception' means a 'uniquely human capacity of knowing',[35] or a holistic epistemological process towards perceiving true humanity:

> [A]pperception is the experience of self-evident self-discovery through which one is drawn into the heritage and the reality of what it takes to be and to stay human in the world. Apperception is the experience of retrospective and prospective immediacy – whatever may be its biological and psychological

---

[29] Lehmann, *Ethics in a Christian Context*, p. 25.

[30] Ibid., pp. 24–5.

[31] Ibid., p. 54.

[32] Ibid., p. 55.

[33] Ibid., p. 54.

[34] Ibid., p. 55.

[35] Lehmann, *The Decalogue and a Human Future*, p. 24.

vectors – which shapes and is shaped by the dynamics of human responsiveness to God, world, and society.[36]

Apperception is that faculty of judgement for the ethical life of human beings. Out of apperception, the congregation perceives the world and discerns what is humanly true or false according to the will of God.

Preaching that aims at helping the congregation gain maturity requires preachers to nurture the congregation's apperception. In order to achieve this goal through their preaching, critical theological reflection and effective communication are essential. I suggest that critical theological reflection be a threefold process. First, the preacher analyses the congregation's existential and socio-political situation and identifies the dynamics of dehumanizing forces in the world. Next, the preacher probes the theological and biblical images of true humanity. And, finally, through theological and biblical images, the preacher interprets and presents a variety of human activities in our world as living parables participating in the politics of God.

In the process of critical theological reflection, biblical stories – especially the story of Jesus of Nazareth – function as a lens to see the world aright. For example, our world in a global economy supported by neoliberal capitalism encourages competition without limits and consequently destroys the communal nature of human existence by denying mutuality and precluding solidarity. However, biblical stories present an image of humanity as relational and communal, genuinely free through their calling by God to a life with and for others. This communal image of humanity justifies neither individualistic materialism nor profit-oriented capitalistic consumerism. Instead, biblical stories remind us that human beings are created in the image and likeness of the communitarian triune God to pursue the common good and the communal welfare with the will of God, whereby justice and peace become truly global.

Regarding effective communication to nurture the congregation's apperception, it is worth noting that Lehmann's *koinonia* ethic is indicative and descriptive. His *koinonia* ethic is not 'the prescriptive and absolute formulation of its claims' but 'a descriptive discipline' for 'the contextual understanding of what God is doing in the world to make and to keep human life human'.[37] In the *koinonia*, states Lehmann,

> the ethical question … is not 'What *ought* I to do?' but 'What *am* I to do?' because in the *koinonia* one is always fundamentally in an *indicative* rather than in an *imperative* situation. There is, of course, also an imperative pressure exerted by an indicative situation. The 'ought' factor cannot be ignored in ethical theory. But the 'ought' factor is not the primary ethical reality. The primary ethical reality is the human factor, the *human* indicative, in every situation involving the

---

[36]    Ibid., p. 23.
[37]    Lehmann, *Ethics in a Christian Context*, p. 14.

interrelationships and the decisions of men. In the *koinonia* something is already going on, namely, what God is doing in the situation out of which the ethical question and concern arise to fashion circumstance and behaviour according to his will.[38]

Lehmann's *koinonia* ethic is indicative because it is grounded in the contextual character of God's incarnation in Christ. Therefore, the primary concern of the *koinonia* ethics is not imperative, instructing the members to '*Do this*', but is fundamentally indicative, directing them to reflect on '*Who am I?*' It calls the people first to be who they are and then to do what they are: 'To do what I am is to act in every situation in accordance with what it has been given to me to be. Doing the will of God is doing what I am.'[39]

Lehmann's *koinonia* ethic is also descriptive because it is based on the descriptive character of the Christian gospel. Through narrative, the Bible tells us of God's saving acts in human history and God's promise for the human future. Moreover, Jesus used a descriptive method when teaching his followers by means of parables. As Lehmann indicates,

> [a]ccustomed as they were to an ethical tradition which moved from precepts to action, from law to behaviour, the disciples were thrown into confusion by Jesus' habit of juxtaposing God's action to the human situation. 'With what can we compare the kingdom of God, or what parable shall we use for it?' ... And his own reply was: 'the kingdom of heaven may be compared,' 'the kingdom of heaven is like ... the treasure hidden in a field, ... like net which was thrown into the sea, ... like a grain of mustard seed ... .'[40]

Lehmann regards even the Decalogue as indicative and descriptive rather than prescriptive and imperative:

> The Decalogue underlines the *indicative*, in distinction from the *legalistic*, the *descriptive* as opposed to the *prescriptive* relation of the Commandments to the human living of human life. The tone of Decalogue is not: 'this is what you had better do, or else!' On the contrary, the tone is rather: 'seeing that you are who you are, where you are, and as you are, this is the way ahead, the way of being and living in the truth, the way of freedom!'[41]

Lehmann asserts that just as the descriptive and indicative moods of language in the Bible have power to invite the readers to live a living parable of God's promise to the world, so the descriptive and indicative in ethical discourse invite

---

[38]    Ibid., p. 131.

[39]    Ibid., p. 159.

[40]    Ibid., p. 346.

[41]    Lehmann, *The Decalogue and a Human Future*, p. 85.

the members of the *koinonia* to participate in the politics of God. In fact, Lehmann uses the indicative and descriptive mood of language in his own sermons. With the persuasive mood of the indicative and descriptive, the tone of his preaching invites the listeners to the eschatological vision and promise. He describes signs in the Bible as the fragmentary foretastes of the kingdom of God in our context and generates a renewal of the listener's apperception at the moment of preaching.[42]

Indicative and descriptive language in preaching has power to disclose God's actions to the listeners so that they may experience the renewal of apperception – a radical shift in perspective, or a new way of looking at life. Indicative and descriptive language functions imaginatively and poetically when the preacher uses such devices as irony, simile, and metaphor that have power to generate enthusiasm and inspiration and stir the listeners from within. The tone of indicative and descriptive language appeals to the listeners' conscience and invites them to voluntarily respond to the sermon. Therefore, preaching based on the indicative and the descriptive invites the listeners to reorient their worldviews and life values by renewing their apperception. Those who accept the invitation participate in God's politics by living out their lives as living parables.

**Conclusion**

Lehmann's *koinonia* ethic reminds Korean churches of what constitutes the real church and challenges them to reconsider their own identity. His *koinonia* ethic also provides them with homiletical insight to understand preaching as a political activity participating in the politics of God. Preaching as the politics of God involves a threefold transformation: that of the individual, of society, and of nature. These are inevitably interrelated because the individual is a component of society, while society and nature are contexts for the individual. Moreover, an individual's predicament and struggles are not separate from social and environmental issues. With the expectation of a new world order for all creation, preaching as the politics of God aims to help the congregation grow to maturity – the new humanity – by nurturing their apperception. This is accomplished through the preacher's critical theological reflection and effective methods of communication. An understanding of preaching as the politics of God invites both preacher and congregation to the authenticity of the Christian message and to the freedom to participate in God's humanizing politics in the age of globalization.

---

[42]    See Paul Lehmann, 'Which Way is Left?' in *To God Be the Glory: Sermons in Honour of George A. Buttrick*, ed. by Theodore A. Gill (Nashville: Abingdon Press, 1973), pp. 83–91, and 'Sermon: No Uncertain Sound!', *Union Seminary Quarterly Review*, 29:3–4 (1974): 273–7.

## Chapter 10

# Christian Ethics in the Morning Sunrise – Living in God's Providential Space

Michelle J. Bartel

In the beginning of *Ethics in a Christian Context* Paul Lehmann paints an intriguing image for us. By tracing the root of the word 'ethics' he arrives at the etymological origin of a barnyard dwelling or stall. That particular structure and space provides safety, sanctuary, a place to eat and be hidden from storms. It is a place where creatures gather and give each other warmth, a necessity for the flourishing of animal life.[1] The proper ethos for human beings is one which provides just such space for human life. For Paul Lehmann, Christian ethics is about a space for flourishing, within the context of the politics of God, that is, God's activity in and among us to bring humanity to fullness. God incarnate in Jesus Christ is made manifest in 'the human situation of what God is doing to make and to keep human life human'.[2] And, if God is about the work of making and keeping space for human life to be human, as Lehmann asserts, then God is a God of infinite providence, love, grace, freedom and tender care. This essay seeks to unfold Lehmann's notion of God's caring and providential space as running richly throughout Christian spirituality, conscience, discipleship and service, humanizing us and allowing us to point to God's humanizing activity in our own lives.

We perceive the broad sweep of God's care as all-encompassing as well as concrete and particular. Jesus in his fierce forgiveness cried out in that angry wail that we hear from folks who are desperately trying to convince their loved ones of a better way: 'Jerusalem, Jerusalem, the city that kills the prophets and stones those who are sent to it! How often have I desired to gather your children together as a hen gathers her brood under her wings, and you were not willing!' (Lk. 13:34). This is God's passion for us, God's persistence in caring for us. What do we read of in Hosea 11, but the love of one who cannot give up on a beloved child, the anger of a betrayed and abused parent that melts into tears of love and compassion?

This passionate love for us is personal. We see this depicted throughout scripture as God takes individuals very seriously indeed. Jesus, for instance, gives the woman at the well a sense of liberation and significance by talking to her and treating her like a disciple. Jesus *knows who she is*. Precisely because God's love

---

[1] Paul Lehmann, *Ethics in a Christian Context* (Harper & Row, 1963), pp. 23–4.

[2] Ibid., p. 99.

is personal, it is also political, for the persons God loves are created as communal individuals, in relationship with God and others. God's persistence in caring for us is nearly a defiant act, for it goes against all our actions to the contrary: we humans abuse each other and the environment, blindly comply in oppressive political and economic regimes, we see each other through bigoted, angry, and cynical eyes, we take grace on the cheap and assume that 'telling the truth in love' means saying anything we want at any time as long as it is factually accurate.

This assertion of Lehmann's, that God is about the work of 'making and keeping human life human', is grounded in an understanding of God that in turn grounds our understanding of what it means to live human life in the space God makes and keeps for the living of human life. Our lives thus become revelatory, pointing towards God's work. Lehmann's point is that this is indeed the nature of Christian ethics, which is founded on the revelation of God's reality instead of a system of prescriptions and prohibitions. Our lives, also, become ones of lived-into maturity, rather than perfected morality.[3] Instead of being arbiter, God is the one in whom 'we live and move and have our being' (Acts 17:28), even as we grow into the body of Christ. God is the one who makes and keeps humanizing space, like those who parent clear the way for the full humanity of the children they nurture.

But our human life in the world is caught up in human and natural capacities for destroying humanizing space. Many forces tear at our spirits and end up violating the sacred space that we are as embodied beings: dwelling places of the Holy Spirit, temples (1 Cor. 6:19). And there are many forces, within and without, that threaten the Church as God's sanctuary, forces that divide the body, member from member so that we forget that 'there is one body and one Spirit, just as you were called to the one hope of your calling, one Lord, one faith, one baptism, one God and Father of all, who is above all and through all and in all' (Eph. 4:4–6). Many forces tear at the world itself, and at all God's beloved creatures, threatening waste, destruction, abuse, starvation, violence and the elimination of any space in which it might be possible for human life to be human.

The Christian's joy remains, though not in blind bliss or wilful ignorance of suffering. In fact, because of God's personal and therefore political love, Christians are called to be ever alert and vigilant, not only attending to what is happening in their homes, neighbourhoods and world, but precisely because these are the contexts in which God is at work to make and to keep human life human. Thus we attend to God who loves the world and is caring for it. The Christian's joy remains in the willing acceptance of a life lived as a believer of Jesus Christ and a member of his church.[4] Gerard Manley Hopkins put it this way:

> THE WORLD is charged with the grandeur of God.
> It will flame out, like shining from shook foil;
> It gathers to a greatness, like the ooze of oil

---

[3]    Ibid., pp. 45, 54–5.

[4]    Ibid., pp. 25, 45.

Crushed. Why do men then now not reck his rod?
Generations have trod, have trod, have trod;
And all is seared with trade; bleared, smeared with toil;
And wears man's smudge and shares man's smell: the soil
Is bare now, nor can foot feel, being shod.
And for all this, nature is never spent;
There lives the dearest freshness deep down things;
And though the last lights off the black West went
Oh, morning, at the brown brink eastward, springs –
Because the Holy Ghost over the bent
World broods with warm breast and with ah! bright wings.[5]

The Christian's joy is in the sheer, giddy relief of the unique comedic nature of the gospel: the Triune God became embodied among us in Jesus Christ, who dwells within us, who created us, loves us and reconciles us and all things to Godself in Jesus Christ.

In a recent unpublished keynote address at a gathering at the Neshaminy-Warwick Presbyterian Church in Pennsylvania, Thomas W. Currie III observed that in classic comedy, rascals and bad folks get their comeuppance, and at the end of the play, the audience is laughing, along with the good characters of the play, at the chastised ones. In the comedy of the gospel, everyone ends up laughing.[6] Karl Barth points to joy this way:

> If you have heard the Easter message, you can no longer run around with a tragic face and lead the humorless existence of a man who has no hope. One thing still holds, and only this one thing is really serious, that Jesus is the Victor. A seriousness that would look past this, like Lot's wife, is not a Christian seriousness. It may be burning behind – and truly it is burning – but we have to look, not at it, but at the other fact, that we are invited and summoned to take seriously the victory of God's glory in this man Jesus and to be joyful in him.[7]

This calls to mind Lehmann's vivid phase about Lot's wife and her 'photoelectric living which always reads backwards. And she has not moved since'.[8] Rather than being frozen in a backward glance, Christian joy looks forward towards Christ who 'for the sake of the joy set before him endured the cross' (Heb. 12:2). This joy grounds a life that sees 'the warm breast' and 'bright wings' of the Holy Spirit

---

[5]  Gerard Manley Hopkins, *The Poems of Gerard Manley Hopkins; A Sourcebook*, Routledge Guides to Literature, ed. Alice Jenkins (Routledge, 2006), p. 131.

[6]  See also Thomas W. Currie III, *The Joy of Ministry* (Westminster John Knox Press, 2008).

[7]  Karl Barth, *Dogmatics in Outline*, trans. G.T. Thompson (New York: Harper & Row, 1959), p. 123.

[8]  Lehmann, *Ethics in a Christian Context*, p. 28.

providing us the space we and others need for our human lives to be human. This joy also looks eastward at the break of dawn, which signifies the hope of the Holy Spirit who never spends nature out, but instead reckons with our searing, blearing and smearing of creation and humanity in such a way that roses grow out of ruins. Looking in that direction and seeing the world through that image of hope, either we stand still or move forward. In such a way is our spirituality, conscience, discipleship and service transformed by the God who broods warmly, rather than conformed to the world that would ignore and even destroy grace and grandeur. The world is charged with the grandeur of God because God created it and stays with it, running around in the wind to gather humanity, like a hen gathers her chicks, under bright wings: this is space for human life, 'For surely I know the plans I have for you, says the Lord, plans for your welfare and not for harm, to give you a future with hope' (Jer. 29:11).

## Discernment – 'The Dearest Freshness Deep Down Things'

Lehmann, of course, presents us with a very basic problem when it comes to consideration of just how we might deliberately live out God's activity to make and to keep human life human. Discernment of how to live out this joy in authentic gratitude and genuine love for God's world can become a dilemma when we consider the problem of agency and action. According to Lehmann God is the ethical actor: it is *God's* activity that makes human life human. This is because God created human beings, and only God can restore them and make and keep the space for human life to be human. It is God at work in the world to do this. Any of our typical categories are turned over on themselves because immediately we realize there are no steps for us to work towards God, to make and keep this space ourselves, or to initiate making and keeping this space for others.

This basic principle – that God is the agent of humanization – is unsettling to many of us Christians even though we commonly invoke Eph. 2:8–9 and assert that it is God who saves us and not we ourselves. More ethical confusion follows in verse 10:

> For by grace you have been saved through faith, and this is not your own doing; it is the gift of God – not the result of works, so that no one may boast. For we are what he has made us, created in Christ Jesus for good works, which God prepared beforehand to be our way of life.

We have been saved by grace; it is not our works that save us; we were created for good works. Or consider the strange passive imperative verb forms found in Rom. 12:2, following the exhortation to offer our bodies as spiritual worship:

> I appeal to you therefore, brothers and sisters, by the mercies of God, to present your bodies as a living sacrifice, holy and acceptable to God, which is your

spiritual worship. Do not be conformed to this world, but be transformed by the renewing of your minds, so that you may discern what is the will of God – what is good and acceptable and perfect.

We are commanded (imperative) to be transformed (passive voice). That is, we are commanded to allow God to do what God is going to do, and this by the renewing of our minds. God is at work even in our minds to seal grace on us, so that we 'may discern what is the will of God'.

Mary, the mother of Jesus, exemplifies such an imperative passive voice. Her story provides context for discerning that our passive 'being transformed by' involves an active participation on our part. Told by the angel that she would become pregnant by the power of God and bear God's son, she ponders the message. She asks questions, as the story unfolds, and then agrees: 'let it be with me according to your word' (Lk. 1:38). As she offers the Magnificat she tenders the history of God's presence with God's people, and the hope of God's historic promises. This is not a young woman who blindly submitted to a greater power but one who recognized what was going on, presented her embodied life as a living offering or sacrifice, her deliberate spiritual worship.

This is the conundrum we face if we take seriously the power and presence of God, especially if we take seriously that power and that presence in the passion of Christ. How can one develop and make manifest spiritual practices? What is the point, if our human spirituality is God's work? What is our conscience if it is not an arbiter of what is permitted or prohibited? What is discipleship if not our decision to follow Christ? How do we serve, as believers in Jesus Christ and members of his church, if we do not, out of our own volition, offer our time, money, effort, and talents?

Mary's story shifts our own stories of life with God into an arena that is uncomfortable for most of us. Her story reveals that life lived in God's humanizing space is comprised in part by surprising possibility, and we often long for predictability and sameness. When it comes to ethics, then, we often prefer following principles that dictate rather than freely obeying the One who freely creates, call, saves and sanctifies us. God is not arbiter, but God is the power of all being and the Author of the story of us all, a story fleshed out in particulars and in community for the flourishing of us all. We long to live with God as arbiter, one who merely passes judgement for the sake of clarity of action and accountability, but as though God was Judge only and not also Creator, Redeemer and Sustainer.

In teaching the work of Paul Lehmann and Dietrich Bonhoeffer to college students I invariably witnessed astonished faces (sometimes with actual dropped jaws) at the thought that ethics is not about figuring out what is right and what is wrong. To throw Christian ethics instead to the more nebulous area of discernment of God's work and will means both that there is nothing to cling to, as to a talisman or good luck charm, and that much more effort goes into the Christian life than previously thought. In the oft-recorded gospel song 'How Can I Keep from Singing?' the singer exclaims that through all the storms of life it is to the Rock that we cling.[9] But this is a Rock that lives, not something we can pocket or dangle on a chain. C.S. Lewis's Aslan was certainly not tame, but he was good, and from such an image of God comes a shocking math, as Phillip Yancey refers to it, that results from the grace of Christ.[10] That is, those who come to class on time and those who skip might actually learn the same amount and get the same grade.

But it is not God as arbiter who allows us to hear the truth of the exhortation that we are, therefore, 'to work out our faith with fear and trembling, for it is God who is at work in us enabling us both to will and to work for God's good pleasure' (Phil. 2:12–13). Instead of arbiter, this comes from God as servant. We are to have the same mind as Christ who emptied himself, counted himself a servant instead of an equal, and gave of himself even to death and was thus exalted. This is the mind we are to have, the mind we are to be transformed into by renewal, the power that is already at work in us for God's good pleasure.

In the end, then, we come to the unexpected realization that trust, joy, and grace are at the root of the Christian ethical life. If we acknowledge our dependence on God for our very existence and as constitutive of our humanness, and if we take seriously our gathered selves as the actual embodiment of Jesus Christ, and if we take seriously the power of God in us and the love of God in us by way of the Holy Spirit that has been given to us, then we are led to a brink. Because of Christ and his trust, joy and grace that are sealed on our hearts by the Holy Spirit this brink is seen as the 'brown brink eastward' of morning rather than the brink of death. We see in the eastward direction of the Holy Spirit who broods warmly over the whole world with bright wings. This is a gift of God and not our own work. Yet it is also our own involvement: we, like Mary, can actively participate in the transformation God is working in us.

And so, as Lehmann asserts, our actions become directional rather than necessary.[11] By this he means that we point to what God is doing in the world to make and to keep the space for human life to be human. Our actions are not necessary to God's work, except as God works through them. We are not required to satisfy requirements for all to be right with the world. On the other hand, because our actions are directional and parabolic – that is, pointing to the story God is playing out in the world – they are no less substantive or creative. As was mentioned above, the broad sweep of God's providential, saving care is not an abstract idea but a concrete and historical reality. Consider two illustrations. One revolves around personal activity; the other is political. Both show how human beings participate in the humanizing space that God alone creates.

---

[9]   Many artists have recorded this song, including Eva Cassidy, Bruce Springsteen, Enya, SheDaisy and Arlo Guthrie.

[10]   Phillip Yancey, *What's So Amazing About Grace?* (Grand Rapids: Zondervan, 1997), pp. 59–72.

[11]   Lehmann, *Ethics in a Christian Context*, p. 14 – 'The present volume seeks to show that the faith and thought of the Reformation provide insights into and ways of interpreting ethics which give creative meaning and concrete direction to behaviour.'

In the first instance, a woman sits in church at worship and hears that a regular attender of the congregation has been in ICU for several days and will remain there for a few more. This patient has a husband who must keep his job and two young boys. So when Sue considers the question (as many Christians do), 'What am I, as a believer in Jesus Christ and a member of his church, to do?' she arrives at an answer that points physically to God's reality of loving care: she brings food for meals. The youth group at a church does yard work for a couple limited by physical difficulties. The teens do not merely point to God's care of this couple and relief of their burdens. They also make manifest witness to God's love and care with their sweat and muscles and time. It is real space that is made and kept for this couple's life to be more fully human, and the teens really do it. The thing is, it is God's reality all along. The actions of the teens are revelatory, pointing to the way God's reality works. Their actions move towards maturity, that integrated community of individuals in which we witness 'the wholeness of everybody in the wholeness of all' accepting themselves while giving of themselves.[12]

The second instance was often repeated in acts of resistance to oppression during WWII. Individuals and even towns pointed to God's reality of 'making and keeping human life human' by sheltering Jews and others who were targets of extermination. The uprising of the Warsaw ghetto similarly points to what is substantively created by refusing to live according to the powers of the world that would separate us from the love of God. When we look to that particular event and note its ending in the takeover of the ghetto, we should notice the more powerfully subversive reality that seems to have had that same mind as Christ, residents of the ghetto choosing to be servants of one another for the sake of common life, recognizing the good of all in the good of each.

In the end, then, questions of how we are transformed by spirituality, conscience, discipleship and service are enduring conversations, useful for our reflection. These modes of formation and transformation have their own role in Christian ethics. They are ways that create space for us to discern and take action in such a way that we point to God's work to make and to keep space for human life to be human. It is to considering some of these that we now turn.

## Spirituality

The 'spirituality' sections of bookstores have exploded in the past decade, taking up far more than one shelf in a corner. Books dealing with spirituality go well beyond straightforward assessments of the term within various traditions and now encompass self-help and a multitude of other interdisciplinary expressions. It is hard to avoid the sense that the consumer thinks spirituality can be bought, and, well, *consumed*. We buy trinkets, symbols, decorations and services along with these books in order to assemble our spirituality.

---

[12]    Ibid., pp. 52–6, 65.

This is good news and bad news. The bad news is that Western society has found ways to commodify the ineffable essence of human being, decorating our inner being as we decorate our homes. Ironically, as with decorating, the sales pitch is cast to our fantasies about individuality: buy this table and really express your uniqueness, and then buy this book and really express your uniqueness. Never mind the same table and book are mass-produced for a mass of consumers. This piecemeal work of spirituality devolves into narcissism and is, ultimately, not spiritual at all, for it does not enable human beings to experience, connect with, or serve any being or purpose larger than themselves that would promote good for the world beyond them, while including them. In addition, individual elements of this vast array of spiritualities – from Orthodox to Buddhist to Quaker, Jewish, Native American or Pagan, etc. – are ripped from their contexts so that the nuances that inform them are lost. Various spiritual elements become calcified, like a brittle bone fragment, and our assembled spiritualities become jangly, fleshless, oddly-pieced-together and lifeless skeletons.

The good news is that this explosion of resources for spirituality means that human beings are hungry for meaning, thirsty for ways to articulate their longing for the great Truth they know is just beyond their grasp. That the books and items are available for purchase can be a benefit, then, a way of meeting a need for exploration, prayer, devotion and service. Just because people look for love in all the wrong places does not mean they are not genuinely looking for Love.

Christians ought to take pause here, and note this revolution as an expression of the constrained space that many people occupy, which cramps human life rather than allowing it to flourish in humanizing ways. In addition, Christians should note here the way this disposable wardrobe of spiritualities are already failing to help human beings. By many counts, suicides are up in most age ranges, with some high schools facing multiple suicides that traumatize entire communities. Lehmann warns us in *The Transfiguration of Politics* that the problem with revolutions is that they end up devouring their young.[13] The freedom sought in the revolution turns into rigid requirements for continued living after the revolution, which results in new oppression. So what do Christians notice in this particular revolution, this groundswell of demand for ways of articulating – and therefore understanding and living out – the meaning of life that means good for them and for the world? What do we see in this revolution?

We see the need not only for spiritual space, or sanctuary, but for this space to be good, true, and beautiful. The emptiness continues if what the individual receives from the newest book or theological fad is mere pablum, or, worse yet, the next hit that feeds an addiction. John Calvin gestures at the architectural integrity of this spiritual space in Book I of his *Institutes of the Christian Religion* when he asserts that piety is 'that reverence joined with love of God which the knowledge

---

[13]    Paul Lehmann, *The Transfiguration of Politics: The Presence and Power of Jesus of Nazareth In and Over Human Affairs* (New York: Harper & Row, 1975), p. 3, *inter alia*.

of his benefits induces'.[14] Knowledge of God is simply not possible without piety, for we cannot know God without knowing that God is good to us and for us. This knowledge of God also consists of knowledge of self, for as Calvin points out in the beginning of Book I, these two are so caught up with one another that it is impossible to know where one begins and the other ends. In other words, the inner experience of God's goodness and love is itself lovely to behold, for God is not only our Judge but also our Redeemer and Sustainer. There is an integrity to this structure of human being and human knowledge in Calvin's thought, a way of encompassing the different trajectories of human experience. For example, we become aware of our sin. This knowledge also becomes part of the integrity of the structure, transformed into beauty by the redeeming death and resurrection of Jesus Christ. Even the knowledge of sin is caught up in our knowledge of God's love for us and desires for our lives.[15]

Within the Christian tradition the definition of spirituality is debated often and earnestly, and within the Reformed tradition the term 'spirituality' is often rejected outright in favour of 'piety'. But spirituality is a term that Christians and others are using, and arguing over the existence of such a category is not helpful. So let us join a biblical description with Lehmann's sense of Christian ethics as revelatory, tending towards maturity, and as safe space for human being: 'Do you not know that your body is a temple of the Holy Spirit?' Yes, this question brings with it a tone of impatience and frustration, for the Apostle Paul is writing to the Corinthians to urge them to abandon lives of wolfish self-indulgence, sexual and otherwise, in the sheep's clothing of Christian freedom. But in bringing this point about our bodies forward, Paul is establishing the basis of a particular exhortation echoed throughout his letters.

This exhortation presses the understanding that if our bodies are temples of the Holy Spirit, then our actions reveal or bury the Spirit's presence. Paul presents an intricate discussion of this presence and our embodied lives in 1 Corinthians 8–10. There, conscience is to be understood as free for the other grounded in Christ's freedom for us: love is revealed in the use of freedom for the sake of the other. Thus, while we might understand perfectly well that eating or not eating meat has no impact on salvation, we either partake or refrain when someone else wrestles with the impact of this knowledge on his or her own relationship with God. In other words, the actions we take in the body point towards the reality of God in Christ in the world, the love of whom has been poured into our hearts by the Holy Spirit. We refrain from eating meat sacrificed to idols in order to support other human beings. Not only this, but our embodied lives are themselves embodied: 'there is one body and one Spirit, just as you were called to the one hope of your

---

[14]    John Calvin, *Institutes of the Christian Religion*, trans. F. Lewis Battles, ed. J.T. McNeill (Philadelphia: Westminster, 1960), p. 41 (I.ii.1).

[15]    For a concise description of Lehmann's thought on the theology of being human, see Nancy J. Duff, *Humanization and the Politics of God: The Koinonia Ethics of Paul Lehmann* (Grand Rapids: Eerdmans, 1992) pp. 11–21.

calling, one Lord, one faith, one baptism, one God and Father of all, who is above all and through all and in all' (Ephesians 4:4–6). The *koinonia* is the context of Christian ethics, for Lehmann, for it is in the body of Christ that we know who we are and are empowered to point to God with our very lives.

So God's incarnation in Christ points to our embodied nature. This was a joyful realization for Thomas Merton:

> In Louisville, at the corner of Fourth and Walnut, in the center of the shopping district, I was suddenly overwhelmed with the realization that I loved all those people, that they were mine and I theirs, that we could not be alien to one another even though we were total strangers … . It is a glorious destiny to be a member of the human race, though it is a race dedicated to many absurdities and one which makes many terrible mistakes: yet, with all that, God Himself gloried in becoming a member of the human race. A member of the human race! To think that such a commonplace realization should suddenly seem like news that one holds the winning ticket in a cosmic sweepstake.
>
> I have the immense joy of being man, a member of a race in which God Himself became incarnate. As if the sorrows and stupidities of the human condition could overwhelm me, now that I realize what we all are. And if only everybody could realize this! But it cannot be explained. There is no way of telling people that they are all walking around shining like the sun.
>
> … Then it was as if I suddenly saw the secret beauty of their hearts, the depths of their hearts where neither sin nor desire nor self-knowledge can reach, the core of their reality, the person that each one is in God's eyes. If only they could all see themselves as they really are.[16]

We are called to 'work out [our] salvation with fear and trembling, for it is God who is at work in [us] enabling us both to will and to work for God's good pleasure'. We read also in Eph. 3:20 that 'God, at work with the power within us is able to accomplish abundantly for more than all we could ask or imagine'. Thus enabled we work out in our daily lives God's good pleasure so that in the midst of all that would deny the self-giving love of God we 'shine like stars in the universe' (Phil. 2:12–15). The promise of Rom. 5:5 is that we have the love of God poured into our hearts by the Holy Spirit who has been given to us. Our bodies are temples of the Holy Spirit, always, not only in our erotically charged moments, as we attend to the context of Paul's exhortation, but in every moment. And so when we encounter the least – whether visiting them in prison, feeding them when hungry, sheltering them when homeless – we reveal the structural beauty and integrity inherent in our embodied temples. Our physical lives reveal one sort of reality or another.

Spiritual practices are key, then, to Christian ethics, because they hone our attention to this internal temple made manifest in daily life. The practice of

16   Thomas Merton, *Conjectures of a Guilty Bystander* (New York: Doubleday & Co., 1966), pp. 140–41.

remembering the Sabbath and keeping it holy directs our vision and action towards the 'brown brink eastward' of morning, toward space for being that God creates.[17] The practice of *lectio divina* likewise hones our attention to God's work in us, in others, and in the world by prayerful attention to scripture as the word of God to us personally. This 'personally' does not refer to atomistic individualism, as though whatever word we hear has no implications for our growth into the body of Christ. Disciplined *lectio* does, however, enable us to focus on God's activity in us and God's word to us, rather than our own word and activity. Subsequently, it has the capacity to train our attention to God's activity and word in the world beyond our own practice. The whole point of *lectio divina* is listening. It would behoove us to bring to mind the origins of 'obedience', which come from the old verb *aubidere* – to hearken or listen. *The Rule of Benedict* begins 'Listen, my son, to the master's [Christ's] instructions, and take them to heart'.[18] There is no obedience without listening.

Speaking about different modes of prayer John Calvin says,

> Moreover, since the glory of God ought, in a measure, to shine in the several parts of our bodies, it is especially fitting that the tongue has been assigned and destined for this task, both through singing and through speaking. For it was peculiarly created to tell and proclaim the praise of God.[19]

The joy of faith is formed at least partly by prayer: 'So true is it that we dig up by prayer the treasures that were pointed out by the Lord's gospel, and which our faith has gazed upon.'[20] So seriously does Calvin take prayer that it is the 'chief exercise of faith', necessary for receiving God's promises and the gift of God's commands to us for a full life with God and others. In all forms of prayer, the initiative for awareness is squarely on God's shoulders. We receive knowledge and are transformed by the renewing of both our minds as well as our hearts. Prayer in all its forms – private, public, communal, individual, petitionary, intercessory, thankful and contemplative – directs us to God's activity in the world to make and keep human life human. Indeed,

> liturgy signals the Creator's celebrative peroration of creation as the prelude to the creature's receiving with thankfulness and praise what is there beforehand. Liturgy gives to sounds and acts the power to point to the ultimate in the immediate, the unique in the common, the memorable in the forgettable,

---

[17] *The Decalogue And A Human Future – The Meaning Of The Commandments For Making and Keeping Human Life Human* (Grand Rapids: Eerdmans, 1995), pp. 145–8.

[18] *The Rule of St. Benedict*, trans. Carolinne White (London: Penguin Books, 2008), p. 7.

[19] Calvin, *Institutes*, III.xx.31.

[20] Calvin, *Institutes*, III.xx.2.

the trustworthy in the transient, the ties that bind amid the singularities that separate.[21]

In his book *Reaching Out: The Three Movements of the Spiritual Life*, Henri Nouwen draws our attention to the ancient practice of hospitality. In his chapter entitled 'Creating Space for Strangers' Nouwen writes,

> Although many, we might even say most, strangers in this world become easily victims of fearful hostility, it is possible for men and women and obligatory for Christians to offer an open and hospitable space where strangers can cast off their strangeness and become our fellow human beings.[22]

Orthodox icons of 'The Hospitality of Abraham and Sarah' depict the biblical story of how the welcomed strangers were actually God making an announcement about Sarah's impending pregnancy. This story makes clear to us not only that we are hosts to others, but that the very act of hospitality makes us guests as well: Sarah, for instance, hosted and entertained by the Lord. Remember, she laughed.

In his poem 'Love III' George Herbert considers that this hospitality is grounded in nothing other than the death and resurrection of Jesus Christ, the abundant pouring out of self for the beloved:

> Love bade me welcome, yet my soul drew back,
>     Guilty of dust and sin.
> But quick-ey'd Love, observing me grow slack
>     From my first entrance in,
> Drew nearer to me, sweetly questioning
>     If I lack'd anything.
> 'A guest', I answer'd, 'worthy to be here';
>     Love said, 'You shall be he.'
> 'I, the unkind, the ungrateful? ah my dear,
>     I cannot look on thee.'
> Love took my hand and smiling did reply,
>     'Who made the eyes but I?'
> 'Truth, Lord, but I have marr'd them; let my shame
>     Go where it doth deserve.'
> 'And know you not', says Love, 'who bore the blame?'
>     'My dear, then I will serve.'

---

[21]    Paul Lehmann, *The Decalogue and a Human Future*, p. 72.

[22]    Henri J. Nouwen, *Reaching Out: The Three Movements of the Spiritual Life* in the book collection *Ministry and Spirituality* (Continuum, 1996), p. 217.

'You must sit down', says Love, 'and taste my meat.'
    So I did sit and eat.[23]

Hospitality is precisely the practice of attention to revolution. Do others have the space in which their human life might be made and kept human? Do our actions point toward what God is doing in the world to make and keep that space, so that all may 'sit and eat'? The practice of hospitality is revelatory, drawing our attention to God's hospitality in accomplishing a peaceable kingdom: 'They will not hurt or destroy on all my holy mountain; for the earth will be full of the knowledge of the Lord as the waters cover the sea' (Isa. 11:9).

Attention to spiritual life supports contemplation of God at work in us, through us, and among us. The connection between contemplation and action is intimate and inevitable, for the Holy Spirit that has been poured into our hearts has been poured into the hearts of others as well. In a recent lecture at the Princeton Institute of Youth Ministry Forum, April 2008, Darrell Guder suggested that Jesus' statement that 'all authority in heaven and on earth has been given to me' (Matt. 28:18) means that the Triune God is at work everywhere. It is not only trust that carries us in our Christian ethical lives but the encounter of a God alive and at work, in Sheol before we ever get there.

> Mysticism and revolution are two aspects of the same attempt to bring about radical change. No mystics can prevent themselves from becoming social critics, since in self-reflection they will discover the roots of a sick society. Similarly, no revolutionaries can avoid facing their own human condition, since in the midst of their struggle for a new world they will find that they are also fighting their own reactionary fears and false ambitions ... . The appearance of Jesus in our midst has made it undeniably clear that changing the human heart and changing human society are not separate tasks, but are as interconnected as the two beams of the cross.[24]

Spiritual practices shape us for lives that reveal this revolutionary work of God to care for us, to make and to keep space for human life to be human amid circumstances that would turn that space into an abyss that separates human beings from God, the Lover of their souls. Spiritual practices are properly built not on the premise that we must 'practice' in order to be spiritual, nor on the presupposition that fellowship with God requires spiritual perfection. Rather, spiritual practices are properly built on the assertion that there is nothing in all creation that can separate us from the love of God in Christ Jesus the Lord. Our understanding of conscience is critical in this regard as it is God's gift for freedom of action and assurance of faith.

---

[23]   George Herbert, *The Country Parson, The Temple* (The Classics of Western Spirituality), ed. John N. Wall, Jr. (Paulist Press, New York, 1981), p. 316.

[24]   Henri J. Nouwen, *The Wounded Healer* (New York: Doubleday Image, 1979), p. 19.

## Conscience

How can the conscience, so commonly understood as an organ of discernment of right and wrong, a voice which is so often limited to permission or prohibition, possibly be a presence of good in the life of the human being? If spirituality is properly built on the assertion that there is nothing in all creation that can separate us from the love of God in Christ Jesus the Lord, is there any convergence with conscience?

Paul Lehmann would respond with a resounding yes. The way in which human beings participate in ethics, according to Lehmann, is as parabolic indicators. By actions in their lives, human beings as ethical actors point to what God is doing in the world to make and to keep human life human. As in the parables, human actions are only indicators of their response to God. Thus, recognition of the ethical and humanizing activity of God is not identical with the elimination of human agency, since it is up to human beings to respond to this activity. For example, violence, riots and revolutions are concrete realities that signal a lack of space for making and keeping human life human.

Christians' responses to these events should not primarily be condemnatory but inquisitive. That is, Christians should ask what these concrete realities signal, a question of discernment. Thus, following Lehmann's approach, 'the primary task of ethics is to discern those forces that break human society apart and to examine what is required to keep human society together in humanizing freedom and order'.[25] For Lehmann, the concrete realities of revolution are signs that the space for being human has become cramped, that the experience of being cramped has turned into the experience of being wronged, that wrong has become experienced as injustice, and finally that injustice has become dehumanization. 'Revolutions signal that the health of society can no longer be deferred but must be set right.'[26]

How do we know what is human? How do we know what is wrong? Defenders of Lehmann's thought have had to face these questions time and again. However, Lehmann's work is certainly no venture in relativism. God is a particular God, who has chosen to be a particular way. Revelation, as has been mentioned above, is of fundamental importance. However, as for Karl Barth and Dietrich Bonhoeffer, revelation is not a propositional reality, comprised of discrete commands intended for casuistical application. Instead, Lehmann draws the distinction between keeping the commandments and obeying them: the distinction of apperception.[27] Lehmann defines apperception in the following way: 'Apperception is the uniquely human capacity to know something without knowing how one has come to know it, and to bring what one knows in this way to what one has come to know in other ways, and, in so doing, to discern what is humanly true or false.'[28] Lehmann

---

[25]  Nancy Duff, *Humanization and the Politics of God*, p. 107.

[26]  Paul Lehmann, *The Transfiguration of Politics*, p. 98.

[27]  Paul Lehmann, *The Decalogue And a Human Future*, pp. 23–4.

[28]  Ibid.

contrasts apperception to the process of learning and understands apperception as a more existential experience, a 'self-evident self-discovery through which one is drawn into the heritage and the reality of what it takes to be and to stay human in the world'.[29] The most important facet of apperception is the acceptance of the knowledge we have.

Without the nurturing of apperception, human response to God and to others is reduced to rote fulfilment of requirements. The commandments as requirements to be fulfilled grow out of heteronomy instead of the commandments as permission to be human rooted in the context of theonomy. If God is indeed the Creator of human beings, then it is in the context of creation by God and in the community of human beings that human flourishing thrives. Heteronomy – the rule of an external other – constricts this flourishing. Lehmann pairs the problem of heteronomy with the problem of autonomy, the problem in which ethical response to God's activity in the world is determined in accordance with my own individual wants. That we ourselves are temples of the Holy Spirit belies such a claim. The 'authority' is not external but instead is the infrastructure of our selves. Created to be individuals in communion with God and one another, we can only understand conscience as an aspect of such communion.

In *Ethics in a Christian Context*, Lehmann proposes consideration of the conscience as properly understood when it is theonomously grounded, moving away from an understanding of conscience that merely forbids or permits.[30] A heteronomous conscience binds the human being to laws as laws, apart from the Lawgiver. This cuts off the possibility that the Christian can freely and joyfully hearken to God's command. The conscience itself is separated from God in this connection, since prohibition and permission have to do with the laws as laws. 'But if the conscience is the bond between *what God is doing* in the world to make and to keep human life human and *man's behaviour*, then the ethical act is the concrete bearer of man's free obedience in the knowledge of good and evil.'[31] In turn, it is apperception, theonomously grounded, which illuminates the conscience and the knowledge in which the human being acts. Apperception is not itself an ethical act. Instead, the nurture of apperception is revealed as a source for Christian discernment since the nurture brings the knowledge of apperception to bear on other knowledge.

Like Karl Barth, Lehmann seeks to underline the absolute freedom of God to move in the world. Thus, God's commands have no existence apart from God, but are bound up in God's dynamic and living freedom *for* making and keeping human life human. Conscience, therefore, understands the law as a dynamic grounded in God's freedom for humanity. We should recall that this freedom for humanity was manifest in the emptying of Christ's self into the form of servant, even though he

---

[29]    Ibid.

[30]    Paul Lehmann, *Ethics in a Christian Context*, pp. 348–51.

[31]    Ibid., p. 351, emphasis added.

was equal with God. This freedom for humanity was exercised in the joy set before Christ and for whose sake he endured the cross.

Understanding conscience in this way is, for John Calvin, a reorientation of vision. It is not one's own self that is the focus (the *cor curvum in se*) but God. God's goodness is all that is seen, and thus is the mark for everything, including the assurance that our sins are not the end of the story.

> The agreement lies in this: that the saints, when it is a question of the founding and establishing of their own salvation, without regard for works turn their eyes solely to God's goodness. Not only do they betake themselves to it before all things as to the beginning of blessedness but they repose in it as in the fulfillment of this. A conscience so founded, erected, and established is established also in the consideration of works, so far, that is, as these are testimonies of God dwelling and ruling in us....For if, when all the gifts God has bestowed upon us are called to mind, they are like rays of divine countenance by which we are illumined to contemplate that supreme light of goodness; much more is this true of the grace of good works, which shows that the Spirit of adoption has been given to us.[32]

Good works are salutary, and the conscience is salutary. For people of faith, revelling in the good grace of God, conscience works to bear witness to who we truly are and how we truly act: as those justified and sanctified by God, founded upon Christ, sealed by the Holy Spirit. Our union with Christ by the power of the Holy Spirit seals us in grace – the sacraments (yes!) are fundamental for nurturing the conscience of the Christian – and so conscience, properly understood is always, finally a good word.

> In sum, they so proclaim God's benefits as not to turn away from God's freely given favor, in which, as Paul testifies, there is set 'length, breadth, depth, and height' [Eph. 3:18]. It is as if he said: 'Wherever the minds of the godly turn, however high they mount up, however far and wide they extend, still they ought not to depart from the love of Christ but should apply themselves wholly to meditating upon it. For in itself it embraces all dimensions.'[33]

Conscience is a blessing from God, because it is a road map of sorts for the pilgrimage, the present life and its helps. Conscience is indispensable for discernment in the life of the Christian, for it is that 'certain mean' which keeps us knowing *with* God. Life with God is salutary for the chaotic life of the human being, bringing order and reasons to rejoice in the sacred nature of one's duties, no matter how noble or base those duties might appear to human eyes. Discernment is not a choice between spirituality and conscience, virtue or obedience. Conscience both

[32]   Calvin, *Institutes*, III.xiv.18.
[33]   Ibid., III.xiv.19.

combines and expands these seeming alternatives. A doxological life, grounded in the grace of God, reveals the conscience to be a dynamic in the fellowship relation with God. Conscience directs ethical considerations to doxology, and shapes a concrete, doxological life in discipleship of the One who 'for the sake of the joy set before him endured the cross'.

## Discipleship

No wonder, then, that Dietrich Bonhoeffer places such emphasis on discipleship as response to Christ's call to 'come and die'. We might remind ourselves of Nouwen's observation mentioned above: 'The appearance of Jesus in our midst has made it undeniably clear that changing the human heart and changing human society are not separate tasks, but are as interconnected as the two beams of the cross.' The way of Jesus is the way of the cross, but it is also the way of life and resurrection. The call to discipleship is not an invitation to destruction, but an invitation to die to self and live for Christ, and in giving up one's life to gain it. This knowledge abounds in daily human life, as individuals find their finest, truest selves when they are ready to give all they have to a certain cause. That deep happiness that is really joy is something we find when we 'abandon ourselves to divine providence'.[34] In the movie *Chariots of Fire* the character of Eric Liddell is explaining to his worried sister just why she should calm down and celebrate his love of running. It is no threat to his calling as a missionary. 'Jenny, God made me for a purpose. For China. But God also made me fast, and when I run, I feel his pleasure.' As Liddell discovered, running in the Olympics brought him to a time of trial, suffering, pressure and even public ridicule as his race ended up being run on a Sunday. The movie depicts the two beams of the cross intersecting as Liddell's human heart intersects with the transformation of his local Olympic society. Liddell listened to his conscience which helped him hearken to God's call, and standing firm he resisted the pressure of the prince of England.

As Dietrich Bonhoeffer reminds us, the life of discipleship is initiated by God alone. We take up that discipleship when we hearken to God's call. Life is shaped by the call, and the grace that is received in the gift of the call is costly both to Christ and to us.[35] The theologian Robert Farrar Capon struggles specifically with Bonhoeffer's analogy here, arguing that grace by definition is gratuitous, that is, free.[36] Rather than resorting to an economic context, however, we could refer to the analogy of the ethos of a generous kitchen and its cook. The pie or roast or

---

[34] This phrase is an adaptation and theme of the book by Jean-Pierre De Caussade, *Abandonment to Divine Providence* (New York: Image Books/Doubleday, 1975).

[35] Dietrich Bonhoeffer, *Discipleship*. Dietrich Bonhoeffer Works Volume 4, trans. M. Kuske and I. Tödt (Minneapolis: Fortress Press, 2001), p. 63, *inter alia*.

[36] Ibid., pp. 43–56. Robert Farrar Capon, *The Mystery of Christ ... and why we don't get it* (Grand Rapids: Eerdmans, 1993), p. 79.

quinoa salad might be freely given, but it does cost something to make: it requires ingredients, time, effort, a bit of planning. But it is freely given and any cook worth his or her salt takes much delight in the delight of others as they enjoy the pie, roast or salad. In the film *Babette's Feast* the French chef Babette, out of gratitude to the two sisters who sheltered her in distant Denmark, spends out all her money, time, artistry and expertise to produce a multi-course meal. It is excellently prepared, with attention to the fine details of seasoning and presentation, set on gorgeous linens, crystal and silver, accompanied by fine wines. It is freely given.

Either one of these gifts could be cheapened. One could walk into the friend's kitchen, grab the pie or roast or salad to go, and be off, thinking the food was freely given, 'so it's mine'. Much of the gift is lost when received this way: none of the fellowship or joy is shared. Likewise, those gathered at the feast that Babette prepared actually tried not to enjoy the food, considering it too indulgent and un-Christian. But they were overwhelmed by the abundance, richness, and fine flavours and their souls were fed along with their bodies. And so it is no wonder that family meals remain quotidian mysteries of delight.

Christ's grace is not cheap. To receive it fully and freely is to receive it facing Christ with an astonished look of delight on our faces, absolute befuddled joy that we have been called, loved, cherished and saved. Discipleship is costly not because it squeezes out every last drop of every last resource, though sometimes it does, but because it is precious and dear, like a lost child restored and reconciled. As God works to bring forth a new heaven and a new earth in which all the families of the earth shall be blessed and we shall gather at the eschatological feast of the lamb, we become aware of how much this must be costing God. And we become aware of the abundant grace that flows out:

> Therefore, since we are surrounded by so great a cloud of witnesses, let us also lay aside every weight and the sin that clings so closely, and let us run with perseverance the race that is set before us, looking to Jesus the pioneer and perfecter of our faith, who *for the sake of the joy that was set before him* endured the cross, disregarding its shame, and has taken his seat at the right hand of the throne of God (Heb 12:1–2 emphasis mine).

While Bonhoeffer did not use the phrase 'doxological life' the sense is the same, nuanced by the socio-political context in which he found himself. As he asserts in *Discipleship*, we are freed from the law for the law.[37] Christ fulfils the law – because Christ does this, we are enabled to join him in this fulfilment. We are freed from an understanding that the law is against us. Martin Luther as well as John Calvin made this clear in their understanding of the Decalogue: it was not merely a reductionistic list of rules marking what was allowed and what was

---

[37]   Bonhoeffer, *Discipleship*, pp. 115–20.

forbidden.[38] In fact, the Decalogue was not a legal tome handed over from an Arbiter God, but rather a narrative of life lived with others and with the God who created a beloved people who God would save over and over again. Thus Luther and Calvin considered the prohibitions to be permissions as well, encouraging us to prosper our neighbours, not just steal from them, to prosper life, not just refrain from killing. The law can be and is cheapened every single day when we take the separate commandments and turn our back on God, treating them as traffic regulations. The warm pie is offered on a plate with cold milk or good coffee, set at a table where the cook herself is sitting, smiling and waiting for us. We can grab it off the plate and dash off. We can take the commandment and dash off. Or we can sit down, share our time and fellowship and delight with our friend in the kitchen. We can turn to face God, dwell with God in time and space by offering ourselves back in joy, living with the freedom for the law given by Christ.

Discipleship begins here, heeding the call, picking up the slice of pie, living the commandments to love the Lord our God with all our heart, mind, soul and strength and our neighbours as ourselves. In this way discipleship is a vital element of a life lived in reflection on the question 'what am I, as a believer in Jesus Christ and a member of his church, to do?' Discipleship is revelatory of grace and doxology, of what it is to live life with the Triune God, indeed, what it is to live life with God in whom 'we live and move and have our being'(Acts 17:28). In this way discipleship creates space by pointing to God who is the Creator of all space.

## Service

Disciples point to this space and manifest God's reality when they serve. We read in Isa. 43:1–13 that God calls all God's children by name, loves them, holds them precious and gathers them from all corners of the earth. And then God sends them out as God's witnesses. There is no calling without sending. Discipleship trains us, coddles and cuddles us, challenges us, feeds us the milk we need until we are ready for solid spiritual food. While spirituality, conscience, and discipleship all continue, we are also sent. All Christians, by definition, are missionaries, ones who are sent out to bear witness. This is why, for Lehmann, how we point towards violence and revolution makes all the difference. To what are we bearing witness and how are we doing it? How does the shape of our lives embody the shape of the cross in our homes, neighbourhoods, and our global village? How do our lives point to God's reality?

In *Ethics*, Dietrich Bonhoeffer distinguishes between 'the last things and the things before the last', the ultimate and the penultimate. Agreeing with Lehmann, Bonhoeffer considers that there is nothing we can do to make God come to us or

---

[38]  Martin Luther, *The Large Catechism* (Minneapolis: Fortress Press, 1959), pp. 9–55 and John Calvin, *Instruction in Faith (1537)* (Louisville: Westminster/John Knox Press, 1977), pp. 28–34.

to others. There is, however, much we can do to make it easier for others both to hear God's call and to respond to it. Thus, penultimate considerations like shelter and food can be critical to one's ability to hear God's call.

> What good is it, my brothers and sisters, if you say you have faith but do not have works? Can faith save you? If a brother or sister is naked and lacks daily food, and one of you says to them, 'Go in peace; keep warm and eat your fill', and yet you do not supply their bodily needs, what is the good of that? So faith by itself, if it has no works, is dead. But someone will say, 'You have faith and I have works'. Show me your faith apart from your works, and I by my works will show you my faith (Jas. 2:14–18).

The writer of James raises a vital point about our faith: it shows. To show it deliberately does not mean that we create our faith or are the source of it. Rather, showing our faith deliberately reveals the truth about God who is at work in us. Simultaneously, in showing our faith, for example, by giving our hungry brother or sister food, our actions are actions of growth into maturity. We recall Calvin's claim from above:

> A conscience so founded, erected, and established is established also in the consideration of works, so far, that is, as these are testimonies of God dwelling and ruling in us....For if, when all the gifts God has bestowed upon us are called to mind, they are like rays of divine countenance by which we are illumined to contemplate that supreme light of goodness; much more is this true of the grace of good works, which shows that the Spirit of adoption has been given to us.[39]

Our interconnectedness is built through the revelation of God's reality at work in our lives, enabling us to 'will and to work for God's good pleasure'. Feeding, clothing, sheltering, teaching, tending, building all create space for human beings. In the Second Helvetic Confession Heinrich Bullinger considers that the providence of God ('making and keeping human life human') does not render our actions futile, as though each act is destined and beyond our responsibility or our participation. Bullinger makes the point that human beings are part of each other's stories and histories of God's care, God sending individuals to one another. We trust in providence, yes. We also live in the joyous expectation that we ourselves might be part of God's care for others, or for creation.[40] In this way, receiving the gift of faith does not remove us from human community or from participating in God's work in the world, for we might be the way (the penultimate) through which God's saving grace (the ultimate) is sealed upon the hearts of others. The work, we see, is God's.

---

[39]    Calvin, *Institutes*, III.xvi.18.

[40]    The Second Helvetic Confession can be found in *The Book of Confessions: Presbyterian Church (USA)* (The Office of the General Assembly, 1999), pp. 60–61.

## Conclusion

Our Christian joy is an affirmation of faith that there is space made and kept for human life to be human: this is the good news of the gospel of Jesus Christ. In the midst of searing, blearing and smearing we lift up our heads to look at 'the brown brink eastward' where we note that instead of the black lights off in the west we see morning, made possible by the Holy Spirit brooding over us all – and the whole world – with 'warm breast and with ah! bright wings'. While in seminary I heard from a number of different people the ultimately hopeless exhortation, 'The future of the church is in the hands of people like you'. If we have faith at all in the Triune God, then we can affirm with Christians of every time and place that God is at work to make and to keep human life human, to work in and through and around us toward the new heaven and new earth. The future of the church is in the hands of Jesus Christ, its foundation, not trained clergy. The future of humanity and its flourishing are in God's hands. The future of all that is is in the hands of God who has reconciled to God's very self all things in Christ.

And so we are freed for good works, testifying with each action to God's dwelling within us. This dwelling within us is like an urn filled with water to overflowing. We are not mere pipes, empty vessels that God runs through. We receive and therefore can give. Discernment of what God is calling us to do flows from this same fountain that fills us: discernment is not something that is possible apart from God 'in whom we live and move and have our being' (Acts 17:28). *All* of life is theonomous, grounded in God, contextualized by God. In the 'brown brink eastward' we see the direction that allows for the actions of Christians to be revelatory as parables, our actions pointing to God's care and work in the world to make human life human. And because actions pointing to God's work reveal God's reality of human life in all its fullness, spirituality, conscience, discipleship and service open us to growth into the body of Christ in the world: 'There lives the dearest freshness deep down things.' Maturity is what we are after, growth into the space that God creates with God's very own self in our world of time and space, 'to make and to keep human life human'.

# Select Bibliography

**Lehmann's Publications Cited**

*Articles and Lectures*

Lehmann, Paul, 'Annie Kinkaid Warfield Lectures at Princeton Theological Seminary' (Princeton, March 26, 1979).
——, 'Betrayal of the Real Presence', *The Princeton Seminary Bulletin* 49 (1956): 20–25.
——, 'Biblical Faith and the Vocational Predicament of our Time', *The Drew Gateway* 23:3–4 (1953): 101–8.
——, 'The Christian Doctrine of Man, I: Man as Creature', *The Journal of Religious Thought* 1:2 (1944): 140–56.
——, 'The Christian Doctrine of Man, II: Man as Sinner', *The Journal of Religious Thought* 2:1 (1944): 60–77.
——, 'The Christian Doctrine of Man, III: Man as Believer', *The Journal of Religious Thought* 2:2 (1945): 179–94.
——, 'Comments on a Critique', *Theology Today*, 22: 1 (1965): 120–25.
——, Paul, 'Evanston: Problems and Prospects', *Theology Today* 11 (1954): 149.
——, Paul, 'The Metaphorical Reciprocity between Theology and Law', *The Journal of Law and Religion* 3 (1985): 187.
——, 'The Politics of Easter', *Dialog* 19 (1980): 37–43.
——, 'Rosenbergs, Then and Now: History's New Light', *Christianity and Crisis* 38:11 (1978): 185–7.

*Chapters in Books*

Lehmann, Paul, 'Black Theology and "Christian Theology"', in G.S. Wilmore and J.H. Cone (eds), *Black Theology: A Documentary History, 1966–1979* (Maryknoll: Orbis Press, 1979).
——, 'A Christian Alternative to Natural Law', in K.D. Bracher (ed.), *Die moderne Demokratie und ihr Recht* (Tübingen: J.C.B. Mohr, 1966).
——, 'Jesus Christ and Theological Symbolization', in E.I. Abendroth (ed.), *Religious Studies in Higher Education* (Philadelphia: The Division of Higher Education of the United Presbyterian Church, 1967).
——, 'Messiah and Metaphor', in E.I. Abendroth (ed.), *Religious Studies in Higher Education* (Philadelphia: The Division of Higher Education of the United Presbyterian Church, 1967).

——, 'On Doing Theology: A Contextual Possibility', in F.G. Healy (ed.), *Prospect for Theology: Essays in Honour of H.H. Farmer* (Digswell Place: James Nisbet and Co., 1966).

——, 'The Standpoint of the Reformation', in J. Fletcher (ed.), *Christianity and Property* (Philadelphia: Westminster Press, 1947).

*Books*

Lehmann, Paul, *The Decalogue and A Human Future: The Meaning Of The Commandments for Making and Keeping Human Life Human* (Grand Rapids: Eerdmans, 1995).

——, *Ethics in a Christian Context* (New York: Harper & Row, 1963).

——, *Forgiveness: Decisive Issue in Protestant Thought* (New York: Harper & Brothers, 1940).

——, *The Transfiguration of Politics: The Presence and Power of Jesus of Nazareth in and over Human Affairs* (New York: Harper & Row, 1975).

**Other Authors**

*Articles and Reviews*

Duff, Nancy, 'Paul Louis Lehmann', *Theology Today* 53:3 (1996): 360–69.

Gustafson, James, 'Commandments For Staying Human', *Christian Century* (December 20–27, 1995): 1247–9.

Kay, James, 'The Word of the Cross at the Turn of the Ages', *Interpretation* 53:1 (1999): 44–56.

McCormack, Bruce, 'Afterword to the 2001 Kampen Conference on Barth's Doctrine of Sanctification', *Zeitschrift für dialektische Theologie* 18.3 (2002): 364–78.

——, 'Barth's grundsatzlicher Chalcedonismus?', *Zeitschrift für dialektische Theologie* 18.2 (2002): 138–73.

Martens, Paul, 'The Problematic Development of the Sacraments in the Thought of John Howard Yoder', *Conrad Grebel Review* 24.3 (2006): 65–77.

Milbank, John, 'Can a Gift Be Given? Prolegomena to a future Trinitarian Metaphysic', *Modern Theology* 11 (1995): 133.

Rutledge, Fleming, 'A Tribute to Paul Louis Lehmann (Sept. 10, 1906–Feb. 27, 1994)', *The Princeton Seminary Bulletin* 15.2 (1994): 165–9.

*Chapters in Books*

Allen, Horace, 'Introduction', in A.J. McKelway and E.D. Willis (eds), *The Context of Contemporary Theology: Essays in Honour of Paul Lehmann* (Atlanta: John Knox, 1974).

————, 'The Life and Ministry of Paul L. Lehmann', in A.J. McKelway and E.D. Willis (eds), *The Context of Contemporary Theology: Essays in Honour of Paul Lehmann* (Atlanta: John Knox, 1974).

Anscombe, G.E.M., 'Modern Moral Philosophy' in R. Crisp and M. Slate (eds), *Virtue Ethics* (Oxford: Oxford University Press, 1997).

Barth, Karl, 'Gospel and Law', in A.M. Hall (trans.), *Community, State, and Church* (Gloucester: Peter Smith, 1968).

Cavanaugh, William, 'The City: Beyond Secular Parodies', in J. Milbank, C. Pickstock and G. Ward (eds), *Radical Orthodoxy: A New Theology* (New York: Routledge, 1999).

Duff, Nancy, 'The Significance of Apocalyptic for Lehmann's Ethics', in N. Duff (ed.), *Humanization and the Politics of God: The Koinonia Ethics of Paul Lehmann* (Grand Rapids: Eerdmans, 1992).

Gustafson, James, 'Moral Discernment in the Christian Life,' in G.H. Outka and P. Ramsey (eds), *Norm and Context in Christian Ethics* (New York: Charles Scribner's Sons, 1968).

Maurice, F.D., 'Incarnation and the Renewal of Community', in *On Christian Theology* (Malden: Blackwell, 2000).

Nouwen, Henri, 'Reaching Out: The Three Movements of the Spiritual Life', *Ministry and Spirituality* (New York: Continuum, 1996).

Ramsey, Paul, 'The Case for Making "Just War" Possible', *The Just War* (New York: Charles Scribner's Sons, 1968), pp. 148–67.

'Second Helvetic Confession' in *The Book of Confessions: Presbyterian Church (USA)* (Louisville: The Office of the General Assembly, 1999).

Taylor, Charles, 'Age of Authenticity' in *A Secular Age* (Cambridge: The Belknap Press of Harvard University Press, 2007).

Warren, Robert Penn, 'The Code Book is Lost' in *Now and Then* (New York: Random House, 1978).

Ziegler, Philip, 'Justification and Justice: The Promising *Problematique* of Protestant Ethics in the Work of Paul L. Lehmann' in M. Husbands and D.J. Trier (eds), *Justification: What's at Stake in the Current Debates* (Downers Grove, IL: Intervarsity, 2004), pp. 118–33.

*Books*

Aquinas, Thomas, *Summa Theologiae*, trans. Fr. T. Gilby O.P. 60 Volumes (Cambridge: Cambridge University Press, 2006).

Aristotle, *Nicomachean Ethics*, trans. R. Crisp (Cambridge: Cambridge University Press, 2000).

————, *The Politics* (Chicago: The University of Chicago Press, 1984).

Augustine, *The City of God Against the Pagans*, ed. R.W. Dyson (New York: Cambridge University Press, 1998).

Badiou, Alain, *Saint Paul: The Foundation of Universalism* (Stanford: Stanford University Press, 2005).

Barth, Karl, *Church Dogmatics* I/1, trans. G.W. Bromiley and T.F. Torrance (Edinburgh: T&T Clark, 1975).

——, *Church Dogmatics* II/1, trans. G.W. Bromiley and T.F. Torrance (Edinburgh: T&T Clark, 1964).

——, *Church Dogmatics* IV/1 – IV/3, trans. G.W. Bromiley and T.F. Torrance (Edinburgh: T&T Clark, 1956–62).

——, *Church Dogmatics* IV/4, *Lecture Fragments*, trans. G.W. Bromiley (Grand Rapids: Eerdmans, 1981).

——, *The Epistle to the Romans*, trans. E.C. Hoskyns (Oxford: Oxford University Press, 1933).

Bellah, Robert, *Habits of the Heart: Individualism and Commitment in American Life* (New York: Harper & Row, 1985).

Benedict, *The Rule of St. Benedict*, trans. C. White (London: Penguin Books, 2008).

Biggar, Nigel, *The Hastening that Waits: Karl Barth's Ethics* (Oxford: Clarendon, 1993).

Blau, Peter, *Inequality and Heterogeneity: A Primitive Theory of Social Structure* (New York: Free Press, 1977).

Bonhoeffer, Dietrich, *Discipleship*, trans. M. Kuske and I. Tödt (Minneapolis: Fortress Press, 2001).

——, *Ethics*, trans. M. Kuske and I. Tödt (Minneapolis: Fortress Press, 2005).

——, *Letters and Papers from Prison* (New York: Macmillan, 1971).

Buber, Martin, *Königtum Gottes* (Heidelberg: Lambert Schneider, 1956).

Calvin, John, *Institutes of the Christian Religion*, trans. F. Lewis Battles, ed. J.T. McNeill (Philadelphia: Westminster, 1960).

——, *Instruction in Faith, 1537* (Louisville: Westminster/John Knox Press, 1977).

Capon, Robert, *The Mystery of Christ. . . and why we don't get it* (Grand Rapids: Eerdmans, 1993).

De Caussade, Jean-Pierre, *Abandonment to Divine Providence* (New York: Image Books/Doubleday, 1975).

Cardinal de Lubac, Henri, *Corpus Mysticum: The Eucharist and the Church in the Middle Ages*, trans. G. Simmonds, R. Price and C. Stephens (Notre Dame: University of Notre Dame Press, 2006).

Currie, Thomas, *The Joy of Ministry* (Louisville: Westminster John Knox Press, 2008).

Drury, John, *The Parables In The Gospels: History And Allegory* (New York: Crossroad, 1985).

——, *Theological Issues in the Letters of Paul* (Nashville: Abingdon, 1997).

Duff, Nancy, *Humanization and the Politics of God: The Koinonia Ethics of Paul Lehmann* (Grand Rapids: Eerdmans, 1992).

Dumont, Louis, *From Mandeville to Marx* (Chicago: University of Chicago Press, 1977).

——, *Homo Hierarchicus: The Caste System and Its Implications*, trans. M. Sainsbury (Chicago: University of Chicago Press, 1970).

Fletcher, Joseph. *Situation Ethics: The New Morality* (Philadelphia: Westminster, 1966).

Fry, Christopher, *The Dark is Light Enough: A Winter Comedy* (Oxford: Oxford University Press, 1954).

Habermas, Jürgen, *The Theory of Communicative Action*, (2 vols, Boston: Beacon Press, 1987).

Holl, Karl, 'Was verstand Luther unter Religion?', *Gesammelte Aufsätze zur Kirchengeschichte*, (Tübingen: J.C.B. Mohr, 1923).

Hobbes, Thomas, *Leviathan*, ed. E. Curley (Indianapolis, IN: Hackett, 1994).

Kittel, Gerhard, *Theological Dictionary of the New Testament* (10 vols, Grand Rapids, Eerdmans, 1964–76).

Lash, Nicholas, *Theology on the Way to Emmaus* (London: SCM, 1986).

Long, D. Stephen, *Tragedy, Tradition, Transformism: The Ethics of Paul Ramsey* (Boulder, CO: Westview, 1993).

Luther, Martin, *The Large Catechism* (Minneapolis: Fortress Press, 1959).

McGrane, Bernard, *Beyond Anthropology: Society and the Other* (New York: Columbia University Press, 1989).

Martyn, J. Louis, *Galatians: A New Translation with Introduction and Commentary* (New York: Doubleday, 1997).

Merton, Thomas, *Conjectures of a Guilty Bystander* (New York: Doubleday & Co., 1966).

Miller, Athur, *Death of a Salesman* (New York: Penguin, 1996).

Morse, Christopher, *Not Every Spirit: A Dogmatics of Christian Disbelief* (Valley Forge: Trinity Press, 1994).

Nouwen, Henri, *The Wounded Healer* (New York: Doubleday Image, 1979).

Outka, Gene and Paul Ramsey (eds), *Norm and Context in Christian Ethics* (New York: Scribner, 1968).

Owen, Susan, *Forgiveness and a Return to the Good*, Department of Religious Studies, University of Virginia (PhD Dissertation, August 1997).

Ramsey, Paul, *Basic Christian Ethics* (Louisville: Westminster/John Knox Press, 1993).

——, *Deeds and Rules in Christian Ethics* (New York: Charles Scribner's Sons, 1967).

——, *The Essential Paul Ramsey: A Collection*, ed. W. Werpehowski and S.D. Crocco (New Haven: Yale University Press, 1994).

——, *Who speaks for the Church? A critique of the 1966 Geneva Conference on Church and Society* (Nashville, New York: Abingdon Press, 1967).

Rilke, Rainer Maria, 'When Catching', in W. Barnstone (ed.), *Modern European Poetry* (New York: Bantam, 1966).

Rousseau, Jean-Jacques, *Émile*, trans. B. Foxley (London: Dent, 1911).

Underhill, Evelyn, 'The Future of Mysticism', in D. Greene (ed.), *Evelyn Underhill: Modern Guide to the Ancient Quest for the Holy* (New York: SUNY Press, 1988).

Webster, John, *Barth's Ethics of Reconciliation* (Cambridge: Cambridge Univ. Press, 1995).

Yancey, Phillip, *What's So Amazing About Grace?* (Grand Rapids: Zondervan, 1997).

# A Paul L. Lehmann Bibliography

## 1930s

Lehmann, Paul, 'The Historical Relation of Barth's Theology to the Lutheran Doctrine of The Word of God' (New York: Union Theological Seminary, 1930).

——, 'The German Church Situation: A Reply to E.G. Homrighausen', *The Christian Century* 50 (1933): 1150.

——, *A Critical Comparison of the Doctrine of Justification in the Theologies of Albrecht Ritschl and Karl Barth* (Union Theological Seminary doctoral dissertation, 1936).

——, 'Theocracy and Liberty', *Radical Religion* 2:3 (1937): 30–34.

## 1940s

Lehmann, Paul. *Forgiveness: Decisive Issue in Protestant Thought* (New York: Harper & Row, 1940).

——, The Authority of the Church and Freedom', *The Review of Religion* 4:2 (1940): 159–69.

——, 'Barth and Brunner: The Dilemma of the Protestant Mind', *The Journal of Religion* 20:2 (1940): 124–40.

——, 'The Use of Christian Words', *The Journal of Religion* 21:1 (1941): 46–8.

——, 'The Promise of Theology in America', *Student World* 35:1 (1942): 70–79.

——, 'Obedience and Justice', *Christianity and Society* 8:3 (1942): 35–9.

——, 'Human Destiny – Reinhold Niebuhr: A Symposium', *The Union Review* 4:2 (1943): 18–20.

——, 'The Christian Doctrine of Man: I. Man as Creature', *The Journal of Religious Thought* 1:2 (1944): 140–56.

——, 'The Christian Doctrine of Man: II. Man as Sinner', *The Journal of Religious Thought* 2:1 (1944): 60–77.

——, 'Towards a Protestant Analysis of the Ethical Problem', *The Journal of Religion* 24:1 (1944): 1–16.

——, 'Christian Foundations of Peace', *Christianity and Society* 9:2 (1944): 36–41.

——, 'Grace and Power', *Christianity and Society* 10:1 (1944): 25–31.

——, 'A Protestant Critique of Anglicanism', *Anglican Theological Review* 26:3 (1944): 151–9.

Richter, Werner, *Re-Educating Germany* (Chicago: University of Chicago Press, 1945). *Preface.*

Lehmann, Paul, 'The Christian Faith and Contemporary Culture', *The Student World* 36:4 (1945): 317–32.
——, 'The Human Prospect', *The Student World* 38:1 (1945): 70–77.
——, 'The Christian Doctrine of Man: III. Man as Believer', *The Journal of Religious Thought* 2:2 (1945): 179–94.
——, 'The Rebirth of Theology', *Religion in Life* 14:4 (1945).
——, 'Contemporary Reflections on the Epistle to the Romans', *The Journal of Bible and Religion* 14:3 (1946): 158–63.
——, 'The Reformers' Use of the Bible', *Theology Today* 3:3 (1946): 328–44.
——, 'The Direction of Theology Today', *The Duke Divinity School Bulletin* 11:4 (1947): 67–76.
——, *Christianity and Community* (Lecture, Chapel Hall: Committee on Convocations and Lectures of the University of North Carolina, 1947).
——, 'The Standpoint of the Reformation' in *Christianity and Property*, ed. J. Fletcher (Philadelphia:    Westminster Press, 1947).
——, 'Justification by Faith and the Disposition of Goods', *Christianity and Society* 12:4 (1947): 12–19.
——, 'Bible Studies', *The Westminster Fellowship Handbook* (September–December 1947).
——, 'Where Liberalism Fails', *Theology Today* 4:4 (1948): 500–506.
——, 'The Bible and the Significance of Civilization', *Theology Today* 5:3 (1948): 350–58.
——, 'Protestants, Liberals, and Liberty', *New Century* (May 1948): 8–10.
——, 'On Being Fit for Freedom', *The Intercollegian* 66:5 (1949): 5–6.
——, 'On the Meaning of Lent', *Discovery* 1 (1949): 16–17.
——, 'Truth is in Order to Goodness', *Theology Today* 6:3 (1949): 348–60.
——, 'The Meaning of the Resurrection', *Counsel* 1:3 (1949).
——, 'The Mindzenty-Spellman Case', *New Century* (Spring 1949): 11–14.


## 1950s


Lehmann, Paul, 'What is Religious Liberty', *Christianity and Society* 15:3 (1950): 10–13.
——, 'The Dynamics of Reformation Ethics', *Princeton Seminary Bulletin* 43:4 (1950): 17–22.
——, 'Renewal in the Church', *Theology Today* 7:4 (1951): 472–85.
——, 'Deliverance and Fulfilment: The Biblical View of Salvation', *Interpretation* 5:4 (1951): 387–400.
——, 'Christianity and Social Change', *The Intercollegian* 69:2 (1951): 7–8.
——, 'The Presbyterian Churches', in *The Quest for Christian Unity*, ed. S. Bilheimer (New York: Associated Press, 1952).
——, 'The Missionary Obligation of the Church', *Theology Today* 9:1 (1952): 20–38.

——, 'Civil Liberties', *Christianity and Society* 17:2 (1952): 5–6.
——, 'The Christian Faith and Civil Liberties', *Social Progress* 43:4 (1952): 5–8.
——, 'The Foundation and Pattern of Christian Behaviour', in *Christian Faith and Social Action: Essays in Honour of Reinhold Niebuhr*, ed. J. Hutchison (New York: Charles Scribner's Sons, 1953).
——, 'Willingen and Lund: The Church on the Way to Unity', *Theology Today* 9:4 (1953): 431–41.
——, 'Biblical Faith and the Vocational Predicament of Our Time', *The Drew Gateway* 23:3–4 (1953): 101–8.
——, *Your Freedom is in Trouble* (New York: National Student Council of the YMCA and YWCA, 1954).
——, 'The Transforming Power of the Church', *The Intercollegian* 71:5–7 (1954): 20.
——, 'Light on Meetinghouse Hill', *Princeton Seminary Bulletin* 47:3 (1954): 17–26.
——, 'Should the Church Speak Out on Social and Political Issues?', *This Generation* 6:3 (1954): 57–59.
——, 'Academic Freedom in the United States', *Student World* 47:2 (1954): 163–71.
——, 'Evanston: Problems and Prospects', *Theology Today* 11:2 (1954): 143–53.
——, 'The Theology of Crisis', in *The Twentieth Century Encyclopedia of Religious Knowledge*, vol. 1, ed. L.A. Loetscher (Grand Rapids: Baker Book House, 1955).
——, 'Anti-Pelagian Writings', in *A Companion to the Study of St. Augustine*, ed. R. Battenhouse (New York: Oxford University Press, 1955).
——, 'Betrayal of the Real Presence', *Princeton Seminary Bulletin* 49:3 (1956): 20–25.
——, 'The Christology of Reinhold Niebuhr', in *Reinhold Niebuhr: His Religious, Social, and Political Thought*, ed. C.W. Kegley and R.W. Bretall (New York: Macmillan, 1956).
——, 'The Changing Course of a Corrective Theology', *Theology Today* 13:3 (1956): 332–57.
——, 'The Context of Theological Inquiry', *Harvard Divinity School Bulletin* 22 (1957): 61–73.
——, 'Law', in *A Handbook of Christian Theology*, ed. M. Halverson and A.A. Cohen (New York: Living Age Books/Meridian Books Inc., 1958).
——, 'Power', in *A Handbook of Christian Theology*, ed. M. Halverson and A.A. Cohen (New York: Living Age Books/Meridian Books Inc., 1958).
——, 'The Servant Image in Reformed Theology', *Theology Today* 15:3 (1958): 333–51.
——, 'Law as a Function of Forgiveness', *Oklahoma Law Review* 12:1 (1959): 102–12.
——, 'The Environment of Authentic Selfhood', *The Intercollegian* 76:6 (1959): 8–9.
——, 'What is a Christian Act?', *The Intercollegian* 76:6 (1959): 11–13.

———, 'Also Among the Prophets', *Theology Today* 16:3 (1959): 345–55.
———, 'Religion, Power, and Christian Faith', in *Religion and Culture: Essays in Honor of Paul Tillich*, ed. W. Leibrecht (New York: Harper and Brothers, 1959).


**1960s**

Lehmann, Paul, 'Then What Did You Go Out to See?', *Harvard Divinity School Bulletin* 25:3 (1961): 4, 8–13.
———, 'Commentary: Dietrich Bonhoeffer in America', *Religion in Life* 30:4 (1961): 616–18.
———, 'Protestantism in a Post-Christian World', *Christianity and Crisis* 22:1 (1962): 7–10, 12.
———, 'Ideology and Incarnation: A Contemporary Ecumenical Risk', *The Seventh Annual John Knox House Lecture* (Geneva: John Knox Association, 15 June 1962).
———, *Ethics in a Christian Context* (New York: Harper & Row, 1963).
———, 'The Formative Power of Particularity', *Union Seminary Quarterly Review* 18:3, pt.2 (1963): 306–19.
———, 'An Ecumenical Venture in the Grand Manner', *Christianity and Crisis* 23:9 (1963): 94–6.
———, 'Integrity of Heart: A Comment upon the Preceding Paper', in *Ecumenical Dialogue at Harvard: The Roman Catholic-Protestant Colloquium at Harvard*, ed. S.H. Miller and G.E. Wright (Cambridge, MA: Harvard University Press, 1964).
———, 'The Logos in a World Come of Age', *Theology Today* 21:3 (1964): 274–86.
———, 'On Keeping Human Life Human', *The Christian Century* 81, 2:43 (1964): 1297–9.
———, 'An Inadmissible Default', *The Christian Century* 81, 2:29 (1964): 908–9.
———, 'The Tri-Unity of God', *Union Seminary Quarterly Review* 21:1 (1965): 35–49.
———, 'Comments on a Critique', *Theology Today* 22:1 (1965): 19–25.
———, 'The Shape of Theology for a World in Revolution', *Motive* 25:7 (1965): 9–13.
———, 'Discussion: Christianity and Other Faiths', *Union Seminary Quarterly Review* 20:2 (1965): 184–7.
———, 'Doing Theology: A Contextual Possibility', in *Prospect for Theology: Essays in Honour of H.H. Farmer*, ed. F.G. Healey (London: James Nisbet and Co., 1966).
———, 'The Function of Conscience in the Making of Decisions', in *Conscience in Crisis* (New Concord: Muskingham College, 1966).

——, 'Paradox of Discipleship', in *I Knew Dietrich Bonhoeffer*, ed. by W. Zimmermann and R.G. Smith (London: Collins, 1966).

——, 'A Christian Alternative to Natural Law', in *Die Moderne Demokratie und Ihr Recht: Festscrift für Gerhard Lieholz*, vol. 1, eds K.D. Bracher, C. Dawson, W. Geiger, and R. Smend (Tübingen: J.C.B. Mohr, 1966).

——, 'The New Morality: A Sermon for Lent', *Dialog* 5:1 (1966): 51–5.

——, 'God in Three Persons', *The Covenant Companion* (March 21, 1966).

——, 'Jesus Christ and Theological Symbolization', in *Proceedings from an Invitational Workshop on Religious Studies in Higher Education* (Philadelphia: The Division of Higher Education of the United Presbyterian Church, 1967).

——, 'Messiah and Metaphor', in *Proceedings from an Invitational Workshop on Religious Studies in Higher Education* (Philadelphia: The Division of Higher Education of the United Presbyterian Church, 1967).

——, 'Ecumenism and Church Union', in *Realistic Reflections on Church Union*, ed. J. Macquarrie (1967).

——, 'Wilhelm Pauck', *Union Seminary Tower* 14:11, 33 (1967).

——, 'Faith and Worldliness in Bonhoeffer's Thought', *Union Seminary Quarterly Review* 23:1 (1967): 31–44.

——, 'Discussion: Communist-Christian Dialogue', *Union Seminary Quarterly Review* 22:3 (1967): 218–23.

——, 'Forgiveness', in *Dictionary of Christian Ethics*, ed. J. Macquarrie (Philadelphia: The Westminster Press, 1967).

——, 'Contextual Ethics', in *Dictionary of Christian Ethics*, ed. J. Macquarrie (Philadelphia: The Westminster Press, 1967).

——, 'The Christian-Marxist Dialogue', *Social Action* 35:3 (1968): 17–22.

——, 'A Theological Defence of Revolutions', *Africa Today* 15:3 (1968): 18–21.

——, 'Faith and Worldliness in Bonhoeffer's Thought', in *Bonhoeffer in a World Come of Age*, ed. P. Vorkink (Philadephia: Fortress, 1968).

——, 'Dietrich Bonhoeffer', in *Four Theological Giants Influence Our Faith* (New York: Union     Theological Seminary, 1968).

——, 'Christian Theology in a World in Revolution', in *Openings for Marxist-Christian Dialogue*, ed. T.W. Ogletree (Nashville/New York: Abingdon Press, 1969).


## 1970s

Lehmann, Paul, 'Karl Barth and the Future of Theology', *Religious Studies* 6:2 (1970): 105–20.

——, 'A Christian Look at the Sexual Revolution', in *Sexual Ethics and Christian Responsibility*, ed. J. C. Wynn (New York: Associated Press, 1970).

——, 'Discussion: Theology and the Philosophy of Religion', *Union Seminary Quarterly Review* 25:4 (1970): 494–9.

——, 'Karl Barth: Theologian of Permanent Revolution', *Union Seminary Quarterly Review* 27:1 (1972): 67–81.

——, 'Eine Politik der Nachfolge', *Evangelische Theologie* 32 (1972): 560–79.

——, 'Contextual Theology', *Theology Today* 29:1 (1972): 3–8.

——, 'Beyond Morality and Immorality in Foreign Affairs', *Theology Today* 28:4 (1972): 489–94.

——, 'Advent, Prisoners, and the Penal System', *Union Theological Seminary Journal* (January 1972): 2–3, 13.

——, 'Theological Perspectives for the Practice of Collegiality in Union Theological Seminary', *Union Seminary Quarterly Review* 28:4 (1973): 287–9.

——, 'Schwartze Theologie und "christliche" Theologie', *Evangelische Theologie* 34:1 (1974): 34–43.

——, 'The Concreteness of Theology: Reflections on the Conversation between Barth and Bonhoeffer', in *Footnotes to a Theology: The Karl Barth Colloquium of 1972*, ed. M. Rumscheidt (Waterloo: The Corporation for the Publication of Academic Studies in Religion in Canada, 1974).

——, 'A Sermon: No Uncertain Sound', *Union Seminary Quarterly Review* 29:3–4 (1974): 273–7.

——, *The Transfiguration of Politics: The Presence and Power of Jesus of Nazareth in and Over Human Affairs* (New York: Harper & Row, 1975).

——, 'A Conference on Law, Theology, and Ethics', *CSCW Report* 33:1 (1975): 17–23.

——, 'Black Theology and *Christian* Theology', *Union Seminary Quarterly Review* 31:1 (1975): 31–7.

——, 'The Transfiguration of Jesus and Revolutionary Politics', *Christianity and Crisis* 35:3 (1975): 44–7.

——, 'De Weg die Tot Vrede Leidt', in *Kerk en Vrede: Opstellen Aangeboden Aan Prof. Dr. J. de Graaf*, ed. A. van der Beld (Baarn: Ten Have, 1976).

——, 'Biblical Iambics for the American Bicentennial', *Interpretation* 30:1 (1976): 60–70.

——, 'Rosenbergs, Then and Now: History's New Light', *Christianity and Crisis* 38:11 (1978): 185–7.

——, 'Black Theology and *Christian* Theology', in *Black Theology: A Documentary History*, eds G.S. Wilmore and J.H. Cone (Maryknoll: Orbis Books, 1979).

—— and Ira Gollobin, 'Stranger within the Gates', *The Christian Century* 89, 2:15 (1972): 1149–52.

## 1980s

Lehmann, Paul, 'The Politics of Easter', *Dialog* 19:1 (1980): 37–43.

——, 'The Commandments and Common Life', *Interpretation* 34:4 (1980): 341–55.

——, 'The Haitian Struggle for Human Rights', *The Christian Century* 97 (Oct. 1980): 941–3.

——, 'Ethics', in *Karl Barth in Re-View: Posthumous Works Reviewed and Assessed*, ed. M. Rumscheidt (Pittsburgh: The Pickwick Press, 1981).

——, 'Continual Invocations of Saint Augustine: Reinhold Niebuhr in American Theology', in *Intergerini Parietis Septum*, ed. D. Hadidian (Pittsburgh: Pickwick, 1981).

——, 'In Memory of Wilhelm Pauck: Colleague and Friend', in *Memory of Wilhelm Pauck: Memorial Notices, Liturgical Pieces, Essays and Addresses*, ed. D.W. Lotz (New York: Union Seminary, 1982).

——, 'Piety, Power and Politics: Church and Ministry Between Ratification and Resistance', *Journal of Theology for Southern Africa* 44 (1983): 58–72.

——, 'Jesus' Temptation, Transfiguration and Triumph', in *Social Themes of the Christian Year*, ed. D.T. Hessel (Philadelphia: Geneva Press, 1983).

——, 'Harvey Cox, Martin Luther and a Macro-Sociological Appropriation of the Decalogue', *Sociological Analysis* 45:2 (1984): 85–90.

——, 'Praying and Doing Justly', *Reformed Liturgy and Music* 19:2 (1985): 77–81.

——, 'Responsibility for Life: Bioethics in Theological Perspective', in *Theology and Bioethics: Exploring the Foundations and Frontiers*, ed. E.E. Shelp (Dordrecht: D. Reidel, 1985).

——, 'Louise Pettibone Smith, Rudolph Bultmann, and Wellesley College', in *Bultmann – Retrospect and Prospect: A Centenary Symposium at Wellesley College*, ed. E.C. Hobbs (Philadelphia: Fortress, 1985).

——, 'The Metaphorical Reciprocity between Theology and Law: A Reply to Mr. Ball', *Journal of Law and Religion* 3:1 (1985): 179–92.

——, 'The Indian Situation as a Question of Accountability: A Theological Perspective', *Church and Society* 75:3 (1985): 51–67.

——, 'Of Faithfulness, Responsibility and the Confessional State of the Church', in *The Barmen Confession: Papers from the Seattle Assembly*, ed. H.G. Locke (Lewiston, NY: E. Mellen Press, 1986).

——, 'The Ant and the Emperor', in *How Karl Barth Changed My Mind*, ed. D.K. McKim (Grand Rapids: Eerdmans, 1986).

——, 'Faithfulness, Responsibility and Justice', *Katallagete* 10:1–3 (1987): 49–55.

——, 'Barmen and the Church's Call to Faithfulness and Social Responsibility', in *Apocalyptic and the New Testament*, ed. J. Marcus and M.L. Soards (Sheffield: Sheffield Academic Press, 1989).

**1990s**

Lehmann, Paul, *The Decalogue and a Human Future: The Meaning of the Commandments for Making & Keeping Human Life Human* (Grand Rapids: Eerdmans, 1995).

——, 'Telling the Truth', *Princeton Seminary Bulletin* 15:3: 254–62.

## 2000s

Lehmann, Paul, *Ethics in a Christian Context*. Library of Theological Ethics (Louisville: Westminster/John Knox, 2006).

# Index